THE RUMBLING VOLCANO

ISLAMIC FUNDAMENTALISM IN EGYPT

Nabeel Jabbour

MANDATE PRESS
Pasadena, California

Published by
MANDATE PRESS
P.O. Box 40129
Pasadena, California 91114
(818) 798-0837

Library of Congress Cataloging-in-Publication Data

Jabbur, Nabil.
The rumbling volcano: Islamic fundamentalism in Egypt / by Nabeel T. Jabbour.
p. cm.
Includes bibliographical references (p. 299).
ISBN 0-87808-241-7 (pbk.)
1. Islamic fundamentalism—Egypt—History—20th century.
I. Title.
BP64.E3J33 1993 93-15796
322'. 1'0962- - dc20 CIP

COVER PHOTO. Thousands of Algerians pray in the streets during Friday prayers in giers outside the Bab el Oued mosque. Jose Goitia, *Wide World Photos* (used by mission).

PRINTED IN THE UNITED STATES OF AMERICA

I dedicate this book to my two sons, Fareed and Nader, who are refreshingly free from prejudice toward Muslims.

ACKNOWLEDGMENTS

I am grateful for the interaction and great help of my two mentors, Prof. Le Roux and Prof. Naude'.

My thanks are due to several people who read my manuscript and gave their expert evaluation and valuable suggestions. Among them are: Ed Hoskins, Waldron Scott, Bob Sparks, Raja Tanas and Abe Weibe.

I am grateful also for Letchmi, my secretary in Egypt, who labored in love as she typed the manuscript. I am also thankful for Ben Hanna's long hours in revising and preparing the manuscript as a dissertation. His expertise on the computer was immensely valuable. I also thank Joyanne Bell for her willing spirit and help with the English language in the final revision before publication.

My wife Barbara along with our son Fareed have also reviewed the manuscript. Their encouragement, along with the encouragement of our younger son Nader, empowered me to use the very early hours of the morning in Egypt to work on this phenomenon of Islamic Fundamentalism.

Above all, I am grateful to God who helped me lay aside prejudice and study this phenomenon of Islamic Fundamentalism from the adherents' point of view and to have a deeper understanding of it.

CONTENTS

FOREWORD

In the autumn of 1992 a violent earthquake shook Cairo, Egypt. It was sudden and totally unexpected. The whole world took note. Yet, there is a "volcano" that has been rumbling in the same region for years, giving ample warning of a violent eruption to come. It is the "volcano" of Islamic Fundamentalism. *Al-Ahrâm*, the largest daily newspaper in the Middle East, has pointed out that the biggest challenges facing Ḥusni Mubârak are a population explosion and the expected eruption of Islamic Fundamentalism.

I was born into the Christian minority in the Middle East and grew up there. I graduated from the American University of Beirut in Lebanon. Then, from 1975 to 1990 my family and I lived in Cairo, Egypt where I had the privilege of being exposed to Islam and the Islamic culture. Reading the books of Ṭâha Ḥusein, Nagîb Maḥfûz, Yousef Idrîs and others became my favorite pastime on our holidays. Soon, books of Ḥasan Al-Banna, Sayyid Qutb and other pillars of Islamic Fundamentalism became the object of my serious study. It was one of the most meaningful experiences of my life to try to see Islam without prejudice and to attempt to get into the mind of the Muslim Fundamentalists and perceive Islam from their point of view.

This book is written to help Western diplomats, politicians and international policy makers to better understand the "strange" phenomenon of Islamic Fundamentalism. It is also written for university students and professors who are concerned about the volatile Middle East. Finally, it is written for people who are not satisfied with the limited news reports about the Middle East and are eager to have a deeper understanding of Islam and Fundamentalism.

Egypt is a strategic country in the Middle East. What happens in Egypt greatly impacts the Middle East and causes ripples in Africa and the Third World. The revolution of Nâşer in 1952 was followed by many revolutions in the Arab world and Africa. If Egypt should one day become an Islamic state, similar to that of Iran, then many other countries will follow.

Islam is considered the fastest growing religion in the world, and Fundamentalism is its spearhead. It is essential that we try to understand this phenomenon.

For readers who are familiar with Arabic terminology, key Arabic words and concepts are presented in the text in simple and readable transliteration. There are appendices with a key to transliteration, glossary of names and terms.

I hope that, as you read this book, you will be intellectually stimulated, informed and challenged as you see and hear the volcano rumbling.

Nabeel T. Jabbour

PART ONE

INTRODUCTION AND OVERVIEW

1

INTRODUCTION

On the 6th of June 1967, on the way to the American University of Beirut (Lebanon),[1] I heard people in the street shouting that the war with Israel had broken out. For days we had been anticipating it, since Jamâl 'Abdul Nâşer inspired within us tremendous hope that the Arabs could beat Israel and help the Palestinians gain back their legitimate rights. I dashed to the university hoping to find someone with a radio. The university was almost deserted. As I entered the cafeteria, there were about forty students huddling over a little radio. The batteries were weak and the sound was very low. As I huddled along with everybody else, I sensed that I was a part of a solidarity, a member of a strong nation—Pan-Arabism. Religious differences were nonexistent at that moment. It was of no relevance whether a person was a Christian or a Muslim. What really mattered was that all of us around that radio were Arabs. Somehow I was able to suppress temporarily that lingering theological view that God helped establish the state of Israel in 1948 in fulfillment of prophecy.[2] But at that moment, nationalism was much closer to the heart than theology.

In the midst of that euphoria of anticipation, excitement and hope a student climbed on a table and frantically started screaming "*Allâhu akbar, Allâhu akbar*" (God is great). The other students joined him in loud voices declaring "*Allâhu akbar, Allâhu akbar*."

A Christian would never use that terminology to praise God. This was Muslim terminology.

There I stood, silent, stunned, cheated and confused. Am I one of them? Is this my war, my cause, or is this cause the monopoly of the Muslim?

That experience of mixed intense feelings was repeated several times over the years. On the one side, an excitement and a sense of belonging to Arab nationalism and the just cause we have, and on the other side, the feeling of being cheated by the Muslims who consciously or unconsciously excluded me and alienated me.

In 1975 a major turning point took place in my life. Just before the civil war of Lebanon started, my family and I moved to Egypt to work with the church. Here I was an Arab and yet a foreigner, having come with "rich experience" in the Christian ministry, yet finding out that very little of what I knew applied to the new situation. I thought that I knew Islam. Because I had studied it, I had "succeeded" in putting it into compartments under labels, and in my mind I had refuted it. Later I discovered that I had been dogmatic, projecting into Islam what I thought it should be.

Over the past few years, as a team of men and I started reading the *Qur'ân* with a new perspective, reading books written by Muslims about Islam, and having meaningful dialogues with Muslims, a new love and understanding of Islam started to develop.

As I studied Watts' book *Muḥammad at Medîna*, I felt a deep respect for Muḥammad and Islam. I envied Muslims for their sense of solidarity as they belonged to the grand *umma* (nation). Through studying Ḥammûda's book *Sayyid Qutb* I began having respect and understanding for the Muslim Fundamentalists. Although it is still hard for me to identify with these men as I see them wearing white robes and black beards, yet as I look at them with respect and dignity, I want to let this phenomenon teach me, affect me, and make an impact upon me. I want to let these men, their thinking and their texts reach out to me in spite of the cultural barriers and differences.

With this undertaking before me, I feel that I am on the verge of the biggest venture of my life. I hope that this study will help the non-Arab in general and the western Christian in particular to see Muslim Fundamentalism with a new and fresh perspective. This is a very hard task, not only because the contents of this book deal with Muslims, but also because they are Fundamentalists. And both these words are loaded with meaning in the western minds.

Dr. Edward Sa'îd, in his book *Orientalism*, describes the stage (the Orient) on which the drama is put together by the dramatist (the western Christian). "In the depths of this oriental stage stands a prodigious cultural repertoire whose individual items evoke a fabulously rich world: the Sphinx, Cleopatra, Eden, Sodom and Gomorrah, Astarte, Isis and Osiris, Sheba, Babylon, the Genii, the Magi, Nineveh, Mahomet, and dozens more; settings, in some cases names only, half imagined, half known; monsters, devils, heroes, terrors, pleasures, desires" (Sa'îd 1979: 65).

Muḥammad does not escape the judgement of the western analysts and critics either. Danté puts him in the Inferno.

> 'Maometto' (Muḥammad) turns up in canto 28 of the Inferno. He is located in the eighth of the nine circles of hell, in the ninth of the ten Bolgias of Malebolge, a circle of gloomy ditches surrounding Satan's stronghold in hell. Thus, before Danté reaches Muhammad, he passed through circles containing people whose sins are of a lesser order: the lustful, the avaricious, the gluttonous, the heretics, the wrathful, the suicidal, the blasphemous. After Muhammad there are only the falsifiers and the treacherous (who include Judas, Brutus, and Cassius) before one arrives at the very bottom of hell (Sa'id 1979: 68).

To this vivid background of imagination and fantasy, the western Christian has been to one degree or another exposed. Recently the picture has turned more to the Arab and the Muslim as the terrorist. It is relatively easy for the western Christian to place people in boxes and label them with stereotypes, and as it were, explain them away. We have to face this phenomenon of Muslim Fundamentalism squarely and let it affect us, speak to us and make an impact upon us, otherwise we are only confirming our own prejudice.

Methodology

It is very easy for any person looking at the Islamic Fundamentalism in Egypt to confirm his prejudice, whether for it or against it. What looks attractive and worthy of admiration for some might look repulsive and offensive to others. The challenge in studying Fundamentalism is to choose the methodology which will best help the researcher discover this "strange" phenomenon, understand it, and then describe it. Phenomenology and hermeneutic thinking, along with the historical approach, seem to be the best methods for this venture.

Many books have been written about Islamic Fundamentalism. They are available and to some extent abundant. Some of these books have been written by the Fundamentalists themselves, or by their sympathizers. Others have been written by Al-Azhar representatives, and a few others have been written by western scholars.

As I read these books covering a broad spectrum of sources, the challenge before me was

> to re-establish contact with the raw material of life itself. It is the effort to re-discover and re-experience life.... Phenomenology wants to learn again how to see clearly and how to describe accurately. It is the attitude of 'disciplined wonder.' A return 'to the things themselves,' as the phenomenological battle cry runs (Krüger 1982: 17).

Islamic Fundamentalism should be re-discovered and should be re-experienced as a phenomenon. It should be allowed to speak for itself, to affect the reader because of its dynamic vitality as "raw material." We should maintain an attitude of "disciplined wonder," where "wonder" and "discipline" will not contradict, but rather compliment one another.

My desire is that we would attempt to understand the world of Fundamentalism from the adherents' point of view (Krüger 1982: 18).

The challenge for us is to see Islamic Fundamentalism from the perspective of Islamic leaders—al-Banna, Qutb, Faraj or al-Khumeini and their followers. The closer we enter "under the skin" and "in the mind" of these men, the more we will be able to observe clearly, and be learners.

In the study of Islamic Fundamentalism, it is very easy for a Christian or a Muslim critic to choose the references that agree with his point of view and attack Islamic Fundamentalism. It is also easy for a Fundamentalist to follow what agrees with his convictions to prove his point. Our temptation is to come to the phenomenon with a mind which is already made up, and manipulate the research to prove our assumptions. Contrary to this, we should emphasize the importance of discipline in suspending our judgements. However, that does not mean that I should become a believer or a convert to be able to make a thorough study using the phenomenological approach, but I should "drown" myself in the other person's culture, without necessarily becoming a believer or a convert (Krüger 1982:18, 52).

Hermeneutics

Hermeneutic Approach

The word "hermeneutics" is derived from a Greek word which means "to interpret." To many, the word "hermeneutics" is understood to mean the interpretation of literary and religious texts from the past, such as Plato's *Republic* and the Old or New Testaments from their original languages. According to Krüger, hermeneutics is more inclusive.

> The word should not be restricted to texts only; it also applies to the understanding of works of art, music and so on. And it should not be restricted to the understanding of the meaning of something in the past; it also refers to the understanding of contemporary things.... Hermeneutic thinking is rooted in the experience of the 'strangeness' of some cultural products, whether they are far removed from us today in time, or whether they are expressed by people who belong to a different culture from our own (Krüger 1982: 20-21).

In the case of studying the phenomenon of Islamic Fundamentalism in Egypt, its "strangeness" is not only because it is removed from us today in time as we consider past and recent historical roots such as Ḥasan al-Banna and Sayyid Qutb. More important than that is that its "strangeness" lies in its being expressed by people who belong to a different culture. The Christian Arab culture is very different from the Muslim Arab culture, and even more different from Islamic Fundamentalism. The Muslim Fundamentalists' religion, their mind-set, their values, their goals and ambitions, their vocabulary, their customs and their dress code are very different from those of Arab Christians, and even more different from western Christians. It is very easy to judge the Fundamentalists' dedication as extremism, their willingness to lay down their lives for serving God as fanaticism, their holistic view of life as rebellion against the state and their hatred of and desire to punish sin as blood thirstiness, their convictions as dogmatism, their solidarity as exclusiveness and their sense of dignity and honor as empty pride. Several orientalists in the past judged Islam and Muslims very severely. Edward Sa'îd says to this effect,

> The Orient 'out there' towards the East, is corrected, even penalized, for lying outside the boundaries of European society. The Orient is thus orientalized, a process that not only marks the Orient as the province of the orientalist, but also forces the uninitiated western reader to accept orientalist codifications as the true

> Orient. Truth, in short, becomes a function of learned judgments, not the material itself, which in time seems to owe even its existence to the orientalist (Sa'îd 1979: 67).

"Respect" is a prerequisite for the success of the hermeneutic process. "To do science of religion in this spirit, is to respect the dignity of whatever I am trying to understand, and to allow it to speak for itself. I become an attentive, humble listener to the human spirit reaching out to me across the barriers of time and cultural differences" (Krüger 1982: 21).

Living in Egypt and knowing the Arabic language has given me an open door to enter the world of Islamic Fundamentalism and to interact with it. People like al-Banna, Qutb, Shukri and Faraj who were assassinated or executed are still present, vital and dynamic through their writings and through the abundance of what has been written about them in Arabic.

By studying Islamic Fundamentalism, I wanted to allow myself to be drawn into its world and get involved with its message. This means that I would not be satisfied with being a cool, calculating, objective researcher, but that I would become an involved participant while at the same time maintaining a critical perspective.

There are various aims of this study. One is to discover the thread that runs throughout the history of Islamic Fundamentalism in the twentieth century and find out whether or not this thread existed from the beginning of Islam. Additionally, we want to find out if it was or was not limited to a particular sect or branch. Another aim is to identify the various factors that motivated and are still motivating people to become Islamic Fundamentalists.

Contents

The first part of the study will give an overview of Islam in Egypt. The second will deal with the earliest divisions that took place in the history of Islam, namely the Kharijites and the Shiites, attempting to identify the causes of these divisions and comparing them with twentieth century Islamic Fundamentalism. It will be helpful to see if this Fundamentalism is "interdenominational," "international," and runs across history.

The third part will deal with the contemporary trends in Islamic Fundamentalism. The Muslim Brotherhood is the major group of Fundamentalists in the twentieth century, with Ḥasan al-Banna and Sayyid Qutb as the two major figures associated with it. In the 1970s three main groups came to the surface. Ṣâleḥ Sariyya's group, Shukri's Society of Muslims and *al-Jamâ'ât al-Islâmiyya* at the universities. Early in the 1980s the al-Jihâd organization became the most famous group as a result of the assassination of President Sâdât.

In this section, following the thread of Fundamentalism from 1930 to 1990 will help us discover the evolution, escalation and development in vision and tactics. What are the causes of this development and is this development limited only to Fundamentalism? Or, is it affecting the whole of Islam in Egypt as well?

The fourth part will deal with the contributing factors to the development of Fundamentalism. These factors could be political, religious, economic, social and psychological. All these factors combined, or the combinations of two or three of these factors, might be the contributing causes that push youth in the direction of Fundamentalism. In this section we want to see in detail these factors in their particular setting, namely the Egyptian society with all its complexities.

The last section of the study will deal with the impact of Fundamentalism. An attempt will be made to give an in-depth application and interpretation of the materials offered in the previous chapters.

In the final chapter, an attempt will be made to look at the future prospects and contemplate what might happen in Egypt in the coming years or decades as a result of Fundamentalism.

In October 1992, an unexpected earthquake shook Egypt, where hundreds were killed, and thousands were wounded. The earthquake was not expected, but the rumbling volcano is on the minds of most people. The rumbling volcano—or Islamic fundamentalism—is the story of this book.

Notes

1 In those days I was a seminary student, taking two courses in Islamic studies at the American University of Beirut.

2 Over the years my convictions regarding that issue have changed dramatically.

2

ISLAM IN EGYPT

A Brief History

In 570 A.D. Muḥammad was born in Mecca in what is today Saudi Arabia. He believed that God had chosen him to be the Apostle of God to proclaim a message of monotheism to the idolators of Mecca. In 622 A.D. the *hijra* (emigration) to Medîna took place. In Medîna the Arab tribes Aus and Khazraj were in constant struggle. The Jewish tribes on the other hand were expecting a Messiah who would deliver them from oppression. As an outsider to Medîna, Muḥammad was accepted as an arbiter to the Arab tribes. He attempted to win the Jews to his side, but later on when they failed to respond, he turned against them.

From Medîna he waged several battles over the years until Mecca came to a full surrender. Within a relatively short time, Islam had spread and the Islamic *umma* (nation) was established in Medîna. The reason for Muḥammad's success was the attractiveness of Islam and its relevance as a religion and social system to the religious and social needs of the Arabs. The contrast was seen "between the feeling of harmony, satisfaction and zest in the Islamic community and the malaise elsewhere; this must have been obvious to many and have attracted them to Muḥammad" (Watt 1981: 70).

In this *umma* (nation) the Christians and Jews were not equal to Muslims, nor were they considered idolators. Instead, they were called *ahl al-kitâb* (the people of the book) and they were required to pay the tribute tax.

In 632 A.D. Muḥammad died and Abu Bakr, his first convert, became the leader of the *umma*. At this time the Persians were in control of Iraq, Iran, and Afganistan. The Byzantines on the other hand were in control of Syria, Palestine, Egypt, a narrow strip of North Africa, Turkey and parts of east and south Europe. The two great empires, the Persians and the Byzantines, were defeated by the Muslims. In one single century an extraordinary marvel came into being—the vast Arab Empire that stretched from Spain to India.

Beginnings of Islam in Egypt

At the time of Caliph 'Umar, one of the war generals called 'Amr Ibnil-'Âṣ entered Alexandria, the capital of the Byzantines in Egypt, and conquered it. As a reward for his victory, he was appointed as the first Muslim ruler of Egypt. With this conquest, major changes started to take place in Egypt. The conversion of many Copts to Islam was one of the changes. A main reason for these conversions was the persecution that the Copts experienced at the hands of the Byzantine rulers because of theological differences on the person of Christ, whether Ḥe had one nature or two (Suleiman 1988: 76-77).

Another change that started to take place was the appointment of Muslim rulers to Egypt by the caliph. Arabic started spreading and by the eighth century it became the official language of the state, gradually replacing the Greek language in the areas of science and knowledge. By the eleventh century Arabic became the language of the people as a whole.

An interesting phenomenon was the inability of the Roman and Hellenic cultures to penetrate the Egyptian culture and change the language of the Copts, although these two cultures occupied Egypt for ten centuries. In contrast to this, within four centuries after the arrival of Islam, Arabic became the language of Egypt (Haykal 1985: 315).

With time, Muslims became the majority and the Christian Copts were considered as *ahl dhimma* (the protected people), as long as they were faithful in paying a tribute tax and adhered to certain commitments. These commitments were laid down in *"Al-Wathîqa al-'Umariyya"* ("The Pact of 'Umar"). This pact described and regulated the relationship between Muslims and Christians. It consisted of two parts: one was the required rules, and the other was the favorable or desired rules.

There have been several versions of "The Pact of 'Umar." An interesting phenomenon lies in the varying viewpoints which these versions reflect. Two samples follow, with the first provided by Qâsem, a Muslim author, and the other provided by Youssef, a Christian leader. As one compares these choices, it is easy to see how two people from different backgrounds will choose various versions of the same document in order to fit their religious and cultural affiliations.

The Required Rules, which were compulsory, include (Qâsem 1979: 26-27):

1. Not to criticize or slander Islam.
2. Not to criticize or slander the *Qur'ân.*
3. Not to mention the name of the prophet in contempt or falsification.
4. Not to commit adultery with a Muslim woman.
5. Neither to proselytize a Muslim to another religion, nor entice the Muslim to consider changing his religion.
6. Not to attempt to kill a Muslim or take his money.
7. Not to take the side of the house of war against the house of Islam.

The Favorable or Desired Rules:

1. A specific dress code for Christians to identify them as non-Muslims.
2. Not to beat the bells of churches loudly, nor raise their voices in chanting Christian songs or scriptures.

3. Not to build the houses of Christians higher than those of the Muslims.

4. Not to display idolatry, crosses, nor display freedom in drinking wine or eating pork.

5. Not to display Christian funerals or mourning for the dead.

6. Not to ride horses.

(Muslim rulers who were moderate put into practice the required rules and ignored the favorable rules.)

In a contrasting version of "The Pact of 'Umar," Youssef quotes the rules and conditions that the Christians in Syria allegedly imposed upon themselves (Youssef 1985: 21):

1. We will pay tribute out of hand and be humiliated.

2. We will not hinder any Muslims from stopping in our churches by night or day.

3. We will beat the *naqûs* (bells) only gently in our churches and not raise our voices in our chanting.

4. We will not shelter in any of our homes a spy or an enemy of the Muslims.

5. We will not build a church, convent, or hermitage, nor repair those that are dilapidated.

6. We will not assemble in any church which is in a Muslim quarter, nor in any of the roads or markets of the Muslims.

7. We will not display idolatry, nor show a cross on our churches, nor in any of the roads or markets of the Muslims.

8. We will not prevent any of our relatives from converting to Islam if they wish.

9. We will not make our houses higher than those of the Muslims.

10. We will not keep weapons or swords, nor wear them in a town or on a journey to Muslim lands.

11. We will not sell wine or display it.

12. We will not strike a Muslim or keep a slave who has been the property of Muslims.

Islam in Egypt through the Centuries

History tends to be prejudiced. I chose to look at the history of Islam in Egypt as Egyptians learn it in their school textbooks. The following is a brief presentation.

During the caliphate of 'Umar, 'Amr Ibnil-'âṣ was the ruler of Egypt, and according to the Muslim scholars he was a ruler who was concerned for the Egyptians. He established peace and security, improved agriculture, reduced taxes and allowed freedom of worship. Furthermore, he made Egypt into a strong military base from which he invaded North Africa. Following 'Amr Ibnil-'âṣ, 'Abdallah Ibn Abi Ṣarḥ ruled Egypt at the time of 'Uthman. He built up an Arab fleet in order to fight the Byzantines in the Mediterranean.

During the Roman and Byzantine reign, Egypt was the richest state in the Empire and the same was true during the time of Islam. To be appointed as the ruler of Egypt was a privilege that meant acquiring great financial gain. In light of this, it is no wonder that during the Omayyad period 31 rulers ruled Egypt, averaging three years per ruler, and during the Abbasid period there were 74 rulers averaging one and a half years per ruler (Haykal 1985: 316).

Following the Omayyad period came the Abbasid period. At this time, Turkish leaders began ruling Egypt. This rule would last for centuries to come. This came into existence because in Baghdad, the capital of the Abbasids, the Turkish soldiers had great power and wealth, to the degree that the caliph's ability to rule was greatly hampered. In order to please these generals, the caliph appointed them as rulers of the various states of the Abbasid Empire. Aḥmad Ibn Ṭolon (not even a general) was appointed as the ruler of Egypt in 868 A.D. Ṭolon built up a strong army of Mamluks (the Mamluks were white slaves who were liberated to become professional soldiers), and declared the independence of Egypt from the rest of the empire. Furthermore, his conquests of neighboring countries included Syria, parts of Iraq and parts of North Africa, making Egypt a strong state. His descendants were weak, however, and this resulted in a decline that led to the conquest of Egypt by the army in 905 A.D. Once more Egypt became a part of the empire.

In 935 A.D. Akhshîd, a Turkish general, was appointed by the caliph as the ruler of the state of Egypt, and later the Arabian Peninsula and Syria as well. His sons tried to maintain an uneasy balance between the independence of Egypt as a state and Egypt as a part of the empire. Kafûr, an Ethiopian liberated slave who became a professional soldier in the Akhshîd army, was later appointed by the caliph as the ruler of Egypt.

After Kafûr's death, the Fatimids, who were in North Africa, attacked Egypt and made it the headquarters of the Fatimid Empire in 969 A.D. The Fatimids grew in strength and their empire included all of North Africa, the Arabian Peninsula and Syria, with Cairo being the capital of that huge empire. During the Fatimid reign, Al-Azhar mosque and university were built. Education, wealth and folk Islam were the marks of this period.

Decline followed as the Saljouk Turks conquered Damascus and the Crusaders conquered the shores of the East Mediterranean. The rulers of North Africa and the Arabian Peninsula declared their independence. Only Egypt remained from the whole Fatimid Empire. During this period a struggle for the leadership of Egypt took place. Shâwer, one of the two competitors for the leadership, called for the help of the Saljouks, and Durghâm, the other competitor, called for the help of the Crusaders.

In 1171 the Fatimid Empire was terminated and the reign of Ṣalâḥ Dîn al-Ayyûbi and his family started. During Ṣalâḥ Dîn's time Egypt became a strong nation and won the approval of the Abbasid caliph. Ṣalâḥ Dîn conquered Libya, parts of Tunisia, the Arabian Peninsula, Syria and parts of Iraq. With this strong nation Ṣalâḥ Dîn surrounded the Crusaders that were in Palestine and along the shores of the

Mediterranean, and in 1187 he conquered Jerusalem and the rest of the Crusaders' strongholds. This stirred the emotions of the Christians in Europe, so waves of armies came "to deliver Jerusalem from the Muslims." In 1192, a treaty was signed by Ṣalâḥ Dîn and Richard the Lion-Hearted which placed Jerusalem under the Arabs. Later, more wars were fought and more treaties were signed until in 1244, King Louis the Nineteenth of France led an army of Crusaders to "crush Egypt." The Crusaders were beaten and the French king was arrested and was released only after a huge ransom had been paid.

At this time the Egyptian army was made up mostly of Mamluks. The Mamluks' strength grew with time, and in 1250 they assassinated the descendent of Ṣalâḥ Dîn and declared Egypt as a Mamluk state. The Mamluks had long wars with the Crusaders that were still on the shores of the East Mediterranean. Another danger was coming not from Europe, but from the East. Under Genghis Khan, the Mongols moved west, starting in parts of China and reaching and taking over Islamic states such as Turkistan and Iran. Finally, under Hulako in 1258, Baghdad, the capital of the Abbasid Empire, was defeated by the Mongols and the caliph was killed. That year the caliphate shifted from Baghdad in Iraq to Constantinople in Turkey, and the Ottoman Empire was established. The Mamluks fought and stopped the Mongol conquest.

A new struggle began. The Ottomans started competing with the Mamluks for the occupation of Syria, and the Ottomans won. The Mamluks experienced their first defeat. By the year 1453 the Ottomans had become the greatest power in the Islamic world. Egypt, under the dictatorship of the Ottomans, suffered for centuries under their oppressive rule.

At this same time, there were two great powers in Europe, the British and the French, which were competing for the spread of their colonies in the various parts of the world. The British had colonized parts of North America, in addition to India and the Cape of Good Hope. Napoleon believed that if

France could possess Egypt, then India would be cut off from the British influence. So, in 1798 Napoleon conquered Egypt. Although Napoleon tried to communicate understanding and respect for Islam, the Egyptians perceived his escapade as "a foreign Christian" occupation.

The British sent their fleet to the Egyptian shores to fight the French, and the French fleet was destroyed near the shores of Alexandria. When the Ottomans wanted to attack the French and take back Egypt, Napoleon moved north to Palestine to fight them. Later, Napoleon, for various reasons, had to go back to France, mainly for the purpose of consolidating the strength of France in Europe. His army was left behind in Egypt to fight the Ottomans and to crush Egyptian resistance. In 1801 the British and the Ottomans cooperated and pushed the French out of Egypt.

During the French occupation a rough plan for digging the Suez Canal was drawn up. From a military point of view, the French conquest demonstrated to the British the strategic importance of Egypt.

After the departure of the French from Egypt there were four powers left: the Mamluks and the British on one side, and the Turks along with the Egyptian resistance, on the other side.

In 1805, Muḥammad 'Ali, a Turk of Albanian origin, was accepted by the Egyptian resistance as the ruler of Egypt. He enforced taxes, pleasing his soldiers and the Ottoman caliph with the money, and thus was able to wipe out the Mamluks and push away their British supporters. Finally, he dealt a heavy blow to the Egyptian resistance that had accepted him and became the sole ruler and dictator of Egypt. In time his ambitions expanded and he added most of the Arabian Peninsula, Sudan, Palestine and Syria to his reign, which aggravated the Ottomans and the British. The Ottomans were annoyed because their empire was challenged, and the British were threatened because their routes to India came under the control of Egypt.

In 1840 the British, along with Europe, forced a treaty on Muḥammad 'Ali that limited his control to Egypt and Sudan and payment of taxes to the Ottoman Sultân was expected.

Ismâ'îl Pasha, the grandson of Muḥammad 'Ali, left one major legacy—the huge debts that Egypt owed to Europe as a result of his extravagant lifestyle. With these debts Europe, and especially Britain, started to hold and pull the strings and interfere with the decision-making process of Egypt. This, in turn, produced a steady growth of the Egyptian resistance. Tawfîq, the son of Ismâ'îl, became the ruler of Egypt and inherited the problems of the debt to Europe. His policy was to please Egypt's debtors and avoid conflict with them, so he was seen by the Egyptian masses as the puppet of the British. 'Urâbi, an Egyptian officer in the army, along with his fellow officers, led the people in a revolt against Tawfîq, and the British came to the shores of Alexandria to protect him. This 'Urâbi revolution was partly motivated by the Islamic teaching of Afghâni, who propagated an Islamic state according to the *Sharî'a* (the legislative code derived from the *Qur'ân* and *sunna*) and encouraged *jihâd* (a holy war) against Muslim rulers they considered to be hypocrites ('Amâra 1985a: 25-28).

The 'Urâbi revolution was finally crushed by the British in 1882 and their occupation of Egypt started. The First World War helped the British strengthen their grip on Egypt, which in turn produced wave after wave of Egyptian resistance.

In 1919, another revolution took place which was motivated by factors that were dramatically different from the 'Urâbi revolution. In the 1919 revolution, Muslims and Christians joined in the demonstrations hand in hand against the British and were united together around the goal of Egyptian nationalism (Sa'îd 1977: 23). In the meantime King Fu'âd, the descendant of Muḥammad 'Ali (Turkish background), cooperated with the British to keep the Egyptians' national movement under tight control.

In 1928 Ḥasan al-Banna founded the Society of the Muslim Brotherhood and had high hopes that the Islamic caliphate, which was terminated in 1924 by the Ataturk's revolution, would be restored. He saw in King Farûq, who was under the influence of *Sheikh* Al-Azhar at that time, a possible hope of becoming the caliph of the Islamic *umma* (nation). Later on, al-Banna discovered that Farûq along with the various prime ministers were either limited by the narrow vision of Egyptian nationalism or were appeasing the British and compromising on Islamic ideals and values. The last few years in Egypt that led to the 1952 revolution were years of disorder and disintegration. There were constant revolts, demonstrations, explosions and some assassinations. This was the boiling climate that paved the way for the national revolution.

With this revolution, royalty was terminated and Egypt became a Republic. For the first time in centuries it was ruled by Egyptians. In 1954 the strong man of Egypt, 'Abdul Nâṣer, ordered the arrest of the leadership of the fundamentalist Muslim Brotherhood. In 1956 he nationalized the Suez Canal and the last control of Egypt by the British was finally terminated.

In 1965 more arrests of Muslim Fundamentalists took place as they openly declared that decadent, liberal Muslim leaders were willfully reproducing the situation before Islam, which was modern-day *jâhiliyyah* (days of ignorance or barbarianism). Sayyid Qutb called for an Islamic revolution because the "Nâṣer regime no longer deserved faithful Muslim obedience. Rather, obedience to Islam necessitated the repudiation of the pseudo-state" (Cragg 1985: 58).

After the death of Nâṣer in 1971, Sâdât became the president of Egypt. Early in his regime he wanted to curb and control the communists and the socialists. He set the Muslims free from prison and used the Muslim Brotherhood as his tool for achieving that control. Some of the Egyptian Muslims that had fled from Egypt during Nâṣer's time went to the Gulf countries and made huge fortunes. With Sâdât's open-door policy, investments were welcomed and the rich Egyptian Muslims returned to the country. In the 1970s, *al-Islâm al-tharwi* (the Muslim "rich") started cooperating with *al-Islâm al-thawri* (the "revolutionary" Muslims), giving Islamic Fundamentalism strength and power. The tool that Sâdât wanted to use to give him stability and strength became the source of instability that finally led to his assassination in 1981.

Mubârak became the president in 1981. By the end of the 1980s the number of Fundamentalist groups exceeded forty.

Reflections and Observations

From this very brief overview of the history of Egypt over the past few centuries, the following observations stand out:

1. Islam and nationalism were always interrelated. When Christians cooperated with Muslims, nationalism became the umbrella that kept them together as Egyptians. When Christians in Egypt associated themselves with western Christians, Islam took the upper hand and became the spokesman for nationalism.

2. The caliphate continued throughout the centuries until 1924. The caliph was the leader of the Muslim *umma* (nation) irrespective of his nationality and his capital. Since 1924 Islam has been like the Catholic Church would be without its Pope.

3. History tends to be biased.

If a Christian Egyptian had the courage to write down the history of Egypt, he would say that from the beginning of Islam until the 1952 revolution, Egypt has always been ruled by foreigners. 'Amr Ibnil-'Âṣ and those who followed after him in the Omayyad period were foreigners. Muslims came from the Arabian Peninsula and were not authentic Egyptians.

A moderate Muslim historian would say that from the end of the Abbasid period until the 1952 revolution, Egypt has been mostly ruled by either Turks, French or British. Rulers that ruled Egypt during the Omayyad period were considered Egyptians, since Egypt as a whole accepted Islam and the Arabic language. This view is the official government view as it is seen in history books taught to Egyptian students (Sayrafi 1984: 67).

A typical Egyptian Muslim, as he looks back at this history, will say that Egypt has been ruled mostly by Egyptians. Only when the French, the British and a few unjust Turkish rulers controlled the state did Egypt lose its independence. A Turk who was a Muslim and spoke Arabic and lived in Egypt was an Egyptian. Muḥammad 'Ali and his descendants were Egyptians although they had a Turkish background. The real issue at stake was whether the ruler was a Muslim or not.

A Muslim Fundamentalist will say that since the *Sharî'a* (the legislative code derived from the *Qur'ân* and *sunna*) ceased to rule the Muslim countries, these countries, including Egypt, have been living in *jâhiliyyah* (pre-Islamic infidelity or barbarianism). The *umma* ceased to exist during the first Muslim century. The issue therefore is not whether the ruler is an Egyptian or not, but whether he is a true Muslim—allowing God to rule. "When God rules," he would say, "people of every nation experience their true authenticity and liberation."

4. A quick glance at the history of Egypt is sufficient to show that "super-powers" competed together for the control of other nations, and usually the smaller nations suffered. At times "super-powers," whether the Ottomans, the French or the British, showed a kind face, but when tested, reality appeared and it was basically self-interest.

5. Along with many other factors which will be discussed later, this history was the cradle for the birth of modern Islamic Fundamentalism.

Manifestations of Islamic Fundamentalism

The manifestations of Islamic Fundamentalism in Egypt are at times quite apparent, and at other times Fundamentalists seem to go underground. But in both cases it seems that Fundamentalism is here to stay. There are various causes for its success, and we will deal with these causes in later chapters. At this point all we want to do is identify briefly some of the most apparent manifestations of Fundamentalism in Egypt these days.

1. According to the B.B.C. television documentary produced in the summer of 1987 called "The Sword of Islam," 70% of the women in Egypt have put on the *ḥijâb* (veil). Twenty-five years earlier young ladies were wearing miniskirts. Perhaps the 70% figure is a bit exaggerated, but certainly there is a clear change in Egypt.

2. More men these days are wearing beards and white robes. There are parts of Cairo where the concentration of Fundamentalists is high and it can be seen because of their distinctive appearance.

3. At the universities, especially during the late 1970s, makeshift mosques sprang up and professors had to accommodate the students by bringing the lectures to a halt so that the Fundamentalist students could pray.

4. In 1988 the Fundamentalists got the votes for student council positions in almost every department at every university in Egypt. Furthermore, the elections for the leadership of guilds and societies, including the Society of Doctors, was won by the Fundamentalists (the Society of Doctors has the highest percentage of Christians of all the guilds).

5. Newspapers claim that there are more than forty various factions of Fundamentalists known to the government. They could be united, at least temporarily, in order to achieve a super-ordinate goal—namely taking over Egypt and turning it into a Muslim state similar to that of Iran.

6. In Egypt there are *Dâr al-Awqâf* mosques (government mosques), and popular mosques. The Imams in *Dâr al-Awqâf* mosques are appointed and supported by the government. The popular mosques on the other hand are built with funds that have been raised by the people. The Imams of these mosques do not report to the government. Popular mosques are some of the places where Fundamentalist youth are trained.

The percentage of the popular mosques has exceeded the percentage of the government mosques since the time of Sâdât.

7. There are various manifestations of an attitude that the Fundamentalists have regarding Official Islam as being fake and unreal. Therefore suggestions made by *Sheikh* Al-Azhar and other leaders are usually disregarded.

8. Early in 1989 the Fundamentalists took control of one of the suburbs of Cairo called 'Ain Shams. They planned to infiltrate the poor suburbs of Cairo in order to surround the rich sections of the city and the parts that they could not infiltrate. A confrontation took place between the police and the Fundamentalists. The government took the upper hand after months of not daring to enter 'Ain Shams, except its main streets.

In April 1989 about 1,500 Fundamentalists were arrested in the city of Fayyûm. In spite of imprisonment, and possibly torture, the convictions of the Fundamentalists are getting deeper and stronger. Although there are big numbers of Fundamentalists in the society that are being watched by the secret police, there must also be huge numbers of Fundamentalists brewing underground which the secret police cannot control.

9. Fundamentalists recruit their contacts mostly among the youth of the universities. They tried to penetrate the army, but all they could reach were the officers of lower ranks, yet these officers are permanently in the military. Rumors say that the Fundamentalists are also focusing on high schoolers

in order to recruit them before they enter the army. Although the numbers of Fundamentalists are small in percentage, they have a clear influence and many sympathizers. When the President of the country makes a major decision, he has to take into consideration the Fundamentalists, although their percentage is not high. In contrast, the Christians, who are 6.3% of the population, are marginal in the President's mind when he makes his major decisions.

10.They have their materials and syllabi which they use in training and equipping recruits. The books of al-Banna, Mawdûdi, Sayyid Qutb, Ibn Taimiyya and Faraj are but a few that are studied in depth.

In this chapter we had a quick and brief overview of Islam in Egypt, past and present. In the following chapters we will have a deeper and more detailed view of the roots and causes of Islamic Fundamentalism.

PART TWO

EARLY HISTORICAL ROOTS

3

THE KHARIJITES

Their Beginnings

Although the Kharijites did not continue as an Islamic sect like the Sunnis or the Shiites, their impact in the early stages of Islam was powerful. They were considered as the conscience of the state. Without them the caliphate would have become an Arab secular state. Furthermore, their continued struggle against the state brought about the collapse of the Omayyads. Today they are not in existence as Kharijites, but their model continues to exist as today's Fundamentalists who are the puritans and reformists of the *umma*.

The last six years of 'Uthmân's reign did not meet the approval of the puritans. 'Uthmân was considered weak, biassed, and was not worthy of being the caliph. Not only did he give certain persons grants of land in Iraq, but he also gave some of the richest governorships to the Omayyads (men of his clan). Furthermore, he was charged with weakness because he failed to carry out some penalties that were prescribed by the *Qur'ân* (Watt 1973: 10).

The nucleus of the puritans was made up of those who had memorized the *Qur'ân* and were called the *qurrâ'*. These *qurrâ'* tended to be mystic, tribal in their outlook to life and saw in the *Qur'ân* the final answer and ultimate solution to all problems that the state or Muslims encountered. The *qurrâ'* were not theoretical in their religiosity, but were dedicated, pious, and perceived issues in black and white with no gray in between. They were not passive or marginal; on the contrary, they were quite involved in the struggles and the opposition. Because of their dedication, and deep involvement in revolts, battles and the opposition, their impact became powerful and they became a force to be reckoned with.

After the assassination of 'Uthmân, 'Ali was appointed by the people of Medîna as the fourth caliph, yet that choice was not universally recognized. In Damascus, Mu'âwiya claimed that he was the right caliph who succeeded 'Uthmân. Mu'âwiya was supported by 'Amr Ibnil-'Âş, the powerful general who opened Egypt to the Islamic conquest. 'Ali, on the other hand, had his capital in Iraq in the city of Kûfa and was the approved and chosen caliph.

The army of 'Ali had the dedicated puritans who saw in 'Ali the hope for an Islamic reformation at its core. It also had some of the nobles of Kûfa, who were halfhearted and went along with what was advantageous for them.

At Şiffîn in Iraq in 657 A.D. a battle raged between the Mu'awiya army led by 'Amr Ibnil-'Âş and the 'Ali army. This battle was perhaps the most controversial battle in the history of Islam. 'Ali's army was almost winning the battle when some religious-minded men from the Damascus army appeared with the *Qur'ân* tied to the tips of their spears, a sign well understood by both sides, namely - to let the disputes be settled by a judgement or arbitration according to the *Qur'ân*.

Two representatives were appointed. 'Amr Ibnil-'Âş, a wholehearted supporter of Mu'âwiya, and Abu Mûsa al-Ash'ari, a halfhearted supporter of 'Ali. An agreement was reached as a result of the arbitration, but this agreement brought shame and humiliation to the puritans in the army of 'Ali. They raised a cry *"lâ ḥukma illa li-llâh"* (no judgement but God's) and withdrew. This withdrawal was one of the reasons why they were called "Kharijites" — the ones that withdrew (Watt 1973: 13).

The name Kharijites can be understood in various ways. The most important four are the following:

1. The Kharijites were those who "went out" or "made a secession" from the camp of 'Ali.

2. They were those who went out from among the unbelievers, "making the *hijra* (emigration) to God and his messenger," breaking all social ties with the unbelievers.

3. They were those who have "gone out against" (*kharaja 'ala*) 'Ali in the sense of rebelling against him.

4. They were those who went out and took an active part in the *jihâd* (holy war) in contrast to those who "sat still." The two groups and the concepts of *khurûj* (going out) and *qu'ûd* (sitting still) are contrasted in the *Qur'ân*. (Sûra 9:83-84) (Watt 1975: 15).

Although the Kharijites called themselves by names such as "The Party of Believers," the names that became widespread were those that were given to them. And most of these widespread names were given to them by their religious and political opponents. The Kharijites finally accepted these names, especially "the Kharijites," and gave them new meaning and a religious significance. Their opponents called them "Kharijites" because they withdrew from the Orthodox theology, rebelled against the leaders of Islam and "went out." They, on the other hand, explained the name to mean that they "withdrew" from immoral, unjust and weak leadership. Thus, their withdrawal was the only proper option available. It was not a withdrawal from Islam, but unto Islam and to the *jihâd* (holy war) (Sûra 9:45-46) ('Amâra 1985a: 14).

The Main Characteristics

The Kharijites were not a bad seed sown in the field of Islam, nor a small unknown plant that grew up in the dark. On the contrary, they were the representatives of the faithfully wholehearted Muslims who had the support of the general public. The following are their main characteristics.

Dedication with Black and White Perspective

The Kharijites could not tolerate hypocrisy or compromise. If they did not go the whole way, it was as bad as not going at all. So lukewarmness was actually worse than being cold. The only right thing to do was sincere repentance. So they repented from the mistake that they had made—namely their initial positive response to the idea of arbitration between 'Ali and Mu'âwiya. They also wanted 'Ali to repent and discard the agreement, or treaty, for it was better to break a "false treaty" rather than to live in sin.

"If two parties of the believers fight, make peace between them, but if one still oppressed the other, fight the oppressive one until it returns to obedience to God" (Sûra 49:9). They considered Mu'âwiya to be the oppressive one, and that 'Ali broke God's commandment in ceasing to fight him. So, when 'Ali refused to "repent" and break the treaty, they rebelled against him and "withdrew" (Wellhausen 1978: 37). They had the courage to challenge all, including the leaders, to live according to God's revelation. The three tests that they applied to the leader, where any of which was sufficient to remove him from his position, were weakness, immorality and injustice. So when 'Ali was too weak to admit that the treaty was bad, and in reality it was an agreement with the devil, he was no more worthy of being the caliph.

Their commitment was to God, not to a person nor a leader. Whenever there was a conflict between the two loyalties, the choice was easy—God.[1] With this theological basis, they dedicated themselves to correct, rebuke and bring about a change of behavior using all means to bring about that reformation. With this black and white perspective, the world was divided into categories. The Kharijites considered themselves to be the only true Muslims, while the other Muslims were in reality hypocrites, even worse than Jews and Christians. As the prophet "withdrew" out of Mecca, so they also withdrew from the "house of war" to the "house of peace" (Wellhausen 1978: 43).

For the Kharijites, issues were simple. There were no gray areas, only black and white. Compromise or neutrality was not wisdom, but hypocrisy and cowardice. Their perspective was one-dimensional. They could not perceive issues from political, economic or managerial perspectives—it was only religious. Mistakes could not possibly be seen as a political error in judgement, economic risk, or mismanagement, but sin. All related to God because their cause was God, and Him alone ('Amâra 1985a: 13-14). The dedication to the "truth" demanded from them obedience and courage, even at the risk of the loss of life.

Men of Action and Involvement

The Kharijites were not dreamy mystics who were satisfied in a life of meditation and prayer. Their meditation and prayer motivated them to action and involvement. They were dedicated and wholehearted soldiers. In many of the battles they were the most courageous soldiers because they fought with convictions, not because of a sense of duty.

Their simplicity in lifestyle, their insistence on a life of poverty and meager means, made them a formidable force of fighters who were free from bonds and domestic responsibilities, and were available to fight for God ('Amâra 1985a: 20).

This dedication made them stand out as men who were honest and religious, who demanded respect and awe. So, before battles, they gave speeches to stir the soldiers to encourage and to fight *jihâd* for God. Actually, from their perspective, faith was demonstrated best by *jihâd* (holy combat) with the sword to lift up God's word and advance His cause (Wellhausen 1978: 36).

Their piety had a political dimension. God demands believers not to be passive when they see something wrong on earth. Therefore, they do not restrict themselves to the duty of doing good and avoiding evil, but they also have a responsibility that this should become widespread on the face of the earth. They have to see to it that people do good and avoid evil. This duty of making people avoid evil was the responsibility of every true believer, by word and by deed. The Kharijites went about doing that, on appropriate and inappropriate occasions (Wellhausen 1978: 41).

Men of Paradox

One of the distinguishing phenomena of the Kharijites was the seeming contradiction in their theology.

Regarding leadership, it was the responsibility of every Muslim to confront the leader when he went wrong, because "*lâ ḥukma illa li-llâh*" (there is no judgement but God's). Therefore, the whole idea of having a king and royal blood is contrary to God's law. The only legitimate authority is when the leadership rules in the name of God and according to His will. As a result of this, the ruler should always be checked by religion and chosen according to his piety, not his family, or tribe, or nationality.

There should be order, harmony and law among God's people. The *Imâm* (leader) must demonstrate to the Muslims and to the world the unity of the Muslim *umma*. Muḥammad was the first *Imâm*. The caliphs who came after him also had authority. Each *Imâm* delegates authority to leaders under him so that law and order would prevail. Each leader, and all the other leaders under him, should be obeyed and submitted to.

On the one hand there was submission to the degree of blind obedience, while on the other hand the ruler should be fought and removed if he did wrong, because there was no judgement but God's—a paradox (Wellhausen 1978: 41-42).

Another area of paradox was how they dealt with sin.

As we have mentioned earlier, the Kharijites were deeply disappointed with 'Ali because he did not repent from his weakness and compromise. Actually, one of the tests they developed for judging the accuracy of theology was to ask the Muslim what he thought of 'Uthmân and 'Ali. 'Abdullâh Ibn Kabâb, a pious Muslim, was questioned regarding his opinion of the two controversial caliphs. When his answer revealed that his theology did not agree with theirs, he was declared a sinner and thus was killed along with his wife who was with him.

And yet it is said of the Kharijites that they had very sensitive consciences. One of them was known to have spat a date out of his mouth when he realized that it was not his. Another paid money to a Christian for a pig that the Kharijites killed by mistake (Wellhausen 1978: 47-48).

On the one hand, extreme love, fairness and a sense of justice. On the other hand, no tolerance with a difference of opinion—a paradox.

Desert Mentality

The ancestors of the Kharijites, and the Kharijites themselves in earlier days, herded camels, lived like nomads and raided other nomads. Later instead of raiding nomads, they participated in expeditions and Muslim wars.

As the numbers grew, a more elaborate organization was needed. Discipline was required and the bureaucracy became heavy for men who had previously enjoyed the freedom of the desert life (Watt 1973: 11-12).

With this change in the social, political and economic structure, tension was bound to increase. This tension, along with the simplicity of the desert mentality, contributed to their black and white perspective. "The Kharijites tended to regard all outsiders, even Muslims of different views, as enemies whose blood might be shed" (Watt 1973: 20).

Not only that, but their perspective on the Islamic community "was closely paralleled by the thinking of the pre-Islamic Arabs about the tribe. This parallelism may be regarded as attempting to reconstitute in new circumstances and on an Islamic basis the small groups they had been familiar with in the desert" (Watt 1973: 36).

Divisions and Splinter Groups

When Muḥammad was establishing and consolidating the Islamic *umma* at Medîna, the revelation that he received fit the particular situation that the *umma* was facing. There was the flexibility of tailoring, since the revelation spoke to the needs of the situation.

With the following generations after the *Qur'ân* was canonized, strict Muslims who adhered closely to the precepts of the *Qur'ân* and did not give room for a variety of *ijtihâd* (interpretations), found themselves in a dilemma. Flexibility was needed, and loyalty to the *Qur'ân* and the model of the *umma* at Medîna were of absolute importance. This gave rise to disagreements and therefore divisions. When there was no room for *ijtihâd* (thinking through issues with an attitude of open dialogue) divisions were bound to happen. In addition to these divisions, categorizing people into spheres was another outcome of this inflexibility. Watt mentions categories with various names, depicting various shades: the people of paradise, the people of fire, the people of war, the sphere of prudent fear, the sphere of mixing, the sphere of Islam, the sphere of monotheism, the sphere of openness, etc. (Watt 1973: 29-31). When tolerance to different ideas was lacking, it became easier to put people into pigeonholes.

Another cause for divisions was the attempts of some groups to arrive at a utopia similar to that of the *umma* at Medîna. In the footsteps of the prophet, they emigrated from the corrupt world into their camp under the rulership of God and whoever He appointed as leader.

> Those who 'sat still' and did not 'go out,' or actively associate themselves with the group prosecuting the struggle against the unbelievers, were themselves

breaking a divine command, and therefore unbelievers. These, with the exception of Jews and Christians who had officially received *dhimma* (protection from the Islamic community as a whole), might lawfully be robbed or killed. The Azraqites (a branch of the Kharijites) for instance, were attempting to form a small body which manifested solidarity in its observance of Qur'anic principles as interpreted by them, and was in state of potential war with all other Muslims (Watt 1973: 22).

With this mentality of a lack of tolerance to differences in opinions, the various groups fought together. Sometimes their disagreement was not whether to "sit still" or to "go out," but when to "go out," and when to "sit still" (Wellhausen 1978: 68). The mere issue of timing became a cause to fight for. The number of splinter groups of the Kharijites, according to Maqrîzi, was twenty-seven.

Because of their dedication and wholehearted commitment to martyrdom for the cause of God, their revolt continued in spite of the shedding of much of their own blood. Whenever they felt guilty about "sitting still," they chose a new leader and that signal led to the beginning of "going out," or a new revolt (Wellhausen 1978: 20).

Their revolts persisted and continued through the years. They fought several wars against 'Ali. After the death of 'Ali and the shift of the caliphate to Damascus, their wars against the Omayyads persisted through the years to the degree that it looked like a continuous revolt (Ṣâdeq 1988: 192-193).

'Amâra cites a detailed account of their wars and battles. In their short history, they participated in twenty-eight major wars under a new leader in each battle ('Amâra 1985a: 23-27).

Although it looks like they did not accomplish a great deal because they were never allowed to rule the Islamic *umma*, their impact was powerful. We will come to this in the next section.

The Significance and Impact

From all of the various sub-groups of the Kharijites, only one group called al-'Abâyeda still exists, especially in 'Umân and Masqat at the Persian Gulf and Algeria, Tunisia and Zanzibar in Africa. This group denies its relationship with the Kharijites because their theology has changed to such a degree that their closest proximity is to the Sunnis.

> But in reality what has not ceased to exist is the fanaticism which calls mistakes by the name of the grave sin of *kufr* (unbelief), and that which is political is analyzed on the basis of religion. Although centuries have passed and names and circumstances have changed, the continuing attitude where issues are judged on the basis of the religious conscience rather than the political mind still remains. Like the pious Kharijites from the time of 'Uthmân and 'Ali, we have the same tendencies today, but under different names ('Amâra 1985a: 29).

That was 'Amâra's conclusion. Watt on the other hand went on to say in his conclusion,

> The Kharijites in their zeal for a community based on the *Qur' ân*, went too far in some directions, as when they asserted that the grave sinner was excluded from the community. Closely connected with this is their view that the community has a charisma. Its charisma is that it is capable of bestowing salvation on those who become members of it. It is in belonging to the community that a man's life becomes meaningful (Watt 1973: 35-36).

Şâdeq points to the main significance of the Kharijites as their being able to stand long enough against the corrupt leadership until the Omayyad Dynasty collapsed. The long wars prepared the grounds for the Abbasid Dynasty to start on the ruins of the Omayyads (Şâdeq 1988: 195 -196).

The Kharijites fought and confronted the system, yet were not able to come up with a new system. They fought the rulers, but could not become the new rulers.

Wellhausen concludes that the Kharijites were dedicated men with deep faith. They were more noble than the Jewish zealots because their cause was not land, but God. Furthermore, they were men of action and thus were more practical than the Christian saints because they sought martyrdom, not at the stake, but on the battlefield (Wellhausen 1976: 59).

The Kharijites and The Fundamentalists of Today

As we look at the history of the Kharijites, we can see many similarities with the Fundamentalists of today. The following are the most important points.[2]

1. The Kharijites gave themselves the right to judge who is a true believer and who is not. Today's Fundamentalists are doing the same.

2. The Kharijites saw in the *Qur'ân* the final answer and ultimate solution to all problems. So it is with the Fundamentalists of today.

3. The Kharijites tended to perceive issues in terms of black and white with no gray in between. The Fundamentalists of today tend to have the same black and white perspective.

4. The Kharijites considered the lifting up of the *Qur'ân* on the tips of the spears as a trick aimed at confusing the judgement of the devout and the pious. The Fundamentalists of today perceive the Muslim leaders appointed by the establishment as tools of the government to confuse the devout youth.

5. "No judgement but God's," was the statement of revolt as the Kharijites withdrew. This same statement "*lâ ḥukma illa li-llâh*" is the slogan of the Fundamentalists today.

6. Some Kharijites made their *hijra* (going out from among the unbelievers to God and his messenger) and broke

all social ties with the unbelievers. One of the Fundamentalist groups that was strong in the late 1970s was given the name "*A-Takfîr Wal-Hijra.*" They broke their social ties with the society (unbelievers) and lived in their own camps. A part of a chapter will be written on this group.

7. The Kharijites were those who "went out" and took an active part in the *jihâd* (holy war), in contrast to those who "sat still." A strong Fundamentalist group in Egypt is called al-Jihad. They are responsible for the assassination of Sâdât. They look down with disrespect at the other Fundamentalist groups that "sit still" and compromise.

8. The Kharijites were the representatives of the faithful wholehearted Muslims who had the support of the general public. So it is with the Fundamentalists of today.

9. The Kharijites had three tests that they applied to the leader to see whether he was worthy of continuing as the *Imâm* of the *umma*. These tests were weakness, immorality and injustice. The Fundamentalists of today use similar tests, and that is the reason why Sâdât was assassinated and the existing president is perhaps on their blacklist.

10.The Kharijites' commitment was to God, not to a person nor to a leader. The Fundamentalists of today have the same claims.

11.The Kharijites dedicated themselves to bring about a change of behavior using all means to bring about that change. Some of the Fundamentalists of today are committed to the same goal *(al-amr bil ma'rûf wa-nahy 'anil munkar)*. At times, we hear stories such as Fundamentalists breaking into a wedding, stopping the dancing and the singing, etc.

12.The Kharijites considered themselves as the only true Muslims. Other Muslims were hypocrites and even worse than Jews and Christians. In some cases in Egypt, the Fundamentalists were, and still are, harder on Muslims than on Christians.

13.The Kharijites could not perceive issues from a political, economic or managerial perspective—it was only religious. There was no political error in judgement, economic risk or mismanagement, but sin. All related to God. This is the same outlook that the Fundamentalists of today have.

14.The simplicity in the lifestyle of the Kharijites, their insistence on a life of poverty and meager means, made them a formidable force of fighters who were free from bonds and domestic responsibilities and available to fight for God. The Fundamentalists of today have a simple lifestyle, live among the struggling majority and have nothing to lose. They are men of courage and are available to take risks for God.

15.The Kharijites lived in the paradox of challenging and rebelling against the leader when he went wrong, and yet blindly obeying the leader when he was right. The Fundamentalists of today are challenging and rebelling against the leadership of the country and teach that their leaders should be submitted to unconditionally.

16.The Kharijites lived with the paradox of being fair, loving and having a sense of justice. On the other hand, they had no tolerance with a difference of opinion. The Fundamentalists of today might be willing to fight other Muslims because they are not "true Muslims," yet tolerate the Christians, although they are of a different religion.

17.When the Kharijites were faced with the dilemma of how to relive the model of the *umma* that the prophet had at Medîna, their lack of flexibility and their strict adherence to the *Qur'ân* made their task almost impossible. Thirteen centuries later, the Fundamentalists of today are trying to establish a "true Muslim *umma*," following the model of the prophet. Their strict adherence to the *Qur'ân* and the *Sharî'a* gives them no room for flexibility.

18.When there was no room for *ijtihâd* (thinking through issues with the attitude of open dialogue) the Kharijites splintered into groups and divisions. The Fundamentalists of today are at least forty splinter groups, and given a particular situation they will start fighting with each other.

19.The Kharijites were involved in many wars and revolts. Although they were never able to have an overwhelming victory that would allow them to rule the *umma* they were a formidable force. The Fundamentalists of today seem to be in a similar situation. Every now and then we hear of more arrests of Fundamentalist youth who have been plotting revolts. Their persistence is remarkable.

In the next chapter, we will go on to another controversial group—The Shiites.

Notes

1 They were called "the men of bruised foreheads" because of their faithfulness in prayer (Sûra 48:29).

2 These facts regarding the Fundamentalists of today are substantiated in later chapters.

4

THE SHIITES

Historical Beginnings

"The *Shî'a* are those who follow 'Ali in particular, and assert his imamate and caliphate by *a-naṣṣ wal-waṣiyya* (appointment and delegation made either openly or secretly) and who believe that the imamate does not depart from his descendants" (in Watt 1973: 57). This is the most comprehensive definition of the Shiites which was presented by Ashahrastâni. The word *Shî'a* literally means party, like a political party. It was used in particular for those that followed 'Ali, but later on it was associated with the theory of *a-naṣṣ wal-waṣiyya*, where the assertion of 'Ali's imamate and caliphate took place by appointment and delegation of the prophet. This theory became clear and defined around the year 732 A.D., when the Imams of the day established it as a theological basis, justifying the existence of the *Shî'a* as an authentic religious sect. Prior to that date, there were several theories attempting to explain the beginnings of the *Shî'a*. One theory claimed that the Shiites started after the death of Muḥammad, when the leadership disagreed on who should be the first of the caliphs. Most favored Abu Bakr, but a few favored 'Ali. Those who favored 'Ali had their good reasons, because 'Ali was the cousin of the prophet, his son-in-law and the father of his grandsons. According to these people, only 'Ali and his descendants were really the worthy successors of Muḥammad.

A second theory attempted to pinpoint the beginning of the *Shî'a* at the end of the Caliph 'Uthmân's time, when a Jew by the name of Ibn Saba' became a Muslim. This man was a controversial figure, because the non-Shiite Muslims who wrote books and articles from a prejudiced and non-scholarly approach blame him for the existence of the *Shî'a.* They claimed that he pretended to have become a Muslim, and then, as an insider, he schemed and plotted to bring about divisions and deteriorations within Islam. The Shiite scholars, in contrast, were satisfied to say that he favored 'Ali, and some even went as far as to say that Ibn Saba' never really existed. From what is known from the reliable sources, Ibn Saba' never referred to the "appointment and delegation" as the basis of *Shî'a*, therefore this theory has no solid theological foundation.

Another theory claimed that the real beginning of the *Shî'a* was around the year 684 A.D. This was the time when the nobles of Kûfa in Iraq came to 'Ali's son Ḥasan after the assassination of 'Ali and wanted him to fight the ruler of Damascus, Mu'âwiya. They assured Ḥasan that he would have the victory because they had recruited an army of 40,000 soldiers. This theory claimed that the real beginning of the *Shî'a* came with the establishment of an army and figurehead and spokesman. Watt called these early beginnings not Shiites, but proto-Shiites.

It looks like the most convincing theory is that which has theological rather than political basis. It could be proven that the division which took place was, in essence, political rather than religious. But in 732 A.D. when the Imams gave a theological basis for the political division through the "appointment and delegation" principle, *Shî'a* proper came into existence ('Amâra 1985b: 199-203).

The history of the *Shî'a* movement is tragic and at times melodramatic. This tragic perspective colored how the Shiites perceived themselves. Right after the death of Muḥammad, 'Ali, the "right" successor, was deprived of his rightful position by an innovation called *shûra* (agreement by majority). Later, during the battle of Siffîn, 'Ali's followers were "deceived" by 'Amr Ibnil-'Âṣ who had the *Qur'ân* lifted up on the tips of the spears, thus forcing upon 'Ali an arbitration that was "not fair" and which deprived him of a sure victory. 'Ali could not please the Kharijites either, and was later assassinated as he was praying at dawn at the mosque. Two others were supposed to be assassinated the same day, at the same time. Mu'âwiya was slightly injured and Ibnil-'Âṣ escaped death as he chose not to go to the mosque to pray. So it seemed that the "righteous suffer and the unjust escape unharmed" (Shah 1987: 63).

After Ḥasan, the son of 'Ali, "sold out" his rights to the caliphate, thus becoming a source of shame to the Shiites, his brother Ḥusein was persuaded to take up the responsibility. After he was given assurances that he had full support in Iraq, he left Medîna and marched to Kûfa. When the news came to him that his close allies had been killed, Ḥusein told his followers to go back home if they chose to because there was a danger of defeat. Many left him at this point and he was left with an army of thirty-two horsemen and forty foot soldiers.

Eighteen of this whole band were his cousins. The battle started at dawn after the time of prayer for both armies, and the followers of Ḥusein bade him farewell, being sure that when they died they would be martyrs and go to paradise. Ḥusein watched the battle as the men died one after the other, until he was the only man left near the tent of the women and the children. For a while, no one dared to kill Ḥusein because he was the grandson of Muḥammad. Finally he was attacked, beaten and stabbed with thirty-four stabs, so that no one person could be blamed for his death. His clothes were stolen, his head along with the heads of his followers were severed from the bodies and sent to Damascus. There in Damascus, Yazîd the competitor for the caliphate, made sport of Ḥusein's head by poking a stick into the mouth.

The Shiites look back at the death of Ḥusein with pain and a sense of tragedy; they see him as a "Christ" who was taken to the cross, a grandson of the prophet being massacred (Wellhousen 1978: 129-137).

Al-Mukhtâr and Al-Mawâli

A further step and a new dimension in the history of the development of the Shiite movement took place with al-Mukhtâr and *al-Mawâli* (the clients). After the martyrdom of Ḥusein, many of those who should have been with him in the battle felt extreme guilt for their failure, cowardice and lack of loyalty to the grandson of the prophet. To compensate for that failure, there were many who were willing to die for the sake of Ḥusein's cause, or for the sake of revenging his death. A key figure appeared at this time who took advantage of this fertile soil, and used it to lead the Shiite movement into broader horizons.

Until 685 A.D. Islam was only among the Arabs. However, with the revolt of al-Mukhtâr, non-Arabs entered Islam, mainly through *al-Mawâli* (the clients). One of 'Ali's sons was called Muḥammad. To distinguish him from another half brother with the same name, he was called by the name of his mother's tribe, Muḥammad Ibn el-Ḥanafiyya. Al-Mukhtâr claimed that he was the trustee and the spokesman of Ibn el-Ḥanafiyya, so he fought battles and led a revolt in his name.

One of the important results of al-Mukhtâr's revolt was helping *al-Mawâli* to arrive into a greater awareness of themselves as a political force. According to Watt, there were three classes of *al-Mawâli*. The first class was made up of those who were incorporated into a patrilineal society. The second class was made up of freedmen who would often be freeborn, but enslaved through capture in war. The third class was made up of people who entered voluntarily into a covenant with an Arab patron as his personal "clients." From this third class, *al-Mawâli* who were non-Arabs entered Islam in big numbers as clients of Arab tribes (Watt 1973: 45).

As a result of this, the Islamic nation was divided into two classes. The class of the nobles—the Arabs, and a second class made of non-Arabs, mostly Persians and Aramaeans, who were treated as second class citizens. These "clients" were about half of the population of Kûfa, the city that al-Mukhtâr wanted to make the capital of the Islamic nation. The clients were controlling the day-to-day means of living, while the nobles were busy in wars and battles. To start with, al-Mukhtâr wanted to please both the nobles and the clients, but with time, the Arabs turned against him, while the clients grasped the opportunity of becoming a powerful political force. (Wellhausen 1978: 151). Al-Mukhtâr, appealing to the penitents and the clients, presented a program of reform, constructing his policy on:

1. The Word of God.
2. The *sunna* of the prophet.
3. Vengeance for the family of 'Ali.
4. Defence of the weak.
5. Fighting a holy war against the unjust and the evildoers.

Al-Mukhtâr pleased the penitents by executing those responsible for killing Ḥusein, and he appealed to the clients when he promised to defend the weak and fight the unjust and the evil doers. *Al-Mawâli* saw al-Mukhtâr as their opportunity to gain dignity and self respect. They were not slaves—Islam set them free, but they were not free men either. They had to be as it were "slaves by choice," which was not really their choice. Finally, they chose to give their full loyalty to al-Mukhtâr and defend him with their lives. This brought about a new dimension in the Shiite movement. It became the sect of the poor, the humiliated, the ones segregated against, the second class citizens, Les Miserables. Yet, blessed were the poor in spirit, for they were the true Muslims. This separation of the Islamic nation into two classes was not something hidden, but became an open issue and was often used as a motivating factor in the battles they fought. In the early stages *al-Mawâli* were not allowed to become horsemen nor carry swords, only wooden staves. At other times the Arab leaders openly motivated the nobles to fight their slaves, otherwise their slaves would lord it over them. So the split in Islam was not only political and religious, but also social and cultural. The issues were fused together to the degree that at times the battle cries were "let us revenge for 'Uthmân" or "let us revenge for Ḥusein," and at other times the battle cries were "nobles, crush your slaves," or "Muslims regain your dignity."

When al-Mukhtâr's army won a battle, *al-Mawâli* were brutal in their revenge on the Arab nobles. After these battles the Shiites increased in numbers, but the nucleus of the army was made up of *al-Mawâli* and the Fundamentalists, while the rest were the "silent majority," the "non-committed," the ones who changed sides and stood with the winners. However, when al-Mukhtâr finally started his downfall the numbers dwindled, and the Arab nobles revenged against *al-Mawâli* by brutally slaughtering them. In 687 A.D. when al-Muktar was killed, around seven thousand of *al-Mawâli* surrendered, and all were executed in one day. It was a blood bath (Wellhausen 1978: 163).

Distinctives of the Shiites

The Need for a Charismatic Leader

Both the Kharijites and the early Shiites were, according to Watt, "reactions to the abrupt change from nomadism to life as the superior military castes of a large empire. In this situation those who first began to treat 'Ali as a charismatic leader were looking for a man whom they could trust utterly to have the wisdom to guide them through their difficulties. In contrast to those who thus looked for an individual with charisma, the Kharijites considered that there was a charisma spread through the whole group of the people of paradise" (Watt 1973: 42). The Shiites discredited the reasoning of the

Kharijites and vice versa. But the significance here was the contrast in the social and cultural backgrounds of both the Shiites and the Kharijites. According to Watt, a high percentage of the early Shiites were from Yemenite tribes. The Kharijites on the other hand came from Northern tribes, where all the adult males were considered equal, and where democracy was highly esteemed.

The early Shiites were mostly Yemenites from South Arabia, the land of ancient civilization. In Yemen, kings ruled for thousands of years and were considered to have "royal blood" and superhuman qualities. Thus, Watt concluded his observations with the hypothesis that

> in time of stress and tension men's conduct was controlled by deep seated urges, varying according to the tradition to which they mainly belonged. In some men the unconscious urge was to rely on the charismatic leader and they eagerly searched for such a person and, when they thought they had found him, fervently acclaimed him without giving too much thought to the evidence of his unsuitability. Others looked rather to the charismatic community, and again assumed too readily that they had found it and understood how it should be constituted (Watt 1973: 44).

Perhaps what we see of the life of al-Mukhtâr gives some evidence to the truth of Watt's hypothesis. *Al-Mawâli* who suffered injustice and lack of worth by their patrons, saw in al-Mukhtâr a new patron who was worth their loyalty. So for them, the issue was not whether they wanted to be clients or not, but whose clients they wanted to be. Al-Mukhtâr offered them that alternative with his charismatic leadership and powerful personality. For although he did not claim to be a prophet, he behaved like one who lived in the presence of the Almighty God. He claimed to have been the special trustee and representative to the hidden *mahdi*, Ibn el-Ḥanafiyya. The sophisticated and educated people were not very impressed with al-Mukhtâr, but the common people adored him, were loyal to him and were willing to die for him. Thus, with his charismatic personality he met their need for a superhuman leader, and with their loyalty they elevated him to a degree of holiness and charisma.

The Shiites' View of al-Imâma

Imâma means the line of leadership of the Islamic nation through history. *Imâm* means a leader, and its root in the Arabic language is *amma*, which means "to lead." It was derived from the presence of a certain man who led in prayer, as those who pray stand in lines shoulder to shoulder, and only one man stands alone about two meters in front of the first row of worshippers facing Mecca with his back to them. This man was called the *Imâm*. He could be a *Sheikh*, a senior citizen, or a devout Muslim, depending on the company which he was praying with.

Today, the Shiites, in spite of their differences, are in agreement about the importance of *al-Imâma*. The principles on which they based this policy are the following.

1. *Al-Imâma* is one of the pillars of Islam. Without it, Islam is incomplete. According to one of their early scholars called Abi Ja'far, there are five pillars in Islam: prayer, alms, fasting, pilgrimage and *al-Imâma*. Another early scholar claimed that this doctrine of *al-Imâma* is as important as that of the Prophethood of Muḥammad (Amîn 1986: 15).

2. In every generation there should be an *Imâm* who will be the successor of the prophet and who will lead the Islamic nation.

3. The *Imâm* is infallible like the prophet. He gets his education either from the prophet Muḥammad, or from the *Imâm* who was his predecessor. He lives without sin and he leads with justice.

4. God commanded that the *Imâm* should be obeyed unconditionally. Disobeying him means disobeying God and honoring him means honoring God.

5. *Al-Imâm* is set apart for this privilege and responsibility through *a-naṣṣ wal-waṣiyya* (appointment and delegation). God appoints the *Imâm* through the prophet Muḥammad or through the previous *Imâm*. As Moses appointed Joshua to be his successor, so the *Imâm* appoints and delegates the new *Imâm* through divine guidance.

6. According to one of the main branches of the Shiite sect there were twelve Imams. The first *Imâm* was 'Ali, and the last was Muḥammad Ibnil Ḥasan who went into *ghaiba* (quiescence—a state of temporary inactivity) more than a millennium ago. The last *Imâm* did not die, and one day he will return like the Messiah, a *mahdi* to rule the world with justice.

7. *Al-Imâm* is the Spoken Word of God, while the *Qur'ân* is the Silent or Written Word of God. Through the *Imâm*, current issues could be addressed through the "right" interpretation of the *Qur'ân* (Amîn 1986: 15-20).

The Persecution Complex, Messianic Hope and Quietism Principle

According to Ṣâdeq, the quietism principle came into existence when the Shiites could not give a convincing answer to the argument, "If 'Ali was appointed by the prophet as his successor, why did he accept the nomination of Abu-Bakr as the first caliph?" The Shiites' response to this hard question was, that 'Ali chose the *taqiyya* (the quietism principle) for the sake of unity. In other words 'Ali sacrificed his right overtly, but deep in his heart he believed that the decision of choosing Abu-Bakr was wrong—all this he did for the purpose of keeping peace and unity (Ṣâdeq 1988: 134).

This principle proved to be useful through the centuries when the Shiites chose to overtly accept the actual circumstances, while covertly they believed the contrary.

Several non-Shiite authors, including Ṣâdeq, Amîn, Shah and Najrâmi, attacked this principle in the Shiite sect as a form of hypocrisy, and a coverup for cowardice. However, in reality this principle cannot be understood unless it is seen in the context of the persecution complex that the Shiites have, and the messianic hope.

The Shiites suffered persecution and bloodshed throughout the Omayyad period. After several active insurrections that resulted in defeats and more persecution, the Shiites went into a state of melancholic introspection (a persecution complex). In that state of mind they knew that rulers of Islam were not true Muslims, and that God in his justice would one day bring a change. So they looked to God in quietism, appearing to be satisfied with the existing situation, but in reality living on the hope of *al-Imâm al-mahdi*, a messiah who would come and deliver them from their suffering. Since God was just, He would have to intervene by sending an *Imâm* who would be infallible like the prophets, sinless, and not chosen according to the whims and worldly wisdom of people, but chosen and appointed by God and His representatives ('Amâra 1985b: 207). Actually, some of their scholars went on to say that Muḥammad Ibnil Ḥasan, the twelfth *Imâm*, went into quietism and vanished in one of the narrow streets of Samirrâ' in Iraq, but one day he would come back to fill the earth with justice ('Amâra 1985b: 210).

The Revolutionary Shî'ism and Al-Khumeini

A Variety of Attitudes towards Al-Khumeini

As we enter this controversial section of the chapter, it is hard to be objective. Revolutionary *Shî'a*, which is associated with *Amal* movement and *Hizbullâh* in Lebanon, and the Kumeini revolution in Iran bring to the minds of westerners images of violence and terrorism. It equally brings to the minds of the non-Shiite Muslims thoughts of suspicion, fear and antagonism. My desire is to look at the revolutionary Shiism in general, and al-Khumeini in particular as a phenomenon, and look at it with "disciplined wonder" without prejudice. Although the Khumeini revolution is a "strange cultural phenomenon," its dignity should be respected and allowed to speak for itself. We need to become attentive, humble listeners and let this "strange" phenomenon affect us (Krüger 1982: 17, 21).

'Amâra, an Egyptian Sunni scholar, approached this phenomenon with objectiveness and scholarship. Others, on the other hand, approached the subject with prejudice, imposing upon al-Khumeini their preconceived ideas and used quotations from his books to prove their arguments. Najrâmi, an Indian Muslim scholar who studied in Cairo and had his book *Al-Shî'a Fil Mizân* published in Saudi Arabia, attacks the Khumeini revolution:

1. He claimed that the motives of al-Khumeini and his followers were bitterness and a reaction against the Shah and all the rest of the secular Muslim presidents and kings. Owing to the banishment and the suffering which the Imams went through, their motive was bitterness and their style was revenge.

2. These Shiites were narrow-minded and dogmatic in their theology.

3. They suffered from an inferiority complex which motivated them to desire to be in the headlines at any cost.

4. They had bitter hatred towards the Sunnis because they were deprived of governing the Islamic nation for centuries.

Najrâmi then appealed to the non-Shiites by pointing out that al-Khumeini and his followers believed that the *Qur'ân* had been changed by Abu Bakr, eliminating verses that spoke about 'Ali, and that Abu Bakr, 'Umar, and 'Uthmân usurped the caliphate and were hypocrites. Furthermore, these Shiites believed that all the non-Shiites were not real Muslims and were living in deception (1987: 160-166).

Nâşer Dîn Shah, in his book *Al-'Aqâ'ed Ashî'iya*, claimed that intelligence agencies of the West planted the

Khumeini revolution in the same way the West planted Israel in the midst of the Arab world, in order to use both to break down the Muslim world and to bring about its disintegration and deterioration. With this hypothesis in mind, Shah went on to prove that al-Khumeini and Israel were cooperating together covertly in order to bring about the downfall of Islam.

In the early months of 1979, the world watched with either distrust or amazement the events that brought about the Khumeini revolution. This was the first successful active insurrection in the history of the Shiites. For centuries the Shiites were satisfied to live in quietism waiting for God to bring about the "right" timing for active insurrection. Al-Khumeini did not wait for God, but brought with his teachings and lifestyle a new type of Shiism. This new Shiism has been germinating since the first third of the 19th century and has come in response to a felt need. The *mahdi* has been hidden for over a millennium, and yet the injustice in the world is ever increasing. The *faqîh*, who is the *Imâm's* representative, has limited authority only in the spiritual realm. This new way of thinking, i.e. revolutionary Shiism, gave the *faqîh* authority not only in the spiritual realm, but also in the totality of life. And so this *faqîh* or *Imâm* started having as much authority as that of the awaited *mahdi*. Therefore, the Shiites need no longer "sit" and wait in passive quietism but they can be active and revolutionary in order to bring justice to this unjust world.

Like the theologians of his sect, al-Khumeini believed that the *Imâm* has authority which exceeds the authority of kings and prophets. In this, al-Khumeini was not an innovator. His innovation came in facing reality honestly and squarely, and in calling for and leading a revolutionary Islam ('Amâra 1985b: 221-224).

The Reality as Al-Khumeini saw It

As al-Khumeini looked at the Muslim world, he faced the issues courageously and honestly. 'Amara relied heavily on al-Khumeini's book *Al-Ḥûkuma Al-Islâmiyya*, and pointed out the following:

1. In the political realm, al-Khumeini addressed the issue of the role of imperialism since the expedition of Napoleon in 1798. Because the West feared the unity of the Muslim world, they saw to it that after World War One the Muslim world was divided into small countries and was put under the mandate of the European countries ('Amâra 1985b: 225).

2. Economically the West sapped the natural resources of these Muslim countries giving the people very little in return. The economic help that the West claimed to have given, was done with the motive to create dependency ('Amâra 1985b: 226).

3. Even in the sale of arms, Europe, Russia and the United States competed to control these Muslim nations. The sale of spare parts for the armaments was always conditional on what was in harmony with the policies of these superpowers. What really mattered was to keep these small and divided Muslim nations dependant on the imperialists and under their control ('Amâra 1985b: 226).

4. In the cultural realm, the West penetrated the Muslim World with schools, hospitals, cultural and proselytizing centers. Through spreading their culture, they wanted to wipe out the Islamic culture ('Amâra 1985b: 226).

5. In the legal realm, the imperialists stimulated their Muslim agents to replace the *Sharî'a*, i.e. Muslim legal system, by European legal systems. They claimed that Islam did not and could not deal with a wide horizon of legal questions and current issues ('Amâra 1985b: 226).

6. In order to tame the Muslims, the agents of those imperialists preached a kind of Islam that had to do only with

prayer and the spiritual realm. They claimed that politics should be left to the politicians and religion should not interfere with the non-spiritual ('Amâra 1985b: 227).

7. They planted the state of Israel in the midst of the Muslim world. This was the way the West chose to humiliate, intimidate and crush the Muslims. Israel became the tool, the police state that the West used and uses to punish the Muslims nations whenever it was "necessary." During the days of the Shah, the Israeli Air Force was invited to have their pilots trained in the broad skies of Iran. Israeli goods flooded the Iranian market, while Al-Aqsa mosque in Jerusalem was under Israeli occupation ('Amâra 1985b: 227-228).

8. In commercial deals, natural resources, especially oil, were sold to the West. The profits went to the West and to the ruling class of these small Muslim nations. The rich got richer, and the multitude of the poor got poorer ('Amâra 1985b: 228).

9. On the local scene, strange expressions of the religion of Islam took place. Pietists called for a life of mysticism and sufism. They called themselves holy ones. Al-Khumeini considered them fools who should be confronted with their foolishness. They were standing in the way of progress and reform ('Amâra 1985b: 229).

10.A major blow against Islam was being made by the Muslim religious leaders who were puppets of the rulers. They took their salaries from these "oppressive" governments, and in return they explained Islam in the manner that pleased the rulers. Al-Khumeini stirred his followers to remove these puppets and reveal their rotten motives. They were tools being used to make Islam a passive religion that could not make an impact on the nation ('Amâra 1985b: 230).

The result of all this was the "catastrophe" that the Muslims were living. What was worse than backwardness and the state of dependency on the imperialists was that the Muslims lost their self-esteem and self-respect. "As Muslims," al-Khumeini said, "we have accepted to become marginal people, living like parasites on the West, being ashamed of our religion and culture. We are in a state of estrangement. Just like the prophet who faced a similar estrangement in Mecca, we should revolt against the oppressors, and make out of this revolution a liberating force that would set the Muslims free and give release to the poor and the oppressed" ('Amâra 1985b: 231).

Al-Khumeini's Answer to the Need of the Hour

Because al-Khumeini was able to look courageously and squarely at the situation, he could see the hope that Islam could offer if its force was released. That force would come from revolution. Some of his ideas were new, and some were merely Jaafarite Shiism that he adhered to.

1. The issue of who has the authority was discussed extensively by al-Khumeini. He rejected the notion that the people were the source of authority, as the democracies claimed. Furthermore, authority did not come from royal blood either. For the *Qur'ân* says, "Kings, when they enter a country, despoil it, and make the noblest of its people the meanest. Thus do they behave" (Sûra 27:34). So the right thing to do was to revolt against the existing regimes that claimed to be Muslim, but in reality have nothing to do with Islam ('Amâra 1985b: 231).

2. The source of authority is neither the people, nor the ruler, but God; neither democracy, nor autocracy, but theocracy. God ruled through His prophet and today He should rule through his Imams. Thus all the authority that the prophet had, *al-Imâm al-waṣi* (the trustee), should prevail in all areas of life. The *Imâm* appoints the president of the country, the head of the army, and the head of the parliament. The Islamic government is not autocratic but constitutional, as the *Imâm* follows the principles of the *Qur'ân* and *sunna*. In democratic and autocratic governments, either the people or the head of

the state legislates, whereas in theocracy, God legislates ('Amâra 1985b: 236-237).

3. As for the *taqiyya* principle (quietism), al-Khumeini went against the main stream of Shiism. He distinguishes between the quietism which was practiced for good motives and the type practiced for bad motives. At times it was good to follow the *taqiyya* principle for the sake of preserving religion, but certainly it was not right to hide one's cowardice behind the principle of *taqiyya*. Actually, Muslims should shake themselves off from the passivity and quietism that they have lived under for centuries. For what is there to lose? If the Muslims get killed, the promise for them is paradise. If they get defeated in a battle they are in paradise, because paradise is not for the cowards. If they should win a battle they would also be in paradise, because they could bring about justice. That is the reason why Muslims should never be afraid, because when one is right there is nothing to fear ('Amâra 1985b: 233-244).

4. Islam as a religion is complete, al-Khumeini said. For it covers ethics, worship, social, legal, economic and political spheres. Islam has the principles, the laws and the systems that are sufficient to educate man and bring him to full maturity. He said to his students and followers, "All that you need, you will find in our Islam, whether it has to do with how to run the country, the taxes, the rights, jurisprudence, etc. You do not need new legislations. You need only to put into practice what God has already given you" ('Amâra 1985b: 235).

5. The role of the *Imâm* was unique and important. This concept was behind the success of al-Khumeini's revolution. According to his Shiite doctrine, the prophet had total authority given to him from God to rule and lead the Islamic nation. After him, all the prophet's authority was passed on to the *Imâm*, namely 'Ali, and then to the twelve Imams. In their absence, all the authority that was given to the prophet and to

each of the twelve Imams was given to the *faqîh*. Yet there were two differences between the *Imâm* and the *faqîh*.

(a) The *Imâm* has a unique position and place of importance before God that no *faqîh* could reach, not even prophets and messengers (Muḥammad was an exception).

(b) The *Imâm's* position is created by God, therefore everyone and everything, including atoms, exist in submission to him. The *faqîh* in contrast has his authority over his followers and not over his equals, the *fuqahâ'* ('Amâra 1985b: 239).

With this thinking, a system of hierarchy was established where the *faqîh* who was appointed by God to lead had authority over all other *fuqahâ'*, and thus became *al-Imâm al-waṣi* (the trustee). Al-Khumeini reached this conclusion in his theology as he pragmatically considered the tragedy that could happen to Islam if they had to wait for another millennium for *al-Imâm al-mahdi* to come. He quoted verses from the *Qur'ân* and quoted from the tradition that went along with his pragmatic theology.

Al-Khumeini, the Phenomenon

In June 1989 when al-Khumeini finally died, many in the world had a sigh of relief. Some rejoiced over his death, and yet others by the millions were grieving with such frantic expression of loss, that they risked their lives to tear a little piece of his coffin for the sake of treasuring it. Why is it that some people loved him so much, and others equally hated him ('Amâra 1985b:225-230)?

1. He was a man who lived a lifestyle that was consistent with his theology. He practiced what he taught his students in Iran and his followers during the period of his banishment in Iraq and France. *Al-Ḥukûma Al-Islâmiyya* (The Islamic Government) was a book he had written which was made up of the lectures he taught in his seminary days. This book

served as his program for toppling the Shah and establishing the Islamic revolution in Iran.

2. He faced the issues with courage and honesty. He had no fear of offending the capitalist or the communist blocks. This gave him clear insight and deep understanding of the suffering of the small nations of the Third World.

3. As he looked at the situation with all the corruption, the social injustice and the intimidation of the weak and the poor, he was sure that the messianic hope which the Shiites waited for was not good enough. Living in quietism waiting for *al-mahdi* to come, perhaps after centuries, might ruin Islam. So he came up with his philosophy of revolution built on a theory of *al-Imâma* which gave *al-Imâm al-waṣi* authority and leadership. This theory helped him put into practice what people dreamed of. He showed a model to Muslim Fundamentalists around the world of what could be done.

4. He succeeded in giving the Shiites a sense of identity and dignity. In Lebanon the Shiites were the oppressed, the weak and the poor. Now they are one of the most powerful forces in Lebanon. In Iran, youth by the hundreds of thousands were willing to give their lives on the battlefield over a period of eight years because they loved him. He gave them a sense of worth and significance, thus loyalty to him was spontaneous and real.

5. He dared to challenge the political system of the Muslim world at the risk of becoming unpopular and bitterly hated. No Muslim leader dared in the past to discredit the kings of Saudi Arabia (protectors of the *Ka'ba*) and the *Sheikh* of Al-Azhar, the recognized authorities in Islamic scholarship. The Persian Gulf countries lived under the tension and the terror of the Khumeini's revolution reaching them one day as it had reached the Shah of Iran.

6. When Muḥammad was establishing the Islamic nation at Medîna, he had all the flexibility he needed. Revelation was still in the process of being received, so what he received was appropriate to the situation. The Sunnis and other sects

of Islam today do not have that flexibility. To remain orthodox in their theology, they are limited by the text of the *Qur'ân* and tradition.

The sect of *Shî'a* that al-Khumeini adhered to believes that the *Qur'ân* is the silent or "written word," while the *Imâm* is the spoken or "living word." That theology gives tremendous breadth in scope and flexibility in action. The *umma* at Medîna was dynamically growing because of the flexibility of Muḥammad. Al-Khumeini had a similar opportunity for flexibility and dynamism. The rest of the Muslim states see in the application of the *Sharî'a* something static, limiting and dangerous.

7. He was exclusive in his theology. If Muslims did not believe in his narrow Jaafarite Shiite tradition, they were considered like the Christians and the Jews. He failed to be a "universal" Muslim that could unite the whole Muslim world under his leadership, and thus was only a Jaafarite Shiite Iranian Muslim.

8. How would *al-Imâm al-waṣi* be appointed? What if more than one claimed to have been appointed by God? The revolution in Iran will continue to be a phenomenon worth studying. Perhaps these questions will be answered in the coming years, not only in theory but in practice as well.

9. Is the seed of death already planted into the Iranian revolution by limiting the ultimate leadership to the *fuqahâ'*? Did al-Khumeini put new wine into old wine skins?

10. When *al-Imâm al-waṣi* could not be challenged nor questioned, what would happen to a nation under such a ruler?

Shiism and Islamic Fundamentalism in Egypt

In the two chapters on the Kharijites and the Shiites, I was dealing with the early historical roots of modern Fundamentalism. The Kharijites have ceased to exist. The Shiites, on the other hand, are still continuing as a sect, but not in Egypt. Al-Khumeini in his dynamic interpretation of Shiism, brought to life the old bones. In his revolution he gave new life to the *Shî'a* movement. There are several parallels between Shiism and Egyptian Islamic Fundamentalism. The following are the most important.

1. One of the slogans of Al-Jihâd Fundamentalists these days says, "Islam is a tree that gets nourished with the blood of the martyrs." The suffering, the imprisonment and executions of the Fundamentalists serve as fuel for more recruits and a stronger fire of commitment. As they looked at their tragic past of suffering, intimidation and oppression, the Shiites also saw that they were the unique and special people of God. Their tragic past motivated them to deeper commitment.

2. The best recruits of the Shiite movement, most of the time, were the poor and the oppressed. *Al-Mawâli* had nothing to lose and had a great deal to hope for. Al-Mukhtâr gave them a sense of identity and dignity, so they were willing to give their lives for him. In contrast, the rich, the educated and the well-off were not that impressed with him. In Lebanon, the Shiites lived in the south for decades as the poor, the underprivileged and the oppressed, in contrast to the Maronite Christians and the Sunnis. When *Imâm* Ṣadr appeared in Lebanon, the *Amal* movement spread like fire among the Shiites. The frustrated Iranian youth, who were deprived of the benefits of the rich natural resources of their country, saw al-Khumeini as their hope and dignity, thus becoming fertile soil for the Iranian revolution.

In Egypt today, the students and young graduates who are aspiring for high ideals see nothing promising in the future. Jobs are not available except to the rich and the privileged. Marriage is not plausible except to those who belong to rich families, because of housing problems. The future is bleak and there is nothing to hope for. Therefore, a revolutionary type of Islam could be the solution. These youth are fertile soil for Fundamentalism.

Al-Mukhtâr promised his followers that he was committed to the defense of the weak and to fighting a Holy War against the unjust and the evil doers. Modern Fundamentalists in Egypt are giving the same appeal today and the response to that call is tremendous.

3. One of the distinctives of the Shiites was their need for a charismatic leader. And once they found him, they obeyed him wholeheartedly and lived in total submission to him.

The Fundamentalists in Egypt, although they come from Sunni backgrounds, are like the Shiites. Charismatic leaders who are fearless and courageous are very appealing. These leaders become *umarâ' al-Jamâ'*at (the princes and leaders) and they are obeyed unconditionally.

Watt's hypothesis regarding the early Shiites could well be applicable in Egypt. "In time of stress and tension, men's conduct was controlled by deep-seated urges, varying according to the tradition to which they mainly belonged. In some men, the unconscious urge was to rely on the charismatic leader and they eagerly searched for such a person and when they thought they had found him, they fervently acclaimed him without giving too much thought or evidence of his unsuitability" (Watt 1973: 44).

Egyptian history in the twentieth century has many illustrations to the truth of this hypothesis. Sa'd Zaghlûl as he led a revolution against the British, Ḥasan al-Banna in the 1940s, Jamâl 'Abdul Nâṣer in the 1950s and 1960s, and Sheikh Sha'râwi in the 1970s and 1980s are a few of these charismatic leaders.

4. Another of the distinctives of the Shiites was their use of the *taqiyya* principle (quietism). It was useful for their survival through the centuries when they chose to overtly accept the actual circumstances, while covertly they believed the contrary. In other words, they were willing to lose a battle for the sake of ultimately winning the war. This same principle is applied, more or less, with all the Fundamentalist

groups today to varying degrees. Whenever circumstances get very tough, many of the Fundamentalists go underground. Actually, in their philosophy, going underground meant the modern term for *taqiyya* and was one of the stages necessary for gaining strength and becoming ready for the Islamic revolution.

5. Another side of the coin to the *taqiyya* principle (quietism) is courage and active insurrection. Al-Khumeini warned against the misuse of the *taqiyya* principle as a coverup for cowardice and passivity. Going underground should not mean despair, but being prepared and getting ready for the Islamic revolution. This is the view of the Fundamentalists today. Although there could be disagreement among the various groups regarding the timing for the active insurrection, there is certainly agreement that the revolution is needed.

6. Like al-Khumeini, Fundamentalists look at the West and see imperialists who want to keep the Muslim world divided, weak and intimidated. They see that the main motive of the West for giving aid to these small Muslim nations is self-interest. The West wants the Muslims to remain dependent, whether through the sale of arms or through their economic policy. The West is seen to have bought through bribes the allegiance of some Egyptians who serve as the agents of the imperialists. Together, they sap the resources of the country.

7. Like al-Khumeini, the Fundamentalists see the West as the one who planted Israel in the heart of the Muslim world. They see that the United States supports Israel unconditionally and intimidates the Muslims by considering Israel as the police state to punish any country that dares to challenge or revolt against the policies of the West.

8. Like al-Khumeini, the Fundamentalists look at the religious leaders in Islam who are supported financially by the government, as the puppets of the regime. They do not recognize their authority and they despise their "hypocrisy."

9. Like al-Khumeini, the Fundamentalists see that Muslims have lost their self-esteem and self-respect. They live like parasites on the West, being ashamed of their religion and culture. They are in a state of estrangement. Like the prophet in Mecca who faced that estrangement, Muslims today should revolt against the oppressors.

10.Like al-Khumeini, the Fundamentalists believe that there should be a return to theocracy like the days of Muḥammad in Medîna. Their famous slogan says, "*lâ ḥukma illa li-llâh*," only God is Sovereign. The *Sharî'a* should be followed, because it is God's complete and perfect system for how nations should be run.

11.The Fundamentalists, to a lesser degree than al-Khumeini, still have room for freedom to interpret the text of the *Qur'ân* in a new and fresh perspective. That relative freedom gives them flexibility, authority and recognition. Unlike the "ordained" Muslim leaders who are stuck within the narrow walls of dead and impotent orthodoxy, the Fundamentalists speak and act with authority and power.

These are but a few of the similarities between the Shiites and the Fundamentalists in Egypt. The doctrinal background of these Fundamentalists is the Sunni sect. Al-Khumeini indicated that Fundamentalists are far more like Shiites than Sunnis.

In the coming section, several chapters will deal with the contemporary trends in Fundamentalism, starting with the Muslim Brotherhood and ending with Al-Jihâd movement.

PART THREE

CONTEMPORARY TRENDS IN FUNDAMENTALISM

5

THE MUSLIM BROTHERHOOD (ḤASAN AL-BANNA)

The Muslim Brotherhood has been the largest Fundamentalist group in Egypt and the Arab world. Its history is the longest, since it started in 1928, and is still continuing today. This organization is strongly linked with the name of its founder Ḥasan al-Banna. Although he was assassinated in 1949, his books are still some of the most popular books among the Islamic youth who are in a state of resurgence and are going back to the roots, the fundamentals of Islam.

In this chapter we will present the Muslim Brotherhood organization with its founder until the year of his assassination.

The Climate into Which Al-Banna Grew

Historical Events

Ḥasan al-Banna was born in 1906 in a village called al-Maḥmûdiya, about one hundred and fifty kilometers north of Cairo. The events that took place during his youth shook Egypt, and some even influenced the mind and the conscience of the Egyptians. Among those who were deeply influenced was Ḥasan al-Banna.

1. In 1914 World War I started with Britain and Turkey taking sides in the war, yet both countries had "interests" in Egypt, to say the least.

2. In 1917 the Belfour Declaration was signed in Britain, preparing Palestine to become the permanent home for the Jews. Their advent into Palestine was not as Jewish people coming to live in that country under the existing governments, but as a Zionist, nationalist, sectarian state. This was a blow for the Arabs, and they have not been able to recover from it. The existence of Israel as a Zionist state in the midst of the Arab Muslim world was and is still "a dashing force against the dreams, aspirations and hopes of the Arab *umma* preventing it from progress, unity and liberation" ('Amâra 1985a: 43).

3. In 1919 the Egyptians united together in a new way against the British. This took place when an Egyptian delegation wanted to go to England to speak for the rights and demands of the Egyptian people to the British government. The British did not give any recognition or weight to this nationalistic Egyptian spirit, and they prevented the delegation from going to England. Furthermore, they banished three *al-Wafd* (delegation leaders). As a result, the "whole" of Egypt, as it were, stood up against the British. There were the students, the workers, the peasants, but most important, the Christians stood side by side with the Muslims. Somehow, the Christians sensed that their place of belonging was with Muslim Egypt rather than with the "Christian" colonialists.

The demonstrations were led by Muslim and Christian religious leaders as they marched arm in arm in the streets of Cairo. It was a clear message to the British, that Christians did not need their protection, and to the Muslims that Copts are authentic Egyptians. I will refer to the significance of this event later.

4. In March 1924, the Islamic caliphate was abolished as Kamâl Ataturk desired to make out of Turkey a modern European state. The last Muslim Caliph Ṣultân 'Abdul Majîd was banished and the Symbol of the Muslim *umma* was removed. Not only the "content" of the caliphate was missing, but now also the "form" was discarded. This event was a

heavy blow to the Muslims who saw the caliph as a remaining sign of unity in the Islamic world. Perhaps they felt like the Catholics would feel if the Papacy was abolished.

5. In 1925 'Ali 'Abdul Râzeq, a graduate from Al-Azhar, published a book called *Al-Islâm Wa 'Uṣûl Ḥukm.* In this book, he gave a thorough study on the issue of the caliphate and tried to prove from the *Qur'ân*, as well as from the *hadîth*, that the caliphate is not Qur'anic. He gave theological legitimacy to what Ataturk did in Turkey, namely abolishing the caliphate.

This book made a large explosion in the intellectual and religious circles in Egypt. Even the uneducated who only heard about the book were shaken. The man was discredited and the book was confiscated.

6. In 1926, Ṭâha Ḥusein published a book called *Fi Shi'r Al-Jâhili* (Pre-Islamic Poetry) in which he used a critical approach of study in analyzing the *jâhiliyya* poetry. In doing so, he placed question marks on the authenticity of this poetry. He went further and tried to study some of the narratives in the *Qur'ân*, like the story of Abraham, with the same approach. This brought about a storm and the book was confiscated. However, the impact continued to shake the foundations of the Muslims and contributed a great deal to the confrontation that was taking place between those who were calling for a return to the caliphate and those who were calling for an enlightenment and open-mindedness.

A Call for the Return of the Caliphate

In the second half of the nineteenth century, the ideas for Islamic unity were crystalized and they greatly contributed to the Islamic resurgence in the twentieth century. The leading figure at that time was Jamâl Dîn al-Afghâni, a philosopher from Afghanistan who travelled and lived in various countries, including Iran and Egypt. From these countries, his influence spread in many parts of the Islamic world.

He was deeply aware of Islam's great heritage during its years of glory, and at the same time he was aware of the factors that brought about regression and decline. He called for a resurgence, so that Islam could face the challenge coming from the West in the form of secularism and materialism ('Amâra 1985a: 25).

In Egypt, 'Abdul 'Azîz Shâwîsh, a leading thinker early in the twentieth century, taught that nationalism and Islam do not go together. Egyptians should demand freedom from the British and should have their own constitution, not within the narrow frame of Egyptian nationalism, but within the larger and only true frame, the Islamic *umma*. This Islamic *umma* is represented by the caliphate. Therefore, the caliphate should be preserved and protected, for in its fall, the whole Islamic world will disintegrate and go into decline (Sa'îd 1977: 24). The caliph is the protector of Islam and the Muslims.

Berger, in his book The Arab World Today, as he reflected on the abolishing of the caliphate in 1924 said, "It destroyed the realistic and geographical foundation of the unity of Islam and brought instead, competitive nationalistic and regional struggles" (Sa'îd 1977: 25).

Immediately after the abolishing of the caliphate, some Egyptian thinkers and Al-Azhar leaders called for a conference to elect a replacement of the banished caliph. The conviction was that Islam, per se, is the nation. It is the Islamic "commonwealth" where all Muslim countries are united together within the boundaries (not geographical) of Islam. Therefore, the caliphate was indispensable. As they called for that conference, their hopes were not only to elect a new caliph, but also to discuss the principles for an Islamic government and an Islamic system of education (Bayûmi 1978: 59).

Wakîl, as he reflected back on this sad history in 1924, came to the conclusion that Britain, in its colonialistic ambition and its awareness of the danger of an Islamic nation, was behind Kamâl Ataturk: shaping his thinking, supporting his secularization of Turkey, and bringing about the collapse of the Muslim dream (Wakîl 1986: 31).

A Call for Enlightenment and Open-mindedness

On one side of the pendulum, there was the call for a return of the caliphate and on the other side there was a call for enlightenment and open-mindedness. These two extremes reacted to one another and caused a greater rift between them.

Ataturk in Turkey made his country into a secular state. He even gave up the use of the Arabic alphabet that was used in the Turkish language and exchanged it for a Latin form of alphabet. He believed that his country was shackled by the bondage of traditional Islam. Once it was set free, there was hope for modernization and progress.

In Egypt, few dared to think like Ataturk, but even fewer dared to express their ideas. Muṣṭafa Kâmel, one of the pioneers of nationalism in Egypt, believed very strongly that Egypt would experience deliverance only when it was set free from both the British colonialists and from the Turkish caliphate. He pointed to the absurdity of those who fight the British in order to evacuate them, only to invite in their place the Turks as the new colonialists. How can the Egyptians ever have independence if they continue to have that mentality (Sa'îd 1977: 23)?

The book of 'Ali 'Abdul Râzeq, the graduate of Al-Azhar, questioned the assumption that Islam is both a religion and a state. He pointed out that the prophet never intended to have either a kingdom or a state. Therefore, Islam should be seen only in the sphere of religion and should not interfere with the matters of the state. Muslims can live good and true Muslim lives without having to have a caliph. He goes on to say, "Actually, the caliphate has been a catastrophe in Islam, and a source of evil and corruption" ('Abdul Râzeq [sa]: 83).

Ṭâha Ḥusein, after earning his doctorate at the Sorbonne in Paris, returned to Egypt to teach at the Cairo University. In his teaching he advocated the use of academic, scientific and objective methods for research and study. Unlike the "narrow-minded" approach that his teachers at Al-Azhar used, he wanted his students and fellow teachers to catch up with the West and be unshackled from the bondage of heavy traditions and superficiality. Those who called for "open-mindedness" were either graduates from universities in the West or had studied in schools and universities that Christian western missions erected in Egypt. Those men believed that the western culture could contribute to Egypt modern alternatives to replace the traditional outdated Islamic values. These western modern principles produced human rights, parliaments, constitutions, specialization, industry and progress in the West. As long as religion and the state are fused together like the Holy Roman Empire, there will be no hope for progress. However, according to those westernized modernists, once religion and state are separated then there is hope for modernization (Bayûmi 1979: 23).

'Amâra criticized both extremes when he pointed out that the "pro-Ottoman" believed that the way to defend oneself from the invasion of the western culture is to go into a shell. These people recruited the masses and invited them to a life of dependency, blindness and regression back to the time of the Mamluks.

The "westernized," on the other hand, appealed to the elite who were impressed and overwhelmed with the civilization of the invader. They believed that the way to recovery was by imitating the West, irrespective of what the distinctives of the Egyptian Muslim culture were. The way to get unshackled from the Ottoman traditionalism, according to the westernized thought, is through becoming European: think like them, live like them, and even copy their mistakes ('Amâra 1985a: 16, 26).

Colonialism

Another main aspect of the climate into which Ḥasan al-Banna grew had to do with the West. The British were the hated colonialists. Christian Europe sent Protestant missionaries to proselytize and erect schools. All this resulted in westernization, whether religious, secular or materialistic, and contributed to humiliating the Muslims and dishonoring the Islamic culture.

Egypt could tolerate the long Ottoman despotic rule, because the caliph was a Turk, and the Turkish rulers of Egypt were Muslims. On the other hand, to face Christian European colonialism was intolerable. The French did not last long in Egypt; only three years ending in 1801. Their motives appeared to be acceptable, at least at the beginning, but the British, right from the start, were seen as despots and opportunists using Egypt, among other things, to protect their routes to India.

Sa'îd, in his book *Ḥasan al-Banna*, quotes a European philosopher who describes religiosity as a "lightning rod." It serves a major purpose by protecting the rulers from social revolts. Religion is a force like the police force or the army, but even more effective and less expensive than both. Religion places a policeman inside the human being, and this policeman can be manipulated by the state to direct the citizens into its schemes and plans (Sa'îd 1977: 46). Sa'îd observed that the British were quite aware of this fact, and they opposed Islam when needed or manipulated it when it was useful.

Bayûmi points out that the British policy during the occupation time was focused on discrediting Islam as a primitive religion which stood against modernization and progress. Associating it with the Ottoman caliphate led to backwardness. So, the British used nationalism as a whip to beat Islam with. Furthermore, the insensitivity of the British soldiers to the values, customs and traditions of the Muslim

Egyptians greatly aggravated and humiliated the Egyptians. In their sense of honor and dignity, the Egyptians sensed that they were defending their country from another Crusader attack (Bayûmi 1979: 20, 34).

Another area where the British manipulated the country was through sowing seeds of discord among the Egyptians. They succeeded in convincing the politicians in Egypt of the importance of having a parliament and competing as political parties. This was presented as a sign of democracy and civilization. The Egyptian politicians fell right into that trap. Instead of being a united front, they split into parties and competed in the elections for the parliament thinking that they were reaching the seats of power, where, in reality the power was in the hands of the British. Furthermore, the constitution that was brought from Europe was foreign and not authentic (Bayûmi 1979: 42).

Ḥasan al-Banna's first hand experience with the British took place at Ismâ'îliyya. He described vividly the situation in that city, as well as his feelings and responses. He described the English camp with its power, authority and exclusiveness. He went on to describe the headquarters of the Suez Canal Company with the beautiful offices and the power it had in taking full advantage of the canal. He described the beautiful houses of the British, the beautiful streets, clubs and gardens. He brought to light the tremendous contrast with the Egyptians. The British were the people in power, the intelligent, the clean and the civilized, while the Egyptians were the poor, the illiterate and the meek workmen who were humiliated and manipulated. The British were in control of the electricity, the water and the policing of the city, while the Egyptians lived under the mercy of the British.

Al-Banna felt very deeply the sense of sadness and sorrow regarding what his beloved country had become. He saw in the British the main obstacle that was preventing Egypt from awakening. He also saw the British as an obstacle that had prevented the Arab Muslims from uniting together over a period of sixty years (Al-Banna 1966: 84).

Wakîl saw the British as a power that manipulated to its advantage the politics of the whole Middle East, from Turkey to Egypt, playing as it were a chess game (Wakîl 1986: 31).

Finally, since Egypt was under the British mandate, this opened the door wide for Protestant evangelism in Egypt. Missions came in with security and safety knowing the British were the ones who were really in control.

Protestant Evangelism

It did so happen, as Ḥasan al-Banna says, that in many places where there were Muslim Brotherhood branches, there were in these same places Protestant missionaries and Protestant schools. This put al-Banna right in the climate of a confrontation with the missions.

All the books written by Muslim authors, at my disposal, are in general agreement about the negative effects of missionaries during the first half of this century. Sa'îd claimed that the main goal of Protestant missionary work was to sidetrack the Egyptians from fighting the colonialists and become involved in side issues, such as sectarianism, which would exhaust the time and the energy of the Egyptians. He seemed to imply that the missionaries were the agents of the British colonialists, or perhaps were unconsciously used by the British as a "lightning rod" to absorb the Egyptian resistance.

He then goes on to say that the strategy of the West was to create beachheads among the Christian minority from which to raid the Muslim population and proselytize.

Then he pointed out that the Protestants had questionable relationships with the foreign powers and embassies. They seemed to work under the umbrellas of these foreign powers. Bayûmi pointed out that these foreign Protestants were not even accepted by their fellow Christians—the Copts. The

Copts were authentic Egyptians (as was seen in the Revolt of 1919), but these Protestants and even their converts were "foreign" to the culture (Bayûmi 1978: 303).

Sa'îd then says that this missionary work aggravated the Muslims and helped produce a strong reaction of reverse proselytizing. This incubated germs of prejudice and hatred between Christians and Muslims (Sa'îd 1977: 28-30, 60). Bayûmi went on to say that the Muslim Egyptians' desire for a return to the Ottoman caliphate grew stronger. Since the occupants were European Christians and the missionaries were also European Christians, it was understandable why the Muslims yearned for the Ottoman days.

Another factor that added to the frustration of the Muslims was the attitude and the strategy of these missionaries. Their aim was to proselytize the Muslims. Their attitude was that Christianity was superior and Islam inferior. Their strategy was to build schools and attract girls and families that were vulnerable, either because of poverty or because of lack of exposure and lack of self-confidence (Wakîl 1986: 71).

The other side of the strategy of all foreign missions, whether Protestant or Catholic, was to erect schools and attract the rich to send their children to study in these schools. Through this strategy they were partially successful in westernizing Muslims and making them despise their own religion and culture. Bayûmi concludes that this mission work was quite close to being another Crusader invasion (Bayûmi 1979: 17, 302-303).

Ḥasan al-Banna was so furious with what was happening that he, with his leadership team, drafted a letter to King Fu'âd. In this letter they requested the following:

1. Enforce strong censorship and control on schools and mission centers that showed evidence of evangelism being carried out.

2. Withdraw work permits of all schools and hospitals that carried out evangelism.

3. Send any foreigner who was evangelizing out of the country.

4. Prevent these mission societies from buying land or raising support from within Egypt.

5. Communicate these requests with all government officials, so that the execution of the above four points would be put into practice.

Carbon copies of this document were sent to the Prime Minister, the Minister of Interior, the Minister of Education, the Minister of Religious Affairs and the Head of the Parliament (Al-Banna 1966: 181-182).

Although we do not know what the results of this document were, it at least communicated to the leadership of Egypt how the Muslim Brotherhood viewed the threat of Protestant evangelism.

Westernization

As the Egyptian nation was beginning to wake up from the long sleep brought about by the Turkish influence, there was a race taking place between two powers for who would fill that vacuum. On the one hand, there was the Islamic resurgence that was taking place through men like Afghâni, Shâwîsh and others, and on the other hand there was the western culture that came to invade Egypt. According to 'Amâra and Ḥasan al-Banna, the western culture won that race and westernization started penetrating the soul and inner being of the Muslim Egyptian.

This westernization process contributed to wiping out the national character and destroying Egypt's Muslim cultural distinctive, or at least distorting it. The purpose of westernization was to make Egypt a subject of European society, militarily, economically, politically and, most important of all, culturally ('Amâra 1985a: 17). As the British came in, they "bought" the raw materials at the cheapest rates. They made Egypt a market for their products. Egypt offered them the cheap labor they needed, and they used Egypt for their military bases ('Amâra 1985a: 44). Their goal was to keep Egypt as a "colony" forever, even if they had to leave one day. They were quite sure and confident of their weapons, the most important of which, in the long run, was westernization.

Afghâni, who made his impact on Egypt towards the end of the nineteenth century, was quite aware of the dangers of westernization. He pointed out that the traitor is not only the one who "sells" his country for his personal gain, but also the one who allows the western invader to put his foot in the door. He persuaded the Egyptians to fight the enemy on all fronts, whether on military, economic, governmental or the management levels. But above all, he persuaded them not to allow the western nations to take any privileges that were usually given to foreigners, such as land, buildings, water, etc. ('Amâra 1985a: 31, 36).

According to 'Amâra, the western culture came in various shapes and colors. It came as capitalism or socialism, and it also came as materialism and secularism. With capitalism, the focus was on the individual and his achievement. This led to individualism, greed, love of power, manipulation and social injustice. Socialism and communism, on the other hand, were a reaction to the social injustices that the capitalism produced. The reaction was no better than the action ('Amâra 1985a: 34).

The "religion" was more dangerous than the economic, political and social systems. Materialism is the "religion" of the West. Its danger is not only on the countries that they have colonized, but also on their own countries and humanity. "The western culture," 'Amâra says, "is a culture with one leg. It emphasized progress in science, technology, specialization in education, industry, etc., but ignores the other leg, which is God and spiritual values. They have missed out 'on the grace that by faith they can have the sense of belongingness to the rest of the universe'" ('Amâra 1985a: 32, 50, 51).

Ḥasan al-Banna pointed out that the moral deterioration in the West was caused by their lack of spirituality. He went into great length in describing the various evidences of this deterioration (Al-Banna [sa]: 59-60, 138).

The other change that came in with the western culture was secularism. "In the West, the domination of the clergy over the people, had to produce an explosion. So the people revolted against the clergy and declared their independence in the form of secularism. In Egypt the situation was different, because Islam is different." 'Amâra goes on to say, "Islam does not give power to the clergy like Catholicism does, but the fooled Egyptians imported the European problem and the European solution to it as well" ('Amâra 1985a: 52).

Those who were fooled were the intellectuals who studied in the West or graduated from schools in Egypt that were erected by western missions. Those intellectuals had a very superficial knowledge and understanding of their heritage and religion. They could see only the corruption that the Mamluk period produced. Furthermore, the influence of the orientalists was great on these intellectuals. They presented Islam to the intellectuals in a negative way, and whatever positives existed in Islam, the orientalists claimed, originated in Greek philosophy.

The other factor was the western universities which introduced these intellectuals to the "gospel" of western education ('Amâra 1985a: 36). Al-Banna described the graduates of these schools and universities as men who were ashamed of their religion, culture, traditions and language, glorying in whatever was western. He distinguished between fruitful cultural interaction with the West versus adopting the shallow imitation and absorption of whatever was western (Al-Banna [sa]: 97-98).

Another danger of secularism is its being universal and international. Not only that, but also its being associated with liberalism and open-mindedness increased its appeal. The sad fact that Egyptians were not aware of was that cultures cannot be transplanted. Once the western culture was plucked off from the West and planted in Egypt, what grew up was empty form with no content (‘Amâra 1985a: 36).

Inner Struggles and Maneuvering

As Ḥasan al-Banna graduated from school and moved to Ismâ‘îliyya, then later to Cairo, and as he visited large parts of Egypt, he was thoroughly exposed to the political, social and religious climate of the time. In the earlier part of this chapter, we looked at the various facets of this climate that al-Banna was exposed to. Now we need to look at the inner struggles and maneuvering that were taking place. The palace, in the person of King Fu’âd, the government, the Copts, Al-Azhar and the political parties were all, with the British, involved in a game called politics. All of the struggles and maneuvering convinced Ḥasan al-Banna of the need of the hour and burned deep convictions within him regarding his call.

To start with, several political parties began forming right after World War I, and these parties represented various trends. Some were for the Islamic league that Afghâni propagated, others for a moderate trend were led by Muḥammad ‘Abdu with Sa‘d Zaghlûl. The former encouraged a revolt against the British with no compromise, the latter was pragmatic and open to negotiate with the British until the British left. All the political parties, whether they had the approval of the palace, the government, the British or the masses, fell short of achieving the ultimate goal which was independence from the British. Actually Bayûmi declared that all of these parties reached bankruptcy (Watt 1979: 38,43).

Al-Banna saw in the political party system an evil influence on the Egyptians. It corrupted the people, broke down social relationships and infected the country with strife. He questioned the wisdom of having several parties when one party could do the job without doing the damage. He pointed out that there was a difference between freedom and democracy and party spirit and strife (Al-Banna [sa]: 180).

Looking back at the picture that Sa'îd used, we see that religion was like a "lightning rod" that could absorb social revolts, provided it was used and manipulated toward that end. There was some truth to that in what happened in Egypt.

In 1924, King Fu'âd, with his aides, tried to maneuver Al-Azhar to plan a conference for the Muslim nations in the world to elect a new caliph. It was advantageous to both King Fu'âd and Al-Azhar if he were elected, but other Muslim nations suspected these hidden motives and the plans collapsed. Furthermore, the relationship between the palace and Al-Azhar continued all the days of the reign of King Fu'âd. So when the king was under the influence of the British, Al-Azhar came under that influence as well, and when the king wanted to put the Prime Minister under pressure, he used Al-Azhar to that end (Sa'îd 1977: 49).

The Copts were feeling insecure because of the Islamic League that Afghâni propagated. They sensed that if the *Sharî'a* which the Muslims were calling for replaced the Egyptian constitution, then the Copts would end up paying taxes as *ahl dhimma*, and not as fellow citizens with equal rights. Some of them called for an Egyptian nationalism based on the pharaonic past. Others called for an African unity rather than an Arab unity or an Islamic league. This produced some friction which appeared in newspaper articles and further increased the Copts' fears (Bayûmi 1979: 311). Some Muslims claimed that the Copts' fears and ideas were motivated by foreign embassies and especially the British. Other Muslims tried to assure the Copts of what the *Qur'ân* taught about *ahl al-kitâb*, and how the Christians had been treated in the history of Islam in Egypt.

Al-Wafd party which followed the secular route recruited most of the Copts to its lines. Al-Azhar, because of its lack of dynamism, lost most of its students and graduates to political and religious parties that offered hope and dynamic involvement.

This was the climate to which Ḥasan al-Banna was exposed and served as the stage set for one of the greatest Egyptians who lived in the twentieth century.

Ḥasan Al-Banna

The First Twenty Years of His Life

Ḥasan al-Banna was born in 1906 in the delta north of Cairo into a devout Muslim family. His father was the *Imâm* of the village mosque, studied at Al-Azhar during the days of Muḥammad ʻAbdu and was a watchmaker by trade. His father, throughout his life, loved to read and continued learning. He wrote a few books on the *hadîth*. Ḥasan was the eldest of five sons. From the age of eight to twelve, Ḥasan joined the *kuttâb* of his village where children were encouraged to memorize the *Qur'ân*. At the age of 12, he joined the regular school and in his first year joined the first of many religious societies and was encouraged by his teacher who had an influence upon his life. The name of the first group was the "Society for Moral Behavior," which was for the purpose of self-discipline and living good moral lives. Soon he became the leader of this society (Sa'îd 1977: 53).

Soon, with some of his friends who exhibited a deeper level of dedication, he formed a new group called "The Society for the Forbidden" for the purpose of reaching deeper into city life and pressuring city dwellers to avoid the forbidden.

During this period, he joined a mystic circle called "The Order of Ḥaṣâfiyya Brothers" as well, and thus was introduced to Sufism which made an impact upon him throughout the rest of his life. He came to know another teenager in this mystic circle of men by the name of Aḥmad Sukkari who later became a co-founder of the Muslim Brotherhood.

He discovered that Sufism was not enough, action was needed. So, with his mates, he formed a new organization called "The Ḥaṣâfiyya Society for Charity." It had two goals: preserving Islamic teaching and resisting the missionaries (Sa'îd 1979: 54).

During his last year at primary school, the outbreak of the revolution of 1919 took place. He joined the demonstration against the British and expressed his nationalistic zeal in the form of poetry with passion (Mitchel 1977: 18).

At the age of 14, he joined the Teachers' Training School at Damanhûr, a town north of Cairo, and was highly influenced by the teachings in Abu Hamîd al-Ghazzâli's book *Ihyâ' 'Ulûm Dîn*. By this time he became fully permeated with the teachings of Sufism.

In 1923 he joined *Dâr al-'Ulûm* (College of Science) in Cairo. As he watched Cairo with the religious eyes of a villager, he was both shocked and moved. Sleepless nights of pondering over the problems of the nation brought down tears of shame and sorrow. The 1920s were years of intense political and intellectual ferment. Political parties were in strife, bringing about disunity. Ataturk's revolt in Turkey encouraged the trend of secularism which attacked the tradition of Orthodoxy and the fundamentals of Islam. All of this, with many other factors, was the climate that al-Banna faced and was like a culture shock to him as he lived in Cairo.

During this period he arrived at a deep conviction that the mosques alone cannot make an impact on the society. Therefore he organized a group of students from Al-Azhar and *Dâr al-'Ulûm* and started training them in teaching, preaching and guidance. They were available to speak at mosques, but more importantly at coffee-houses and other popular meeting places.

Some of these students were sent out to villages and towns as resident lay preachers and teachers. So the "para-mosque" idea came into existence in Egypt among the Muslims as he purposed to bridge the gap between the day-to-day practical living and the teaching and preaching of Islam (Sa'îd 1977: 56).

In his final year at *Dâr al-'Ulûm*, his class was asked to write an essay on the subject, "Explain your great hopes after the completion of your studies, and show how you will prepare yourselves for their realization." In this essay, al-Banna put down on paper his dreams, ambitions, analysis of the situation and his solemn promise that he would be completely dedicated to God and to this cause. God and his teacher were witnesses to that promise (Mitchell 1977: 22-23).

In 1927 he moved into Ismâ'îliyya to start his work as a teacher of the Arabic language in the government primary school. There, he began his call and vocation and the Muslim Brotherhood was born.

Ḥasan Al-Banna - The Charismatic Initiator

Ḥasan al-Banna was not one of those who "sat still" and hoped things would get better. Nor was he a man who rationalized and made excuses for the state of corruption and deterioration that Egypt had reached. On the contrary, he was a man who knew the people. He visited them, lived with them, knew their agonies and analyzed the causes for their suffering. Their suffering became his suffering and their hopes and dreams became his goals.

He worked as a teacher, and therefore had the flexibility during the summer months to travel and get acquainted, through firsthand experience, with what the people were going through. Although the summer months were quite hot, especially in the south of Egypt, he travelled by train, boat, car and donkey to towns and villages all over the south. He went to places where he knew no one.

If he discovered that there were feuds and competition among the leading families in a village, he stayed with the poor so that he would not be forced to take sides. If he, on the other hand, was invited to stay at the home of an influential person in another village, he would use that home as a platform to preach the relevance of the fundamentals of Islam. If nobody invited him, he would sleep at the mosque, using his little case as his pillow.

Over the months and years, he came to know individuals, families, relationships and names by the thousands. Actually, all the books at my disposal agree that he had "personal" relationships with tens of thousands. Many could boast of the fact that they were personal friends of Ḥasan al-Banna. Sa'îd says that the wide net of personal relationships that al-Banna had was the real cause of his success as a leader (1977: 72).

He learned to speak with people in their own languages. He knew the accents and dialects of the various parts of Egypt, and he knew the vocabulary of the rich, the poor, the educated, the peasants and the workers. As he visited the south, he wore a white robe like everybody else, made himself approachable, and incorporated within himself the suffering of the people—his people. Thus, he became their spokesman, their friend, their relative and their leader.

No wonder, then, that he had sleepless nights pondering the state to which "his people," and his beloved country reached. He analyzed the causes and came up with answers and a strategy. His analysis of the situation was not puritan or worldly. It was rather comprehensive, for it included the various dimensions, such as the social, the economical, the political, the historical and the religious. Therefore, his answers were comprehensive and found their full scope in Islam.

Islam, for him, was a state, a place of belongingness, a nation and a government. Islam was the record of creation, of God's power, His mercy and justice. It was a culture and a code of justice. It included guidance on how to deal with money, how to make it and how to dispose of it, how to possess it, but not get possessed by it. Islam was not only a holy war *(jihâd)*, a call and an army, but was also a pure doctrine and a system of worship (in Bayûmi 1979: 141).

In his view, the Muslim should be like a "monk" at night, praying and worshipping, but during the day like a "knight," courageous, strong and involved. If Muslims got satisfied with a life of prayer and worship, and left the matters of politics, administration and government to people who were corrupt, that would be escapism and not Islam. Islam is *dîn wa dunya* (religion and life). Politics, holy war and social involvement are in the heart of Islam, and the Muslim who does not believe in that is shortsighted.

Ḥasan al-Banna was not "shortsighted," but followed a comprehensive strategy to implement Islam and make it relevant. As soon as he started his teaching in the primary school in Ismâ'îliyya, he started teaching in the mosques and the coffee houses as well. With an attractive style of preaching and teaching, he presented the fundamentals of Islam as the need of the hour. Those eager ones who stayed behind asking questions, demonstrating genuine desire for learning, he took aside and formed groups. Those small groups were for discipleship, and out of these groups he believed the future leadership would one day emerge.

There were other dimensions to his strategy as well. Not only did he reach people who went to the mosques, coffee houses and meeting places, but he also had his eyes on the key and influential people in the city. He knew that once these men responded to the call, their followers would come as well.

Another dimension to his strategy was seen at Ismâ'îliyya and was repeated in several other places in Egypt. He raised money and built a mosque, then a center, then a school for boys, then a school for girls, then a club. In some places he had a clinic and an economic project as well. He attempted to create a model where a Muslim could experience the totality of Islam in a genuine setting (Sa'îd 1977: 61, 94-95).

His objective in the first three to four years was expansion, and he gave himself to that task. Although he was wholehearted in Ismâ'îliyya, he did not forget Cairo. His eyes were on Cairo, its sins and its hopes (Mitchel 1977: 27). When the right time came, he moved to Cairo and established the headquarters of the Muslim Brotherhood there. From Cairo, expansion spread to many parts of Egypt, while at the same time the framework of the structure of the organization was growing. In his strategy, he had a thorough system of discipleship and leadership development that we will get into later in this chapter. His vision was clear, he aimed for the individual. His aim was to help him become a real Muslim, in his relationship with God and in his relationship with those around him. The next circle was the family, then the following circle was the society. And once you had a truly Muslim society, sooner or later the government would follow the *Sharî'a* and the whole country would live under Islamic rule. Al-Banna then looked further, not only to Egypt and the Arab world, but to the whole Muslim world, the Islamic nation. The next circle in his vision included countries that used to be Muslim but had turned away from Islam, such as Andalos in Spain. Finally, the whole world needed to know about Islam, for in it was the hope for humanity (Al-Banna [sa]: 85-86).

His vision was not building castles in the air, but was implemented by action and practical steps. He knew, for instance, that the army was a key and influential segment of the strategy. So he gave the time and the effort to think through how he could penetrate it. Articles were written defending the abused soldiers who were manipulated by some officers as domestic helpers. These articles won the hearts of the troops. Furthermore, al-Banna was always anxious to take advantage of ceremonies, social get-togethers and celebrations of religious occasions, to be there, to speak and to meet officers and high ranks. At one of these occasions Sâdât heard him and was impressed, and later sought him (Bayûmi 1979: 246).

Although his strategy and vision included the use of violence when necessary and to resort to revolution at the right time, he still managed not to alienate the masses. Part of the reason was his non-judgemental attitude. Unlike other Fundamentalist group leaders, he did not declare that the whole society was apostate ('Amâra 1985a: 59, 80).

Bayûmi quotes an American writer named Robert Jackson who interviewed Ḥasan al-Banna in the 1930s.

> This week I visited a man who might become one of the greatest men in current history, or he could go into the shadows, if circumstances prove to be too big for him. Although he spoke no English, he was empowering. He was kind, quiet, secure and very confident in the truth of his convictions and the legitimacy of his aspirations. If he takes over the leadership one day, it will not be only in Egypt but in the whole East as well. This man believed that Islam was a force which dwelt in the conscience and inner being of the East, and therefore Islam could give to that part of the world, life and dynamism (Bayûmi 1979: 76).

The Man and the Organization

Identity and Uniqueness of the Muslim Brotherhood

In March 1928 in Ismâ'îliyya, six men who worked at the British camp came to al-Banna. Their words were descriptive of the level of loyalty, obedience, availability and the depth of relationship that existed between al-Banna and his followers. Mitchell pointed out that what these men actually said could not be verified, but it served the purpose of showing the type of loyalty that was evidenced by the men and desired by the leader. With the statement of these six men, the Muslim Brotherhood organization was born. Al-Banna said that these men came to him, and after thanking him for his teaching said,

> We have heard and we have become aware and we have been affected. We know not the practical way to reach the glory *('izza)* of Islam and to serve the welfare of Muslims. We are weary of this life of humiliation

> and restriction. Lo, we see the Arabs and the Muslims have no *manzila* (status) and no *karâma* (dignity). They are not more than mere hirelings belonging to the foreigners. We possess nothing but this blood...and these souls...and these few coins.... We are unable to perceive the road to action as you perceive it, or to know the path to the service of the fatherland, the religion and the nation as you know it. All that we desire now is to present you with all that we possess, to be acquitted by God of the responsibility, and for you to be responsible before Him for us and for what we must do. If a group contracts with God sincerely that it lives for His religion and dies in His service, seeking only His satisfaction, then its worthiness will assure its success, however small its numbers or weak its means (Mitchell 1969: 8).

Al-Banna accepted the responsibility very seriously and the men took an oath to God to be "soldiers for the message of Islam." As they wondered about what they should call themselves, al-Banna said, "We are brothers." Therefore, they decided to call themselves "the Muslim Brotherhood."

Although what these men said could not be verified, especially that they spoke it rather than wrote it, though al-Banna wrote it down at a later date, it is quite significant for the following reasons:

1. These men echoed and reflected what al-Banna had been teaching and preaching. He "reached their souls." It was a test to show how much he had communicated and to what depth.

2. These men began to see the situation of Egypt, the Arabs and the Muslims from his perspective.

3. They were moved and stirred enough to the point of getting unshackled from their state of "sitting still," to a state of righteous indignation.

4. They recognized that al-Banna was a man with a special calling and vision. He could see what they could not see.

5. They trusted him and believed that he was sent to them by God.

6. They were willing to live and die for God, and this commitment level was demonstrated by loyalty and obedience to al-Banna. Obeying al-Banna was obeying God who sent al-Banna to be their leader.

7. Since al-Banna gave so much importance to this incident, it must have seemed as the perfect model of loyalty and obedience.

Al-Banna relied heavily on the writings of Mawdûdi regarding the type of the relationship that should exist between leader and followers. He became fully convinced that it was not the majority that made a decision right or wrong. It was what goes in line with God's will and God's leading, irrespective of the majority. Al-Banna took from Mawdûdi as well *qasam al-bay'a* (the oath of loyalty). The contents of the oath and the setting at which it was taken were both significant. The content of the oath pointed to the depth of loyalty and obedience that were demanded, while the setting of the oath contributed to the seriousness of that decision. At times the men would take the oath by putting their hands on the *Qur'ân* and a pistol in a dark room, in the presence of al-Banna (Sa'îd 1977: 78-79).

Regarding the identity of the Muslim Brotherhood, al-Banna wrote a letter of farewell in 1943, thinking that the British were planning to banish him in the near future. In this letter *(wathîqa)* he warned his followers of the persecution which was coming and lifted up their morale by clarifying to them their identity. He said:

> My brothers: you are not a benevolent society, nor a political party, nor a local organization having limited purposes. Rather, you are a new soul in the heart of this nation to give it life by means of the *Qur'ân*, you are a new light which shines to destroy the darkness of materialism through knowing God; and you are the strong voice which rises to recall the message of the

> prophet.... You should feel yourselves the bearers of the burden which all others have refused. When asked what it is for which you call, reply that it is Islam, the message of Muhammad, the religion that contains within it government, and has freedom as one of its obligations. If you are told that you are political, answer that Islam admits no such distinction. If you are accused of being revolutionaries, say 'We are voices for right and for peace in which we dearly believe, and of which we are proud. If you rise against us or stand in the path of our message, then we are permitted by God to defend ourselves against your injustice....' If they insist on pursuing their oppression, say to them, 'Peace be upon you, we will ignore the ignorant' (Mitchell 1969: 30).

In this letter we see how al-Banna conceived the Muslim Brotherhood to be:

1. Although they did benevolent acts, and were involved in politics, etc., that did not make them a benevolent society or a political party. They were far more than that. They were "the new soul in the heart of the nation to give it life by means of the *Qur'ân*...."

2. The Muslim Brotherhood was a risky task that demanded courage unto death. It was a task that all others shrank from because of fear or lack of conviction.

3. The Muslim Brotherhood Society was the voice of Islam. It was on the offensive and no one could stand in its way. *Jihâd* revolution was permissible.

With these words and others, al-Banna inspired his followers to see their dignity in being Muslims and belonging to the religion that had the final and ultimate truth. Not only that, they had dignity because they were brothers in a society that was translating the fundamentals of Islam into practical expression in daily life, whether in politics, economics, or other areas of life. The age of Islam, according to al-Banna, had come again, because that band of men united by brotherhood was taking God and His message seriously and were willing to die for Him.

The Organizational Structure

Ḥasan al-Banna's genius was not only in his vision, dedication to God and love for his fellow Egyptians. There were others in the history of Islam in Egypt who had similar qualities. What made al-Banna unique was the way he translated his vision and convictions into action and into an organizational structure.

Having been in the circle of the Sufis for several years helped him keep the value of worship and disciplined training in focus. This was reflected in the training programs that he came up with, forming the skeleton, giving strength and coherence to the organizational structure.

The chief instrument and cornerstone for training, recruiting and mobilizing the loyalty of the members was cell groups, or *'usar* (families). This was the place where the recruit became an inseparable member of a small band of men that studied, prayed and shared together. They had one meeting per week, where they spent a good part of the night in prayer, *Qur'ân* recitation and a study of commentaries. During these sessions, members shared transparently about their activities, their work, and their finances. There was an accountability relationship to edify and build one another up. The main purpose of these cell groups was to transform the depth of the relationship of the member to the organization, from loyalty out of duty to loyalty out of convictions and dedication to God.

In 1945, al-Banna presented a comprehensive set of statutes which became the basic constitution of the Society.

> This gave formal recognition to an informal operative system of administration and control based on a theoretical delegation of power to, and distribution of function and authority among the Leader, the General

Guide, the Advisory General Guidance Council, and a Consultative Assembly. Similarly, the statutes provided the framework for administrative and technical operations and established a concrete field apparatus and hierarchy (Mitchell 1969: 36, 177).

That was the view from the top of the organizational chart. Whereas looking from the bottom up, there were the "families" or cell groups, where the solid work of discipling was going on. Every four families constituted an *'ashîra* (clan) and every five clans constituted a *raht* (group) and the five groups formed a *katîba* (battalion). All these together formed a branch, and there were several branches and several specializations.

Out of the pool of the families, special promising members with potential were set apart for a special function that needed special training. These men were called *al-jawwâla* (the rovers). They were trained in physical fitness and deeper indoctrination with the discipleship program. They were trained in unconditional obedience and ultimate sacrifice. Their function was to be available as a task force for a variety of activities. At times they served as police. At other times, they worked in programs of educating the illiterate or worked as public health agents in dealing with a cholera epidemic. Still at other times they served as bodyguards or to scare off opponents in the political parties. At the peak of their strength they were about forty thousand.

Above all, the Rovers served as a pool out of which very special and promising members with high potential were set apart for a very special function. These men formed a group called *anizâm al-khâs* (the special section), but they were called by the outsiders *al-jihâz al-sirri* (secret apparatus of the Muslim Brotherhood). Most probably the "special section" was formed around the beginning of 1943, but the idea must have been germinating in the mind of al-Banna for years.

Since the principle of *jihâd* was very central in al-Banna's theology, this commandment had to find a channel for its expression. So the members of the "special section" were highly trained especially in military techniques. They were commandos available to die for the cause of Islam and in obedience to the leadership. Their training programmed them to believe that their highest goal in life was to die for the sake of God (Sa'îd 1977: 203).

Mitchell summed it up by saying,

> inspired in the first instance as an idea by the concept of *jihâd*, formalized into an organization under the pressures of nationalist agitation, the 'secret apparatus' was almost immediately rationalized as an instrument for the defense of Islam and the Society. Later on, it began to play the role of defender of the movement from the police, the rival political parties and the government (Mitchell 1969: 32).

As the members of the "special section" were reinforced and encouraged with statements such as, "You are the soldiers of God and you are the defenders of His religion," and "on your shoulders alone will be the salvation of the Islamic nation and doctrine," their morale went up very high. In 1948 their numbers increased to around 1,000 (Sa'îd 1977: 205). High morale and youthful enthusiasm were the cause of big mistakes they made, such as political assassinations that put the whole movement in jeopardy (Bayûmi 1979: 119-121).

Something went wrong and al-Banna's tight control of the organization was lost. Persecution and imprisonment were like a dark cloud creeping slowly along, announcing the advent of the decline.

The Decline

Schisms within the Organization

Just before al-Banna left Ismâ'îliyya to go to Cairo, he witnessed the first internal schism in the Society. This schism was described in detail by al-Banna himself, and therefore it described the problem from his perspective. Furthermore, some of the same issues which were raised in this first schism were repeated in following ones.

Al-Banna nominated an *Imâm*, who was a carpenter by trade, and this nominee won the votes. According to Bayumi, we understand that a competitor, who was more educated and believed himself to be more qualified for the job, started spreading rumors that the elections were illegal and needed to be repeated. Furthermore, this competitor pointed out that he could do the job as a volunteer without a salary, while the carpenter would need to be paid. So, al-Banna had the elections repeated and the carpenter won the votes a second time. Then the competitor again made an issue of the carpenter's financial need. In response, al-Banna raised funds to pay the carpenter's salary. (Bayûmi 1979: 275-276).

Some of the dissidents preferred legal charges claiming that al-Banna had misused money which was supposed to be sent to the Palestinians, instead distributing it among some of the branches of the Muslim Brotherhood, especially the branch which his brother led in Cairo. The public prosecutor cleared al-Banna of the charge. Al-Banna then became convinced that these dissidents should be dismissed. Before he could dismiss them, they resigned and started spreading more rumors about al-Banna, claiming that the Society did not allow "freedom of expression" and it was too secretive. Upon al-Banna's arrival in Cairo, some of these dissidents attempted to discredit him in the new school he was moving into, so his supporters beat them up (Mitchell 1977: 28-29).

The prominent trends in this first schism were:

1. Al-Banna saw a need and went about working on it, expecting to be treated by his followers as the leader who was more spiritual, wise and who had a clearer perspective on things. Therefore, his suggestions or decisions must be more correct. Furthermore, he was aware of the impure motives of some of the members.

2. People who wanted to have more to say in the decision-making process felt they had been ignored and unappreciated.

3. Al-Banna acted to accomplish what he felt should be the society's goals, whether or not the membership approved of his methods.

4. When dissidents were defeated badly, they tended to become more bitter and resentful. Al-Banna had won the argument, but did not win their hearts.

5. Al-Banna envisioned himself as the "founder of the Society" who knew where and how money should be spent. He believed that he had a special calling from God, and as God's appointee he did not need to give reasons for his decisions regarding money and how it should be distributed. Perhaps he felt that God did not want him to be rigid and legalistic, but that God desired al-Banna to have the freedom and flexibility to do what was right.

6. Hesitancy in dismissing people at the most strategic time put him in difficult situations where dissidents became more bitter and more open in their confrontation.

7. His men used force with dissidents, for when reasoning did not produce results, force did.

The second major schism took place in 1943, resulting in the birth of a splinter group called "*Shabâb Muḥammad*" (Muḥammad's Youth). The reasons for the defections, according to one of its leaders, were:

1. Al-Banna became loyal to the king and to the prime minister 'Ali Mâhir and thus started to contradict himself and compromise on values he once claimed to believe in when he said, "avoid involvement with 'notables' and 'names,' 'parties' and 'societies.'"

2. Al-Banna was too free to "play around" with the money of the Society.

3. He refused to allow others to share in the decision-making process, and thus, with time, he became more and more a dictator.

4. He sheltered some of the members and was not decisive in dismissing those who were living immorally (Sa'îd 1977: 168).

Al-Banna defended himself on each of these four points, but the dividing factor in this particular schism was the theological differences between al-Banna and some of the Youth.

> Having joined the Society in defense of Islamic values, some members took this commitment in a literal sense, encouraged by the Society's emphasis on discipline and training, in the physical as well as the spiritual and moral areas. As the Society grew more powerful...some of the members became inclined to demand the fulfillment of its mission. For this group, its mission was clear and not confused by political considerations; it was the moral salvation of Egypt, if necessary with the force of the hand (Mitchell 1969: 18).

As "Muḥammad's Youth" defected, they took with them the *Al-Nadhîr* magazine. But this schism, although significant in its theology, did not shake the society nor its membership.

The third major schism took place in 1947 as a result of the lack of al-Banna's decisiveness. The General Secretary of the society, 'Âbdîn, was al-Banna's brother-in-law. 'Âbdîn seemed to have lived an immoral life, and in spite of being judged eight to one that he should be dismissed from the society, al-Banna put his weight into it, maneuvering for months to prevent this. Finally, it boomeranged with the resignation of a key leader in the society.

Another factor in the schism of 1947 was the dismissal of Sukkari, his close friend and co-founder, from the society. According to Bayûmi, both al-Banna and Sukkari were in agreement regarding the importance of involvement in Egyptian politics. Their disagreement, though, was on leadership. Sukkari desired to become the political leader, and he wanted al-Banna to be the spiritual leader only. Al-Banna could not envision two separate types of leadership, but one man who was gifted and qualified in both areas, spiritually and politically. After all, in his judgement, there was no separation between religion and politics (Bayûmi 1979: 280).

With these schisms al-Banna's weaknesses came to the surface.

Al-Banna's Weaknesses

If we stop to think about the strengths of al-Banna, we might find that the greatest two were his vision of Islam as being inclusive of all aspects of life, and his vision of himself as the leader whom God had chosen to bring about a resurgence in Islam, starting with Egypt.

Strengths can become weaknesses if a person does not check himself. Al-Banna's greatest weaknesses, according to his critics inside and outside the organization, had to do with his strengths. His vision of Islam, as the way of life which was all inclusive, was interpreted by his critics as a rejection of having a definite program, a running away from the responsibility of accountability by stating issues in very broad terms and thus being a colorless leader.

Al-Banna defined the scope of the movement as a "*salafiyya* message, a Sunni way, a Ṣûfi truth, a political organization, an athletic group, a cultural-educational union, an economic company, and a social idea" (Mitchell 1969: 14). Sa'îd saw this as an illustration of al-Banna's running away from the responsibility of being specific. This style of using very broad terms was his subtle way of taking sides with any group or party at a time when it served his ends, teaming up against that same party, if his ends could be served somewhere else. According to Sa'îd, al-Banna attempted to deceive the palace, the government, the political parties and the public by the use of his broad and contradictory terms. On the other hand, the society, in al-Banna's view, was a political organization, and yet unlike the other political parties. It was a religious organization, but did not fall under the authority of Al-Azhar or other religious bodies. Furthermore, the Muslim Brotherhood, according to Sa'îd, at times was in full agreement with the government and worked closely with the existing regime, and at other times it suggested some changes in the constitution to make Egypt a truly Islamic state. Still at other times, it considered the state as being very far from being a Muslim state, and in reality close to being a Jahelite rule (Sa'îd 1977: 130, 140).

Considering the other strength of al-Banna, which was the vision he had of himself and the task he was chosen to fulfill, there was also a weakness, he considered himself to be indispensable.

Because of his deep dedication to God and to the task that he was entrusted to, unity in mind and spirit within the ranks of the society were of utmost importance. "The opinion of the one (meaning himself) should be the opinion of all.... Those who disagreed and rebelled were under the influence of the devil, and these dissidents were Kharejites." Al-Banna went on to say, "It is sad that we have been greatly influenced by mediocre systems that shoot attractive terminology at us such as democracy and personal freedom." Al-Banna also said, "The ideal Muslim brother is one who does not have an independent view." As he reflected on two branches of the society in a certain town that seemed to have taken a different style, he said, "These two branches will be of no use to us anymore because their training is not my system of teaching and training."

As he pondered about the shortage in leadership, al-Banna said, "I wish there were men by my side that have understanding and management abilities so that I could give them the responsibility of leading the Society, and have that peace of mind that I need. But where are these men?" (in Sa'îd 1977: 74-76).

It seemed that Al-Banna made himself so much the "vine" that the branches could not survive without him. The theological and organizational basis on which he built the society made him indispensable. In the third general conference of the society, he was given full authority over all the branches and committees of the Society. Al-Banna's understanding was that the *shûra* council (the advisary board) had no authority over the General Guide (the leader of the Muslim Brotherhood). The advice he received from this council was not binding (Sa'îd 1977: 74-76).

It seems by 1945 al-Banna's power and authority became quite a burden on the rest of the leadership of the society. "The regulations formulated during that year were admittedly designed to herald a gradual abdication by al-Banna of his position, and the distribution of his power and functions to appropriately established governing units" (Mitchell 1969: 54).

But it seems that the process did not occur fast enough, because al-Banna was going deeper and deeper into the quick sand of Egyptian politics. The events that followed brought al-Banna and the society to some of its hardest times, as he seemed to be unable to keep his head above water in the tough political game.

The Overwhelmed Politician

It is so easy to forget that al-Banna, who had such a magnitude of power and such a momentous task, was still very young in age. In 1949, the year he was assassinated, he was only forty-three years old. His involvement as a politician kept him at a disadvantage. The people he had to deal with and maneuver around were men with years of experience and were experts at the political game. Ten years earlier, when al-Banna began getting into the political game, he was in his early thirties and had to deal with politicians that perhaps were well into their fifties and sixties.

Farûq, at the age of sixteen, was put under the guidance of two strong men; Marâghi, who was *Sheikh* Al-Azhar, was the spiritual counsellor and trainer of the future king; 'Ali Mâhir was Farûq's trusted counsellor and later was assigned as the Prime Minister.

Farûq, at the age of eighteen rather than twenty-one, was crowned as King as a result of the maneuvering of the two men. Furthermore, they planned an "Islamic celebration" to present Farûq as the "good Muslim Ruler." Al-Banna, who was seen as the man of potential, leading a society which was fast growing, became an ally of 'Ali Mâhir. No wonder then that the whole fourth Conference of the Muslim Brotherhood was set for one purpose, to plan for and discuss their role and participation in the crowning ceremony of King Farûq.

From al-Banna's perspective, perhaps this crowning celebration was the fulfillment of a dream which was a return to the Islamic caliphate. The last caliph was in Turkey and was corrupt. Farûq, in contrast, was in Egypt, he was young and teachable and was under the influence of al-Banna's "friends." After the crowning ceremony, the men of the Society stood in front of the palace shouting slogans of loyalty to the king, assuming that he was going to rule according to God and his Prophet.

As al-Banna was naively following the track of the caliphate, the king's advisors were viewing al-Banna and the society as a tool to use against the *Wafd* Party which had great popularity among the masses. 'Ali Mâhir, who was holding the strings, was able to see that only the Muslim Brotherhood could compete with the *Wafd* Party for influence on the masses. So, al-Banna fell into the first trap. What made it worse was that al-Banna, with very few, were the privileged ones to have those confidential get-togethers with the politicians. This possibly left the rest of the Brotherhood envious, suspicious, trusting blindly, wondering, or angry at this change of the policy of the society. This was one of the main factors that brought about the schism which resulted in the formation of the splinter group called "Muḥammad's Youth."

The puritans saw al-Banna as a man who got sidetracked from the real goal and spiritually regressed to politics.

What ‘Ali Mâhir started became a model that other people in power followed in the years to come. Şudqi, the Prime Minister in 1947, used the society as a tool against the communists and the Wafdists. The society started to grow rapidly in numbers and its presence became felt as a major political force. In the meantime, the old ideals of spiritual training started to erode and the huge skeleton was not as coherent as it used to be. According to Sa‘îd, al-Banna had to resort at times to the "secret apparatus," using force to keep the society together. Furthermore, the masses could not understand why al-Banna and the society refused to cooperate with the other parties to form a strong national front against the British. All these factors, whether growth in numbers and form, or weakness in spirituality and unity, made the society a huge giant that even al-Banna could not control. King Farûq and his aids were the first to "open that box to let the giant out" to help them check the popularity of the Wafdist. The giant turned out to be a huge giant that was more threatening than the *Wafd* Party and the communists. "As the giant stood straight, looking tall because of his Islamic foundation, and looking strong and reckless because of his "secret apparatus," even the one who wanted to use him became terrified of him" (Sa‘îd 1977: 210).

The schemes of the politicians to use al-Banna were too intricate for al-Banna to fathom. More and more he discovered that he was getting entangled in a web called the political game. He lost control of his men and discovered that he had no control over the politicians.

From 1945 to 1948 a stream of violence shook Egypt, where the society was not the only party involved, but was the most dramatic. These events convinced the government that the society was planning a revolution.

In 1948, a series of events took place that resulted in the society being dissolved. The charts, maps and secret documents that were confiscated with a huge number of weapons convinced the government that it was high time that the "giant" should be trapped and killed. During that year, huge numbers of the Muslim Brothers were arrested, among them were the leadership of the "secret apparatus." Al-Banna, in contrast, was left free. There he was, separated from his men, powerless, and agonizing for the suffering of the thousands of prisoners and their poor wives and children. His "prison of freedom" was harder than the prison of his men, especially as he heard how his men, one after the other, confessed in detail the secrets of the society and were not able to resist the torture that they were going through.

There was al-Banna, in the past a strong man who was invited to eat with the king, now a weak man, begging for an appointment with the Prime Minister and being denied it.

Sa'îd described al-Banna in this time of life as a man who was being hunted down. The hunters were two men (agents of the government) who played the role of the "go-between." The trap was to get al-Banna to write statements condemning what his men had done. These statements were to be in exchange for the promise that the Muslim Brothers would be released from the prisons. He was tricked into believing that the mere writing and signing of these declarations would set his friends free. What was happening was a different story. His declarations were shown to the prisoners, making them furious. Thus, they were willing to fully cooperate with the police and tell all that they knew. Furthermore, he was enticed to write another declaration called "A Declaration to the People" in which he called his own men terrorists, stating that they were not true Muslims.

There was al-Banna, caught between two sides. On one side there was the anger of his men in prison as they saw him disintegrating, and on the other side was the government slowly cutting him off from all power and support. There was also the pressure of guilt and shame from within when he found himself saying of his brothers and fellow soldiers in the army of God, "These men are neither brothers nor Muslims." Going as far as praising the government and the king, and advising the masses to be loyal to them, made the burden even greater.

There was al-Banna, the overwhelmed, beaten, powerless politician, wanting to believe the illusive promise that his men would be released and that the society would be recognized again. However, deep in his heart he must have known that the end was coming. On February 12, 1949, al-Banna was assassinated on the birthday of King Farûq. Perhaps his assassination was a birthday gift to the king, who was believed to have ordered the assassination.

The question is, when was the real date of the death of al-Banna?

— Was it on February 12, 1949 when he was shot down?

— Or, was it when he wrote the declarations saying of his men "they are neither Brothers nor Muslims" (Sa'îd 1977: 228-236).

— Or, was it when he decided to get into politics making himself a target and stooping down from his privileged position of being the "dignified leader"?

Conclusion

Al-Khumeini did not allow himself to become the front line of defense. He maintained his dignified position as "the leader" in the spiritual, political and all other realms. He appointed presidents, prime ministers, and helped create the Revolutionary guard.

He did not need to order the arrest of the Americans at the American Embassy and take them hostage, the revolutionary guards did it for him. He only "blessed" it. It was below his dignity to get into mundane matters like that.

In spite of his magnitude and power, he allowed untested and younger men to take responsibility for running the country and become the political leaders. They could make mistakes and learn, but if the mistakes were major, then he removed these men, directly or indirectly, and appointed others.

Al-Banna was a great and a charismatic founder of the Society of the Muslim Brotherhood. In contrast to al-Khumeini, he did not know how to maintain his dignity and stature. He did not allow his men to take over, to take the responsibility and the leadership. He failed to see the advantage of keeping aloof and dignified while his men took the role of the negotiators, meeting with the politicians and then reporting to him.

He failed to construct several lines of defense, where he would be the last and final one. In contrast, he put himself on the front line, which made him vulnerable and open to attack. He was a charismatic founder, but a poor politician—an amazing beginning but a sad end.

Finally, as we look at the Society of the Muslim Brotherhood, we see the "trunk of the tree" of Fundamentalism in Egypt in the twentieth century personified in al-Banna. From this one tree came two huge branches. One was the Neo-Muslim Brotherhood, the branch of infiltration through the proclamation of the message. The second branch was Sayyid Qutb, the branch of the philosophy of militant Fundamentalism. Both branches were from the same trunk in the tree of Muslim Brotherhood.

In chapter five we concentrated on the trunk, the Muslim Brotherhood, as it was personified by its first leader al-Banna. In chapter six we will have an overview of the Muslim Brotherhood from 1949 until the end of the 1980s, covering the Neo-Muslim Brotherhood but concentrating on the philosopher of militant Fundamentalism, Sayyid Qutb.

6

THE MUSLIM BROTHERHOOD (SAYYID QUTB)

One year preceding the assassination of al-Banna, the struggle between the society and the government escalated to a climax. In December of 1948 the society was dissolved by the government. Twenty days later the Brotherhood assassinated al-Naqrâshi, the Prime Minister. On the 12th of February 1949 al-Banna was assassinated in one of the main streets of downtown Cairo. Arrests and torture continued until January 1952, when a new government formed by the *Wafd* party stopped the wave of torture and released the prisoners. So *al-miḥna al-'ûla* (the first calamity) of the Brotherhood was over; but was this calamity really over? According to several analysts, the calamity continued on because the imprisonments and the torture of the Brethren were not the main marks of this calamity, rather the outstanding feature was the assassination of al-Banna, the great leader of the Brotherhood. 'Amâra and others believe that the loss of al-Banna was so great that the Brotherhood never recovered from that catastrophe, namely the shortage of great leadership ('Amâra 1985a: 145).

As was mentioned in the previous chapter, al-Banna failed to train replacements, and the gap between him and the middle leadership was large. Even before his death, a great vacuum of leadership, organization and vision was beginning to emerge. With his death a stage in the history of the Brotherhood was over and a new stage began.

In this new stage, the outstanding figure was not a charismatic leader similar in style to al-Banna, nor was he in a position of leadership as the General Guide. The outstanding figure was a philosopher, a thinker, a model of a brother who lived what he preached, a courageous man who was willing to lay down his life for his convictions. Although Sayyid Qutb was hanged by the Nâşer regime in 1966, his influence continued through the years and was a main fountain of inspiration for several new groups and organizations of the Fundamentalist movement. Both al-Banna and Qutb emerged from the Fundamentalist movement and the Islamic League. Out of this movement, al-Banna, the charismatic leader, the trainer of men, the visionary founder and organizer, was the trunk of the tree of the Muslim Brotherhood. The two main branches were Sayyid Qutb, who contributed a new philosophy to modern Fundamentalism, and the other branch was the Neo-Muslim Brotherhood. Smaller branches which have emerged over the years from this thriving tree were offshoots from Qutb and the Neo-Muslim Brotherhood. In chapter five we focused on al-Banna as the main figure, and in this chapter we will cover the Neo-Muslim Brotherhood but focus on Sayyid Qutb.

The Brotherhood After Al-Banna

Al-Huḍaybi the Successor of Al-Banna

After the death of al-Banna, the society, while still illegal, was regrouping under the leadership of Şâleḥ 'Ishmâwi. It survived and continued because it operated and stayed together as an organization within the prisons. About 4,000 of the Brothers were concentrated together in a few prisons.

Some escaped by leaving Egypt and going to the Gulf countries to work and make money. Others proclaimed the message of the society in countries like Syria, Jordan and

Pakistan, winning the sympathy of many supporters as they reported about the torture and imprisonment of their brothers in Egypt.

The main task before the Brothers in Egypt who were not imprisoned was to make the society legal. For them to do that, they had to cooperate with the *Wafd* party—their previous enemy and competitor in the mobilization of the masses.

One of the distinct marks of this period is the search for a leader to succeed al-Banna as the General Guide. 'Ishmâwi, who had been the deputy of al-Banna since 1947, was a likely candidate. Other candidates included the brother of Ḥasan al-Banna, but the choice fell on none of the likely candidates. Instead, it fell on a judge who was relatively new to the leadership of the society. In 1950, Huḍaybi was chosen as the General Guide for the following reasons:

1. His election would not cause splits and divisions in the society like the other candidates, who had their followers and supporters.

2. His election might help in restoring the relationship with the palace, since Huḍaybi was a relative of the chief of the royal household.

3. Because he had been a judge for twenty years, his election might help the society with its legal problems and might help its image in the sight of the legal system.

In short, what was needed for the position of the General Guide was a man who was well-known, respected and with no stigma associated with his name.

Huḍaybi was born in 1891 (fifteen years older than al-Banna), and as a child he memorized the *Qur'ân*. Instead of joining Al-Azhar, he went into secular education which finally ended with his graduation from the school of law. After working as a lawyer for nine years he was appointed as a judge, and for decades he served in the judicial system in various cities in Egypt.

In 1943 Huḍaybi met al-Banna for the first time, and after several long and private discussions with al-Banna, he committed himself to the cause of the Muslim Brotherhood. Furthermore, he became an intimate friend and close supporter of al-Banna. Yet this friendship, loyalty and commitment were not translated into open active membership in the society so that his job as a judge would not be jeopardized. This he did in accordance with the advice of al-Banna (Wakîl 1986: 131-134).

In 1950 as he started preparing himself for the elections of a new General Guide, he resigned from the judicial system.

Huḍaybi was known to be a man who disliked violence, and he believed that the society should not seek to govern Egypt until the nation turned to Islam wholeheartedly.

He was not like al-Banna, and when compared to al-Banna, he always fell short. "He did not and could not live up to the extraordinary image that al-Banna bequeathed to the Society. He himself is said to have warned the Society of the futility of a comparison when he first took over al-Banna's job. The curt, phlegmatic judge who publicly noted his distaste for the ebullience of political demonstrations, who curbed excessive enthusiasm at public meetings, who spoke quietly neither visibly moved nor visibly moving—failed to fit the mantle passed onto him, partly because it might have been impossible for any man to do so" (Mitchell 1969: 300).

Instead of visiting the south of Egypt in the hot summer months, he went there only in the winter, and during the summer months he moved to Alexandria, the most popular summer resort. Furthermore, he was known to swim on the beaches of Alexandria. In the pious and devout minds of the conservative Brothers in the society, this was unthinkable and outrageous.

His relationships and contacts included people who were considered enemies of the society, and this was offensive to the hard-liners. Critics in the ranks wanted him to have a different title because he was unlike al-Banna, but Huḍaybi insisted on being called the General Guide (Mitchell 1969: 188).

During the twenty-three years that he served as General Guide, he spent many years in different prisons and under house arrest. In 1953 he was imprisoned for two months. In 1954 he was imprisoned for one year and then was placed under house arrest until 1961. In 1965 he was imprisoned for the third time. After a release of 15 days, he served an extended sentence and was not released until October 1971. Two years later he died (Wakîl 1986: 133).

The Political Struggle during Huḍaybi's Time

After they were released from the prisons in 1951 and after gaining back their legality, the Muslim Brothers went back to being actively involved. The Tuesday evening meeting in the central headquarters where al-Banna used to preach started again. The new General Guide was the speaker, and at times Sayyid Qutb lectured. Branches of the society reopened all over Egypt, and the society came back to life.

At this stage, a magazine called *Al-Da'wa* (The Proclamation) was started and was considered then as the spokesman of the society. The members of the society continued their religious, social and intellectual activities. But above all, they participated in the battles of Palestine and in the underground resistance against the British in the canal cities. The membership in the society started to increase again, and their impact on the universities became noticeable. King Farûq's reign began to weaken as a result of the defeat of the Arabs in Palestine in 1949, the clash between the British and the Egyptians in the city of Suez on Jan 25, 1952, and finally because of the burning of central Cairo on January 26, 1952.

The relationship between the society and the Free Officers (those responsible for the 1952 revolution) started with Sâdât and al-Banna in 1941. The relationship later continued through other officers, including Nâṣer. Several of these officers even joined the "secret apparatus" of the society and took the oath of the Brotherhood in a dark room, laying their hand on the *Qur'ân* and a pistol. With time it became clear to both sides that they needed one another if the revolution was to succeed. At times the relationship between these two partners was smooth and fruitful. At other times there was tension and distrust. It was very clear that the society contributed immensely to the preparation for the revolution, but their role was minimal in the takeover on July 23, 1952. The agreement between the society and the Free Officers regarding the role of the Brotherhood in the takeover process included the following.

1. The Brotherhood had the responsibility of guarding the foreign community, the minority groups, the churches, the synagogues, the strategic centers and the central offices in the cities. This responsibility was to be carried out in order to safeguard the revolution from being used and abused by the wrong people.

2. The Brotherhood had the responsibility of closely obeserving all possible traitors, keeping them under control.

3. In case the masses did not respond enthusiastically to the take over, the society had the responsibility of igniting the masses with enthusiasm and vocal support of the revolution.

4. If the police failed to cooperate with the army in the take over, the rovers of the society would take the place of the police.

5. If the takeover failed and the revolution collapsed, then the society had the responsibility of giving protection to the Free Officers and helping them escape arrest.

6. If the British got involved and stood against the takeover, the society then had the responsibility of declaring open war against the British.

This agreement was kept secret, and only a very few leaders of the Society were aware of it. The reason for this secrecy was that they did not want to give the British an excuse to crush what appeared to be an "Islamic revolution." There were other motives in the minds of the leading Free Officers as well, especially Nâşer.

The secrecy deprived the Brotherhood of the joy and pride of being seen as partners in the revolution. Members of the Brotherhood, as they reflected back on the agreement, sensed that they were used, since they were invited to become partners in the cross, but not partners in the glory (Mitchell 1977: 168-170).

On July 23, 1952, the revolution took place and the ordinary members of the society felt that this revolution was the final outcome of their long and tedious years of struggle. They naturally expected that it was an Islamic revolution, and Huḍaybi demanded that the foundation of this revolution should be the Islamic *Sharî'a*. To start with, there was a short honeymoon stage between the revolutionaries and the society. Shortly afterwards, mutual lack of trust, disappointments and resistance to one another led to confrontation. Thus, the revolutionaries began taking active steps to rid themselves of this unpleasant and stubborn partner that had become a *markiz quwwa* (center of power), or a nation within the nation. Secularism and Arab nationalism were far more attractive and more uniting than the goals of the society. Huḍaybi, on the other hand, distrusted Nâṣer right from the beginning (Wakîl 1986: 142). Along with a few of the leaders of the Brotherhood, Huḍaybi began to criticize the leadership of the revolution openly. Others in the society supported the revolution, so the leadership was divided. Huḍaybi had secret meetings with a British representative regarding Egypt's independence from the British. This was seen by the leaders of the revolution as another demonstration of Huḍaybi's desire to be a *markiz quwwa* (center of power), and they requested that the "secret apparatus" of the society be abolished, and that the membership of the society should be put completely under governmental control. Those who supported the revolution were considered by the government as the real and genuine Muslim Brotherhood, while Huḍaybi and his followers were considered to be a band of rebels. In 1954 the confrontation and open struggle were reaching a climax. Huḍaybi, during a trip which he made to Saudi Arabia and other Arab countries, openly criticized Prime Minister Nâşer and the treaty that was reached with the British. Immediately after his return he was arrested and imprisoned.

The "secret apparatus" of the society, continued functioning illegally, and schemes were made to assassinate Nâşer. Soon its schemes changed to a plan for a national uprising, leading to the overthrow of Nâşer's regime and giving the authority to Nagîb, a man the society believed in.

On October 26, 1954, in Alexandria, an attempt on Nâşer's life was made. One of the members of the society shot six bullets at Nâşer, missing him. Nâşer, who was giving a speech that was being broadcast all over Egypt, used the incident with such spontaneity that he became a hero of the masses. As a result of that assassination attempt, another wave of arrests took place, and torture in prisons was common practice. The government claimed that the assassination attempt was sufficient proof of the society's treason, while those who were sympathetic with the society claimed that the whole assassination plot was faked by the secret police of Nâşer's regime. Nâşer's critics gave convincing reasons for that claim.

Whatever the truth might have been, the consequences that followed were very clear. Nâşer became the hero of the masses and the president of Egypt, while the society was considered as a band of fanatic Muslims who deserved imprisonment. So, a wave of persecution of the Muslim Brotherhood took place. This was *al-miḥna a-thâniya* (the second calamity). Many of their centers were burned, the society was disbanded and many were imprisoned and tortured. On November 9, 1954, the trials began and the judge "conducted himself rather as chief prosecutor. He freely interrupted the answers of the witnesses if the answer displeased him, he put words into their mouths and forced—sometimes by threats—the desired answers. His questions were phrased to preclude any answer but that sought by the court. At times he engaged in an exchange of petty insults with the witnesses, in most cases the insults came from the court alone" (Mitchell 1969: 155). These court proceedings were in marked contrast to the court proceeding that took place in 1981 after the assassination of Sâdât, where the legitimacy of the whole judicial system was questioned by the prisoner's defense for its not being based on the Islamic *Sharî'a*.

The destruction of the society in 1954 had failed to extinguish the flame that was started by al-Banna. Inside the concentration camps of Nâṣer's regime, new strategies were developed. While he was in prison, Sayyid Qutb, who was later hanged by Nâṣer in 1966, produced a work which analyzed the government in terms of Qur'anic categories.

Sympathizers of the Muslim Brotherhood outside the prisons began meeting again. Charitable efforts for the families of the prisoners, and later on for the prisoners themselves after their release, kept the members of the society together and contributed to the emergence of new nuclei. These nuclei, that had arisen in various governorates, included mostly young men who dreamed of avenging the 1954 events. The writings of Sayyid Qutb started providing them with fuel for thought and motivation. In 1964 the society was secretly reconstituted, and Qutb's book *Ma'âlem Fi Ṭarîq* (Signposts on the Road) was its manifesto (Kepel 1985: 30).

In 1965 there were two trends in the society. The young generation aimed for seizing power and bringing down Nâṣer's dictatorship by the use of violence. The pacifists, on the other hand, favored a change in the country that would come as a result of Islamic education. Only after the majority of the population returned to Islam would the timing be right for a justifiable takeover.

The Brothers had come together again but could not agree on a political strategy. In their lack of unity they were easy prey, used again by Nâṣer as a scapegoat to unite the country and to raise its morale.

In 1966, Nâşer's regime attacked the society again. But this time Sayyid Qutb's *Signposts on the Road* provided the Brethren with theology and convictions, and charted for them the "signposts" on the road to the destruction of the state, and its replacement by a Muslim state.

In 1967, the Six-Day War with Israel brought about the beginning of the collapse of Nâşer. Through the introspection following that humiliating defeat the conclusion was reached that this was God's punishment of Muslims for forsaking Islam. In 1973, when they fought the October War with Israel with the battle cry of "*Allâhu akbar,*" God gave them the victory.

The Neo-Muslim Brotherhood

In 1970 Nâşer died and Sâdât became the president of Egypt. With Sâdât's presidency certain landmarks were established.

1. He started releasing the Muslim Brotherhood prisoners gradually. He wanted their public support and their endorsement of his regime. He was wholeheartedly endorsing their call as Muslim individuals, but he was unwilling to resurrect the society out of fear of its potential power.

2. With Sâdât's economic open-door policy, the Muslim Brothers of the 1953-54 persecutions who went to the Gulf countries and made their fortunes returned to Egypt and invested their capital. *Al-Islâm al-tharwi* started to become a formidable force in the financial support of Fundamentalism.

3. "*Allâhu akbar,*" the battle cry of the war of 1973 with Israel, brought the conviction that God gives the victory, and faithful adherence to Islam is the solution to Egypt's problems.

4. Sâdât's regime competed with the Fundamentalists in attempting to prove that his state was a Muslim state. Education and mass media were used as channels for spreading the call of Islam.

By the time Sâdât took over, al-Huḍaybi was an old man, and the Muslim Brotherhood was split into two main directions. One group was made of *Jamâ'ât al-Ikhwân al-Muslimîn.* Those were the young militant Fundamentalists who later splintered into various groups. The other group was the Neo-Muslim Brotherhood, which was made up of moderates and became the bulk of the society. The Fundamentalist militants were mostly influenced by Sayyid Qutb and were eager to use violence to bring about an Islamic state. Their existence in the society brought embarrassment to the leadership. Although al-Huḍaybi, in 1962 after his first reading of Qutb's notes of *Signposts on the Road*, endorsed Qutb as the hope for the future of Islam, he later wrote a book called *Preachers Not Judges*, where he indirectly criticized Qutb and *Signposts on the Road.* The militants did not like the new structure of the society, so they splintered and formed other groups. The moderates saw the militants as a threat to the wise and slow, but sure strategy. The main figures who stood out in the Neo-Muslim Brotherhood were Ṣâleḥ 'Ishmâwi, Muḥammad al-Ghazzâli and Talmasâni. Al-Ghazzâli was the theologian of the society. 'Ishmâwi, who was expelled from the society during Nâṣer's time, was responsible for continuing a line of open communication with the state, even during the time of Nâṣer. The magazine *Al-Da'wa* (The Proclamation), which he published, was the voice of the expelled Brotherhood during the dark years of Nâṣer's time.

In 1967, 'Ishmâwi gave this most important and most influential Islamic magazine to Talmasâni, the new General Guide. *Al-Da'wa* appeared sporadically for a period of five years, between 1967 and 1981. Talmasâni, the new Guide, led the society with two clear goals: legal recognition of the Society, and the application of the *Sharî'a.* In a special column in *Al-Da'wa*, Talmasani wrote about the past and the current activities of the Society. He praised Ḥasan al-Banna as he wrote about the history of the society. Then he pointed out that in current activities "our movement exists within the framework of the Muslim mission.

1. We educate the people, in particular the youth, in an Islamic manner set by the Muslims.

2. We proclaim the truth, and urge all the people to rally to it, and to support it in all circumstances.

3. We gather people together, to tell them what they must do and from what they must abstain.

4. We warn the people against secularism masquerading in Islamic garb in an effort to alienate Muslim youth from their religion through discourse as mellifluous as it is poisonous.

5. In educating the youth we base ourselves on God, through the *Qur'ân* and *sunna*" (Kepel 1985: 126).

These were the guidelines that Talmasâni had for the Neo-Muslim Brotherhood.

Talmasâni, along with 1,500 Muslims and about 120 Christians, was arrested and imprisoned one month before the assassination of Sâdât in 1981. Almost a year later, he and all the others were released in stages by Mubârak. The Neo-Muslim Brotherhood continued to press on with the goals of regaining their legal recognition as a society and applying the Islamic *Sharî'a*. Their demands were taken up even at the time of Sâdât. In 1977, Ṣûfi Abu Ṭâleb, "an astute jurist trained in law schools in Paris, was elected President of the Peoples' Assembly (parliament). Abu Ṭâleb repeated unceasingly that Egypt would apply the *Sharî'a* some day soon, but first, he said, a titanic labour of codification of this Muslim law was necessary in order to adapt it to the conditions of contemporary society.

The demand for participation in political life, first by entering the Parliament, and then by bringing repeated pressure on the deputies to apply the *Sharî'a*, sharply differentiated the strategy of the Neo-Muslim Brethren, from that of the other tendencies of the Islamicist Movement" (Kepel 1985: 126-127).

In 1987, the Neo-Muslim Brotherhood managed to have a large number of representatives reach the Parliament as they united with existing political parties and joined the elections. Legally the society was still not in existence, but practically and discretely they were in existence as they had a strong voice in the Parliament (Foda 1989: 14).

Talmasâni died in the late 1980s, and the new General Guide who was elected was Ḥâmed Abu-Naṣr. The new Guide was an old man with poor health and weak leadership, but new leadership was emerging, especially in the person of Seif al-Islâm, the son of Ḥasan al-Banna. The Neo-Muslim Brotherhood failed to capture the spirit of the society at al-Banna's time. Furthermore, the youth were more attracted to the radical tendencies of the Fundamentalist movement. However, the core of the society still believes that an Islamic state will sooner or later "fall into the lap" of the Muslim Brotherhood, as the Islamicization of the nation comes to full maturity and fruition. Wisdom in gradual penetration and control of the society is the slow but sure strategy for reaching the desired objective. Perhaps the promise that God gave to Israel in Deuteronomy 7:22-23 best describes the Neo-Muslim Brotherhood strategy. "The Lord your God will drive out those nations before you, little by little. You will not be allowed to eliminate them all at once, or the wild animals will multiply around you. But the Lord your God will deliver them over to you, throwing them into great confusion until they are destroyed."

The Neo-Muslim Brotherhood is one type of Fundamentalism in Egypt. The other type is seen through the existence of more than forty splinter groups of militant Fundamentalism. All of these groups are offshoots from the Muslim Brotherhood, and they all branch from the second main branch who is Sayyid Qutb, the *'ustâdh* (master), the philosopher, the thinker, the model and the martyr.

Sayyid Qutb and his Impact

Qutb, A Synopsis of his Life

Like al-Banna, Sayyid Qutb was born in 1906 and was exposed to the social, religious, political and cultural milieu of his time. Like al-Banna, he memorized the *Qur'ân* at the *kuttâb* of the village, then joined a secular school, and later moved to Cairo, joining the teachers' training college and *Dâr al-'Ulûm*, a modern teachers' training institute founded to compensate for the deficiencies of Al-Azhar. Unlike al-Banna, Qutb was not a charismatic personality, nor an eloquent speaker, nor an organizer, nor a great leader of men. Instead, he was an *adîb* (man of letters) who became the philosopher, and the ideologue of the Muslim Brotherhood, and the *'ustâdh* (master teacher) of Islamic Fundamentalism in Egypt.

As a child, he was exposed to the political ideas of his day because of his father's involvement in Muṣṭafa Kâmel's National Party. At a young age, he developed strong feelings of anti-British nationalism. He was also exposed to secular books which he bought from the local travelling bookseller. In 1921 he moved to Cairo and lived with his uncle who was a journalist and a supporter of the *Wafd* party. At the age of twenty-seven, he graduated from *Dâr al-'Ulûm* in 1933 and started his career as a teacher. According to several writers, Sayyid Qutb lived a secular life for many years. Qutb described that period as the stage of atheism in his life (Ḥamm̂ûda 1987: 50). From 1940 to 1948, he worked as an inspector for the Ministry of Education. During this time, he became interested in nationalism and in political and social problems. In 1948 he was sent to the United States to research the American educational system. It was expected that this trip would make him a believer in the American dream and the western way of life. Instead, even while still on the deck of the ship on the way from the port of Alexandria to the

United States, he had a "conversion" experience that brought him to a deep faith and commitment to the God of Islam. He started praying faithfully five times a day and began motivating the fellow Egyptians on board to love God and avoid sin. Very soon after that "conversion" experience, a half naked drunken woman entered his cabin and made herself available to him. He violently refused the invitation, and for the coming two years in the United States, he avoided with embarrassment and disgust the sexual promiscuity that was around him.

During his stay in America, he witnessed the enthusiasm of the West for the establishment of the state of Israel. He also witnessed the rejoicing of the Americans for the assassination of Ḥasan al-Banna. Those experiences deeply hurt him and motivated him to study America with a critical eye. He was impressed with the advanced technology, the efficient management, and the value of work and success, but he was very critical of the role of advertising and entertainment that made America a lie (Ḥammûda 1987b: 90).

According to Qutb the Americans' dedication to materialism, pragmatism and superficial religiosity made them a material body that had no soul or spirit. Their genius in industry and management was accompanied by primitiveness in spiritual and ethical values. Qutb returned from America to Egypt a dedicated Muslim, who was convinced of Islam, intellectually, spiritually and emotionally. He was critical of the American society, to the degree that he was forced to resign from the Egyptian Ministry of Education.

In 1951 he was recruited to the Muslim Brotherhood, and a year later was elected to the leadership council of the society and given major responsibilities. With his joining the society, he went through a deeper religious experience in becoming a part of the solidarity of like-minded brothers.

During the short honeymoon stage that followed the 1952 revolution between its leaders and the society, he met with Nâşer regularly. Later in 1953, when the confrontation between Nâşer and Huḍaybi took place, Qutb sided with

Huḍaybi, and as a result he had his first prison experience for three months.

After the attempt on the life of Nâṣer in 1954 by one of the Muslim Brotherhood, Qutb, along with thousands of the Brethren, was imprisoned and considered an enemy of the state. He was sentenced to twenty-five years of hard labor, but because of his poor health, he was moved to the prison's infirmary. Later, in 1964, he was released in response to a plea made by the visiting President of Iraq. During his imprisonment, he produced his major work, the Qur'anic commentary *Fi Dhilâl Al-Qur'ân* (Under the Shade of the *Qur'ân*), along with several other works. In 1962, he started writing his highly influential book *Ma'âlem Fi Ṭarîq* (Signposts on the Road) and had parts of it smuggled outside the prison infirmary.

After his release, *Signposts on the Road* was published and within six months was reprinted five times, after which it was banned. In 1965 a conspiracy was uncovered, and Qutb was found to be the leader. He was imprisoned, and one year later was hanged along with two companions. "If you want to know why Sayyid Qutb was sentenced to death," wrote the Muslim Sister Zaynab al-Ghazzâli, "read *Signposts on the Road*" (Kepel 1985: 42).

Sayyid Qutb, the Author.

According to Ḥanafi, a professor of philosophy in Cairo, the life of Sayyid Qutb as a man of letters can be divided into four stages. These stages are not clear-cut and defined, but they flow back and forth into one another (Ḥanafi 1988: 168-298).

The first is the literary stage, the second is the social stage, the third is the philosophical stage and the last is the political stage.

The literary stage, from 1930 to 1950, was the longest. During this stage, he wrote poetry, short stories, novels, biographies, and literary criticism. In his view, poetry was a supreme art, and the poet was a philosopher. Also he was a journalist who was aware of the social and political problems of Egypt. He also wrote autobiographies. In his first, *The Child of the Village*, he described in detail his village life, the poor farmers, the injustices and folk Islam. In his second autobiography, he wrote about his family, mainly his two sisters and his brother. In his third autobiography, *The Thorns*, he uncovered his deep feelings of disappointment, after the failure of a love affair, which resulted in his resolution to remain a bachelor. However, his greatest works during this period had to do with his exegesis of the *Qur'ân*. As a child he memorized it and was fascinated by it, but as an adult, reading the commentaries on the *Qur'ân* left him cold and dry. Then he returned to the *Qur'ân* itself and was overwhelmed with the beauty of its *al-taşwîr al-fanni* (artistic imagery), to the degree that he burst out saying, "Thanks be to God, I found the *Qur'ân*" (Ḥammûda 1987b: 69).

Kenneth Cragg described Sayyid Qutb's ability and gifts as going beyond the mere theology to the beauty of literature found in the *Qur'ân*.

> His deep emotion is of course utterly authentic and played a great part in his exegesis. His early interest (as well) in literary analysis and criticism promoted him to a more technical awareness of the *Qur'ân's* literary virtues than the ordinary believer could attach to the Fundamental doctrine of its matchlessness (Cragg 1985: 56).

The second, or social stage, was from 1951 to 1954, which coincided with the alliance of the society with the Free Officers in the breaking forth in the revolution. If the honeymoon had been allowed to continue between the two and not ended abruptly, this stage with Sayyid Qutb would have continued. It would have coincided with the social reforms of Nâşer in the 1960s. Perhaps Qutb would have become a revolutionary social reformer like Mao Tse-tung, Che

Guevara or Karl Marx. Instead it was the shortest stage in his life. Here he started with literature and ended with Islam as a religion. He searched the *Qur'ân* and wrote about social justice in Islam, the battle of Islam with capitalism, and world peace. In the 1940s he searched the *Qur'ân* for literary values; while in this stage, he searched the *Qur'ân* for answers to social issues and nationalism.

As he analyzed history, he evaluated the western culture that included both Christianity and communism, comparing it with the Islamic culture. He found that Islam was more just and practical than both communism and Christianity. Both communism and western Christianity will end up in bankruptcy one day, Qutb pointed out, and the future is for Islam. Because in Islam there is a return to God alone, "*lâ ilâha illa Lâh*," and in returning to Him alone there will be hope for emancipation and liberation from materialism, modern idols and slavery to the super powers.

In this stage, he bitterly criticized what he called the Modern Crusaders—right-wing dispensational Christian theology and Zionism. He pointed out that both were the enemies of Islam because they cooperated together and "placed the state of Israel as a thorn in the back of Islam" (Ḥanafi 1988: 202).

The third stage in Sayyid Qutb's life, as a man of letters, was the philosophical stage which extended from 1954 to 1962 and took place in prison. His search in the *Qur'ân* shifted from the social issues and nationalism to a purely philosophical study of Islam as it was contrasted to capitalism and communism. He philosophically dealt with four areas: capitalism and communism as two elements of western culture, the future and Islam, distinctives of the philosophy of Islam and *ḥâkimiyya* (the sovereignty of the *Sharî'a*). The impact of the Pakistani Islamicist Mawdûdi started affecting his thinking and conclusions, but that influence was limited. During this stage, his major accomplishment was the writing of the Qur'anic commentary *Under the Shade of the Qur'ân.*

With the beginning of another round of persecution of the Brethren, the fourth stage in Sayyid Qutb's life started, the political stage, from 1963 to 1965. During this stage he shifted from the study of the philosophical distinctives of Islam, to the study of the practical persecution and martyrdom theology, which clearly identified for him the "signposts" on his road. He went through his Qur'anic commentary and chose the sections that he included in his book. In this period his writings were saturated with a set of theological themes such as divinity, lordship, sovereignty, judgement, obedience and *jâhiliyyat al-mujtama'* (barbarianism of the society).

What he wrote during this stage has made the greatest impact on Islamic Fundamentalism in the decades that have followed.

Sayyid Qutb's Signposts on the Road

Ma'âlem Fi Ṭarîq (Signposts on the Road) is a short book made up of thirteen chapters and is highly motivating. It is an excellent tool for discipleship, since its major themes are repeated in waves, driving the convictions deeper and deeper in the minds of its readers. Actually, this little book is a main syllabus that is used to train new disciples in Islamic Fundamentalism.

After its first printing in 1965 it was immediately banned. However, when President Nâṣer read it he gave permission for its distribution. Shortly afterwards Nâṣer's regime became aware of the impact of this book and banned it again. During Sâdât's time it was allowed to be reprinted, and for some people in Egypt today it could be equated with the Red Book of Mao Tse Tong to the Chinese.

Kepel, in his book *The Prophet and the Pharaoh*, gives an excellent translated summary of Sayyid Qutb's *Signposts on the Road*. In the first chapter Qutb points out that

> humanity today stands on the brink of the abyss...because of its bankruptcy in the domain of the values.

> Both individualist and collectivist ideologies have failed. Now it is the turn of Islam, of the *umma* (community of believers) to play its role. God has accorded man his lieutenancy over the world and as a means of worshipping God and of realizing the aims of human existence (Kepel 1985: 34-44).

Humanity will not listen to an abstract belief, but if Islam is embodied in the society as *umma*, then the world will listen. Qutb goes on in his book and deals with issues such as *jâhiliyya*, *ḥâkimiyya*, *'ubûdiyya*, and *jihâd* and their implications. For him, *jâhiliyya* could best be translated as barbarianism, since it described the pre-Islamic society of the Arabian Peninsula. The people were ignorant of God, worshipping idols, and were in a state of barbarianism until Muḥammad's mission. The whole world today according to Qutb is in a state of *jâhiliyya*. This world of barbarianism includes the communist world and the nations that worship idols, such as Buddhism and Hinduism. The third group are the Jews and the Christians around the world that "got diverted from the truth." And finally, the *jâhiliyya* is also spread in all the so-called Muslim countries (Qutb 1987: 98-101). When man unduly arrogates to himself "the right to establish values, to legislate, to elaborate systems, and to take positions, all without regard to divine ethics," he is in a state of modern *jâhiliyya* (Kepel 1985: 45).

True Muslims should view their societies as the prophet viewed his society. The prophet withdrew from Mecca to Medina when he found himself in a weak position and returned to conquer the city later. So must the vanguards do in their societies.

Sayyid Qutb did not indicate clearly that the withdrawal should be physical as others thought that he meant. The separation he talked about is a moral, spiritual and social aloofness, so that the vanguards will not be polluted with the world. The Muslim can continue dealing with the world in the daily needs of work and living, but he should be separated in his heart and mind. The reason for this separation is the fact that he has been uprooted from the society of *jâhiliyya* and transplanted in the *umma* (Qutb 1987: 20).

Because "*lâ ilâha illa Lâh*" (there is no god but God), any attempt of some men to become gods for others is a transference of sovereignty. Only God is *Rabb* (Lord). Only He has the right to rule and be sovereign. Thus *ḥâkimiyyat Allâh* (sovereignty of God) was the corner stone of Qutb's theology.

> The necessary and sufficient criterion for determining whether a given society is Muslim or belongs to *jâhiliyya* therefore, lies in the sort of *'ubûdiyya* (worship) and *ḥâkimiyyah* (sovereignty) that may be observed within it. In Muslim society God alone is worshipped and holds sovereignty, while in *jâhiliyya* societies, that status is held by someone or something other than the one true God (Kepel 1985: 51).

When Nâṣer made Pan-Arabism the cause of his regime and he became its god, he had led the Arab world into *jâhiliyya*. Instead of worshipping God *('ubûdiyyat Allâh)*, people worshipped Nâṣer. The only option that was left was *jihâd* (holy war) against a kind of *jâhiliyya* which included both the rulers that ordered the torture of the true Muslims and the whole society that accepted worship of the rulers and passively did not raise a finger against what the rulers were doing. So not only the rulers were in *jâhiliyya*, but the whole society as well. Therefore, the starting point was to go back and start from the very beginning, just like the prophet did ('Amâra 1985a: 148-154).

The process of walking in the footsteps of the prophet, according to Sayyid Qutb, goes in the following steps.

> A man has faith in his credo, which emanates from a hidden source and is enlivened by the power of God alone; the virtual existence of the Islamic society begins with the faith of this one man. This one man, however, receives the revelation not in order merely to turn in on himself, but to carry its spirit too." The one

> becomes three, and these three become the "new society, an independent Islamic society, separate from the *jâhiliyya* society. The three become ten, the ten a hundred, the hundred a thousand.... What characterizes both the Islamic credo and the society inspired by it, is that they become a movement or *Ḥaraka* that would allow no one to stand apart. The battle is constant and the sacred combat or *jihâd* lasts until the Judgement Day (Kepel 1985: 53-54).

Qutb goes on to say that this holy combat *(jihâd)* is characterized by the following:

1. A holy combat *(jihâd)* is against the devil within one's heart to free oneself from the pollution of the world. Furthermore, one must discipline himself to rely on one source which is the *Qur'ân*; otherwise, the purification process will not occur.
2. A holy combat *(jihâd)* is against the rulers that made themselves gods and gave themselves the right of sovereignty. This holy combat is not against the society but against the rulers that enslaved the society.
3. Once the holy combat *(jihâd)* has set the society free from the tyranny of the rulers, then and only then, would the proclamation of the message to the society be useful. (In this Qutb departed from the teaching of Ḥasan al-Banna).
4. The holy combat *(jihâd)* should spearhead the proclamation to the uttermost parts of the world. There will always be confrontation with cultures and religions, and Islam should not compromise. These societies should either come to Islam, or surrender to Islam by paying the taxes. Then the individuals in these societies are really free to respond to the proclamation of the message of Islam, one way or the other. No force is needed to compel people to become Muslims *(lâ ikrâha fi dîn)*.
5. When people are set free from the tyranny of the rulers then their nature *(fiṭra)* that was created by God, will be set free to respond to God by the exercise of the will.

6. No political program is needed in advance. This is a trick that people will use as they ask the vanguards, 'What is your political program?' *Jihâd* (holy combat) is the starting point, and once the *umma* is being formed the program will emerge as it occurred with the prophet in Medîna (Qutb 1987: 66-91).

Sayyid Qutb, A Deviant or The Master

In the eyes of his admirers, Qutb was a model of courage, insight and integrity. In the eyes of Nâṣer's regime, he was a traitor. By Al-Azhar, his heretical genealogy was traced all the way back to the Kharijites, and Qutb was declared a deviant *(munḥarif)*. *Sheikh* Al-Azhar responded to *Signposts on the Road* chapter by chapter and pointed out that it was blasphemous to describe as *jâhiliyya* any period other than the pre-Islamic society of the Arabian Peninsula. Qutb, like his ancestors, the Kharijites, used the concept of *ḥâkimiyya* to motivate Muslims to rebel against the rulers, even the Muslim rulers, while Islam teaches clearly that rulers should be obeyed.

Qutb, like his ancestors the Kharijites, also used the concept of *jihâd* in a wrong way. He interpreted the holy combat *(jihâd)* to mean a fight against all those who disagree with his interpretation. His books are dangerous because they mix truth and falsehood, and they delude the simple-minded and turn them into fanatics.

These were the views of *Sheikh* Al-Azhar who was seen by the Fundamentalists as the puppet of the rulers. He merely said what his gods *(ṭawâghît)* wanted him to say.

As for the Neo-Muslim Brotherhood, they evaluated Qutb with mixed feelings. They had secret admiration for him, but they feared the consequences of his impact on the militant youth. Talmasâni declared that Sayyid Qutb's writings did not represent the teachings and ideology of the Muslim Brotherhood. Huḍaybi, in 1962 upon his exposure to the first draft of *Signposts on the Road*, declared that this book vindicated all the hopes he had placed in Sayyid Qutb, who now embodied the future of the Muslim mission. A few years later in 1965, Huḍaiby, in his book *Preachers Not Judges*, explicitly criticized Mawdûdi and so indirectly criticized Sayyid Qutb (Ḥammûda 1987b: 181).

Ḥammûda, 'Amâra and several other writers, on the other hand, see Sayyid Qutb as the *'ustâdh* (the master). They see his impact continuing in shaping and forming the minds of the young militants, and perhaps one day affecting the future of Egypt.

His impact started through his writings and his discipling a few men within the Muslim Brotherhood. Neither his sickness nor his imprisonment prevented him from putting into practice what he wrote about, namely a movement *(ḥaraka)* which would continue with the years.

With his writings, he transformed the Muslim Brotherhood in the 1960s from being a society that cared for prisoners and their families, and struggled to prove its existence, to a society that had a nucleus of men who were on the offensive and were getting equipped and trained to become commandos and vanguards who would make an impact on the whole society. The tortures in the concentration camps produced an ideology that was colored by martyrdom.

Sayyid Qutb was not allowed to live for long. In 1966 he was hanged and thus became "a martyr *(shahîd)* and therefore a hero, a model, a master, a teacher and a man not of this world" (Ḥammûda 1987b: 184).

In conclusion,

> the martyrology of the Nâşer period, is of the utmost importance for the subsequent Islamicist movement. The halo of persecution suffered in defense of a faith and a social ideal, confers a status of absolute truth upon Islamicist discourse. Within the movement itself, this martyrology sharpens the contradictions between competing tendencies, which are divided according to

their ideological reading or non-reading of Qutb's *Signposts on the Road*. Shukri Muṣṭafa, for instance, preached *'uzla* (withdrawal from society) as a means of avoiding the horror of the camps and gallows. Others took the road of political commitment in a multitude of ways either collaborating with the regime in an attempt to Islamicize it, or entering the world of politics as a sort of opposition, in the hope of avoiding, partly through ties with the regime itself, the specter of torture and extermination. Still others organized for the forcible seizure of power, hoping that next time they would be able to act before the state could strike back. This was the view of the members of 'Abdul Salâm Faraj's group, who assassinated Ṣâdât in 1981 (Kepel 1985: 35).

In the next chapter we will consider Shukri Muṣṭafa and his group, who favored *'uzla* (withdrawal from society), and in the following chapter we will consider 'Abdul Salâm Faraj and the al-Jihâd group who assassinated Sadat.

NOTES:

1 From an Arab point of view, in contrast to the 1967 defeat, the 1973 war against Isreal ended in victory. As a result of this war, Isreal was willing to negotiate and give up the Suez Canal and later on the whole of Sinai. This would not have been possible without the relative victory of the Arabs in the 1973 war.

7

ATTEMPTS AT ESTABLISHING A MUSLIM SOCIETY

Sayyid Qutb was hanged in 1966. A year later there was war with Israel and the humiliating defeat which followed. Nâşer, who was hated by the Muslim Brotherhood, was broken, beaten by the defeat in the war, and his political career was almost finished. In 1970 Sâdât became the new president after the death of Nâşer. His presidency started with a honeymoon stage with the Neo-Muslim Brotherhood and with the Fundamentalist groups at the universities. He opened the prison doors, and the Muslim Fundamentalists imprisoned by Nâşer were released.

In October 1973 the war with Israel was fought under a Muslim battle cry, and Sâdât's popularity in Egypt and the Arab world was at a climax.

Yet, two ill-timed attempts took place at establishing Muslim societies. The first was started in 1971 by Şâleḥ Sariyya and was aborted in 1974. The other was started in 1972 by Shukri Muşṭafa and was aborted in 1977. These were the first actual attempts at creating and establishing Muslim societies in centuries, and they are a phenomenon that is worth looking at with wonder.

Unlike the Islamic League of Afghâni, the Muslim Brotherhood of al-Banna, and the ideology of Qutb, these men went a step further in actually creating defined Muslim societies. Sariyya, through an attempted coup, wanted to establish an Islamic republic. He was so confident of success that he had his declaration of the new republic ready to be televised with the signature "President of the Islamic Republic." Shukri, through creating a commune for his followers, established a special Muslim society that had its own value system and lifestyle.

What were the odds, and why is it that in spite of it all, these attempts at establishing Muslim societies took place?

There were several factors opposing these attempts:

1. In contrast to the 1967 war which was fought in the name of Arab nationalism and socialism, the 1973 war was fought during the month of *Ramadân* and under the battle cry of "*Allâhu akbar*." Why is it Sariyya and Shukri were not satisfied?

2. Both attempts took place before the surprise visit of Sâdât to Jerusalem, and before the Camp David accords, which were considered by Muslim Fundamentalists as high treason.

3. Both attempts took place during the time of Sâdât, who released the prisoners from Nâşer's time, including Shukri himself, the leader of the second attempt. Furthermore, Sâdât's regime was cooperating with the Fundamentalist groups at the universities. Why is it that even when Sâdât was in full cooperation with the Muslim Fundamentalists, the plots were being hatched?

4. The Egyptians during this period were not ready for any revolution or coup d'état. They were quite pleased with the accomplishments of Sâdât, whether at the military or political levels. Furthermore, the people were still overwhelmed with the beginnings of the economic open-door policy which was very promising. After years of deprivation and poverty, all of a sudden money started to circulate and western products were allowed to flow into the country and flooded the market.

So why is it, that in spite of the assurance of no popular support, these attempts at establishing Muslim societies took place? This is the question that we hope will be answered as we look at these two men, Sariyya and Shukri.

Ṣâleḥ Sariyya

In addition to the problems that have been mentioned earlier, Sariyya had two more that further complicated the phenomenon of wanting to establish a Muslim Society.

1. He was not imprisoned or tortured, so his ideology was not the product of the concentration camps like that of Sayyid Qutb or Shukri. What was his motivation for wanting to establish a Muslim republic?

2. Because he was Palestinian, the probability of the success of his coup was very slim. Egyptians would have found it extremely difficult to be ruled by a non-Egyptian after all the centuries of occupation. Furthermore, as a non-Egyptian, he was doomed never to have a large following because foreigners tend to be treated with suspicion and caution. Why did he risk his life by going against all these odds?

Sariyya was born near Ḥaifa in Palestine in 1933 in the same hometown of the founder of the Muslim Fundamentalist party called the Islamic Liberation Party. This party was founded as a reaction to the establishment of the state of Israel and the assassination of Ḥasan al-Banna. Sariyya was highly influenced by the ideology of the party, which in turn was influenced by the Muslim Brotherhood and al-Banna.

Sariyya obtained his doctorate degree in education from a university in Cairo. He lived in Jordan, then in Iraq, having to leave both places because of his religious and political activism. Finally, he came back to Egypt where he worked in the education section of the Arab League, which had its headquarters in Cairo.

Sariyya's Document of Faith

When Sariyya was arrested and executed in 1974, a sixty-page book that he had written was confiscated and banned. This book which he called *Risâlât al-Imân* (Document of Faith) is still banned and is not available. Only after Rif'at Aḥmad wrote about it in the *Al-Yaqza Al-'Arabiyya* magazine, using extensive quotations, did people become aware of the philosophy and ideology of Sariyya. His "Document of Faith" was banned because the government considered it dangerous because it "unsettles social and political stability" (Aḥmad 1986: 84-103).

In order to understand Sariyya's ideology, it will be fruitful to have him compared and contrasted to Sayyid Qutb.

1. Like Qutb, Sariyya was a specialist in education.

2. Like Qutb, he tried political parties, and finally ended in Islam.

3. Like Qutb, he considered all the governments of all the Muslim nations in the world as forms of *jâhiliyya* (barbarianism)—not only the governments, but their Muslim societies as well.

4. According to Qutb, the manifestations of *jâhiliyya* were seen in people's doctrines, values, customs, traditions, educational systems and contents, literature and law.

For Sariyya, the manifestations of *jâhiliyya* were seen in the obvious social relationships and daily behavior, such as dancing, swimming, drinking alcohol, adultery, gambling, lying, etc. These were sufficient evidence and enough proof that the society had reached the state of barbarianism.

So, while Qutb dealt with principles, Sariyya focused on behavioral manifestations.

5. According to Qutb, *jâhiliyya* comes as a result of usurping God's authority over men. "There is no God but God," and when people observe this truth and live accord-

ingly, there will be an Islamic nation and social justice will be established.

According to Sariyya, *jâhiliyya* comes as a result of *kufr* (pride against God and blasphemy), and whoever blasphemes should be excommunicated. This blasphemy has its roots in the false assumption that religion means only worship. So when the so-called Muslim kings and presidents observe prayer, fasting and elements of worship and assume that this is Islam, they are in reality blaspheming and thus are naturally excommunicated.

6. According to Qutb, *jâhiliyya* includes all humanity, except for the selected few that are vanguards in God's kingdom.

According to Sariyya, *jâhiliyya* is more of a description of the governments and the establishments. As for the society, individuals who are in agreement with their governments are living in *jâhiliyya*, while those who are in opposition and in disagreement with the establishment are the believers.

7. Qutb's strategy involved training and development in the stages of faith, then *tamakkun* (gaining strength discipleship), and then *jihâd* (holy combat). The disciples of Qutb had to have convictions and thorough training.

Sariyya's strategy involved the stages of a revolutionary takeover of the government, then enforcing the Islamic law, and then working on establishing the Islamic nation. Sariyya's disciples were trained not primarily in convictions, but in blind obedience to the leadership (Ḥammûda 1987a: 48-50).

Sariyya's Attempted Coup

Since Sariyya was convinced that rulers are the ones who block the spread of an Islamic mode of society, the starting point for him was at the top, a coup d'état.

As he arrived in Cairo in 1971, in addition to making contacts with the leadership of the Neo-Muslim Brotherhood, he started training youth and preparing them for enforcing a takeover of the government. The youth that he recruited were mostly university students from Cairo and Alexandria. He made sure that the cell group members observed secrecy and did not know other cell group members. By 1974 he had approximately one hundred committed recruits. Training in obedience was high on his list of qualities that he wanted to build into the lives of his recruits. Their obedience was tested when he would command them to do something courageous, heroic and which involved the risk of being caught by the police.

Sâdât's religiosity in front of the cameras did not impress Sariyya. He viewed him as a *kâfir* (blasphemer) who lived in deception, making Islam sheer "religiosity" with no impact on economics, politics, the legal system and everyday living. The TV stations began showing more programs on Islam during Sâdât's time, and yet the latest American TV serials were televised as well. The call of the minaret or a sermon from the *Qur'ân* was followed by a ballet program. What hypocrisy and blasphemy. Pan-Arabism and the liberation of Palestine were shortsighted goals that could blind the masses from the real goal—Islam. To Sariyya, Sâdât's regime was more dangerous than secular regimes. It had in it the power of deception, of appearing to be a Muslim regime, thus splitting life into *dîn wa dunya* (a time for God and a time for practical living). What blasphemy. Sâdât must be toppled, even while he was at the climax of his popularity, because his evil impact on the masses was at its climax.

Sariyya, along with a very few of his supporters, planned to occupy the Technical Military School in Cairo, and April 18, 1974, was the chosen date. The plan was to drug the guards, occupy the school quietly, dress like soldiers, and use military trucks the next day to go to the Peoples' Assembly (The Parliament) where Sâdât was supposed to give a speech.

The rest of the plan was a surprise attack at the Peoples' Assembly, killing Sâdât and taking the leaders of Egypt as hostages, then reading the first declaration right in front of the TV. The declaration which was supposed to be televised had nine points and the signature of the president of the Islamic Republic.

As one reflects on this plan, it looks too simplistic. If it had worked, history in the Middle East would have been different. Another simple plan worked out in 1981 and resulted in Sâdât's death in spite of very tight security in comparison with 1974.

However, the plan did not work. The drugs placed in the tea which the guards drank was not strong enough. The quietness that was required was soon interrupted by the sound of bullets, and the men of Sariyya were arrested. The next day Sariyya was arrested as well, and on October 11, 1974, he was executed along with his top assistants. Twenty-nine recruits were imprisoned (Ḥammûda 1987a: 41).

Ḥasan al-Banna had multitudes of recruits and a powerful organizational structure. Sayyid Qutb had a thorough ideology, but neither of them reached far enough in attempting the execution of a plan to Islamicize Egypt overnight. Sariyya in contrast was compelled to act urgently and not just "organize" or "write books."

Shukri was another man who was compelled to act, but his action took a very different form.

Shukri Muṣṭafa and the Society of Muslims

After the execution of Sariyya, one of his men joined Shukri's group and became one of the close men on his team. Another of Sariyya's men started his own new splinter group and started recruiting some men from Shukri's followers. So these two groups overlapped in thought, as we shall see, and overlapped in time as well. Sariyya's mission was from 1971 to 1974, and Shukri's mission was from 1971 to 1977.

Shukri and His Ideology

Shukri Muṣṭafa was born in 1942, the son of the *'umda* (mayor of a village) of Abu Kurûs in the vicinity of Asyût, in the middle of Egypt. His mother had a previous marriage. Two years after the birth of Shukri she was divorced and moved to Asyût and married another man. Abu Kurûs was a distant village at the foothills of the Libyan mountains, at the outermost limits of the agricultural zone. There were a great number of caves in the mountains near the village, and these caves have long provided hideouts for smugglers, hashish dealers, and outlaws. Only in the late 1970s was a military road opened along the ridge of the mountains so that the authorities could penetrate that distant haven of outlaws.

Before the road was constructed, the police came to that area, perhaps once a year, trying to arrest the criminals, and in those attacks villagers fled to the caves in order to escape the violent and harsh treatment of the police. Ḥammûda made quite an issue of these hideouts and caves in the mountains and attempted to explain Shukri's later behavior in light of his childhood experiences of fleeing from the police along with the rest of the villagers (Ḥammûda 1987a: 173-174). I do not know what a two-year-old child can remember, but perhaps stories that he heard later on in life about his village and the police attacks affected his thinking and formed some of his views.

In Asyût, his step-father, although he was rich and could have afforded to send him to a good school like the American Protestant school, sent him to a school run by an Islamic charity, where all the fellow students were poor and from the lowest classes of society.

His high school grades were poor, he was a mediocre student throughout his school days, so his best option was to enter the School of Agriculture in Asyût University.

In 1965, while a student at the university, he was arrested by the police for distributing Muslim Brotherhood leaflets. To start with, he was imprisoned in Ṭurra prison in Cairo, and a year later he was moved to the "concentration camp" at Abu Za'bal. Although it was called a prison, in reality it was like a concentration camp.

While his classmates were studying agriculture for the sole purpose of having a degree, and not for the purpose of using it in agriculture, Shukri was at another university. He was in the "concentration camp," studying the "philosophy of life" at the feet of Mawdûdi and Sayyid Qutb. At the concentration camp he was in contact with like-minded prisoners who were exposed to torture, humiliation and injustice. He had the opportunity to discuss, filter through ideas and reach his own conclusions and convictions. To start with, he joined an Al-Azhar graduate by the name of 'Ali 'Abdu Ismâ'îl who formed a new group called the Society of Muslims. Ismâ'îl's black and white perspective to issues attracted Shukri, and thus Shukri became his most dedicated follower.

At the concentration camp, the prisoners discussed together their ideas and interpretations of Sayyid Qutb, and various conclusions were reached. The older prisoners like Huḍaybi and other Neo-Muslim Brotherhood leaders, preferred the approach of penetrating the society before Islamicizing it. The youth, on the other hand, were in agreement about the need for the true Muslims to detach themselves from the society, since the whole society is living in *jâhiliyya* (barbarianism). Yet, the youth were divided into two groups on the meaning and the application of *hijra* (detachment). One group held the view that withdrawal from the society meant only spiritual detachment. The other group understood *hijra* to mean total separation and withdrawal. Shukri was among the second group.

So there was this "open university" inside the "concentration camp" filled with people who had paid quite a costly "tuition"—imprisonment and torture—and as equals they all sought to understand God's mission in a sick world ruled by *ṭawâghît* (dictators) who behaved like *aṣnâm* (idols). Unlike the university in Asyût that prepared graduates for disguised unemployment, these men in the "concentration camp" were being prepared for a mission and a calling which demanded not only their time, but their money, and even their lives as well.

Huḍaybi, a fellow prisoner, met with the youth and tried to reason with them from the *Qur'ân*. He was able to help some of them to move into broader perspectives and more moderate conclusions.

One of those influenced by Huḍaybi was Ismâ'îl, the leader of the Society of Muslims, who believed in total separation and withdrawal from the society. On a summer day in 1969, after leading his group in prayer, Ismâ'îl renounced his views on detachment and *takfîr* (excommunication) quite dramatically, by throwing off his white *gallâbiyya* (robe) and declaring that he was renouncing his wrong views and casting them off just as he had cast off his robe. His sect fell apart, and with time Shukri became the sole member of the society. In 1971 Shukri graduated from the "university of the concentration camp" to start his mission and call in life of establishing the Society of Muslims, just as the prophet had done fourteen centuries before.

The release of the prisoners in 1971 took place as a result of Sâdât's desire to win the Muslim Fundamentalists to his side. The Naserites were very strong, especially at the universities. In government offices, no one dared to take down the picture of Nâṣer, so they had the picture of the new president next to the picture of Nâṣer. Furthermore, the jokes of the day about Sâdât presented him as a weak and small dwarf trying to occupy a huge throne. So Sâdât used the Muslim Fundamentalists to crush the Nâşerites and the communists at the universities. At the same time he started a honeymoon stage with them, hoping to keep them as a formidable force at his side.

Shukri was not at all attracted to Sâdât's appealing offers. From Shukri's point of view these offers were shortsighted goals. The real issue was not resolved by the beginning of a new regime and the end of the old because the whole country was still in *jâhiliyya*, including the so-called Muslim Brotherhood that turned "liberal," the president who wanted to appear like a good Muslim, the government and the whole of society. Shukri's conclusions were crystal clear, so lesser goals were not attractive at all.

Shukri's ideology could be summarized in the following points:

1. *Hijra* (total withdrawal from society) is the necessary first step during the stage of *istiḍ'âf* (weakness). That was the model of the prophet who withdrew from Mecca and established his new society of Muslims in Medîna, preparing them for the stage of *tamakkun* (power) that would finally result in *inqiḍâḍ* (attack and conquest).

Hijra (withdrawal) was the necessary first step. And for *tamakkun* (power) to be achieved, one must start with an authentic and genuine starting point. Not with spiritual, cowardly halfhearted detachment, but with radical, courageous total withdrawal and separation. This separation was a temporary situation until the goal, which was the conquest of society, was achieved.

2. *Takfîr* (declaring the society as living in barbarianism and therefore excommunicating it from true Islam) was his second major pillar in his ideology. The mass media used these two ideas and called Shukri's group *A-Takfîr Wal-Hijra* instead of calling it by its real name, the Society of Muslims.

3. During his school and university days, as he reflected on the whole system of education in Egypt whether secular or religious, he was not satisfied.

> Since there is no science or knowledge except in God...the Muslim is obligated to seek his path and knowledge before God alone, and the so-called knowledge, which is actually no knowledge at all because it is not founded in the Lord, is forbidden. Indeed the *Qur'ân* teaches (Sûra 2:216, 232) that God knows and you know not. This means, according to Shukri, that everything which came after the Book and accounts of the Traditions of the Prophet *(sunna)*, is excluded from the domain of legitimate knowledge. The four great legal schools of the Sunni Imams, Abu Ḥanîfa, Ibn Ḥanbal, Mâlik, and Shâfi'i in particular are null and void. Shukri told the court: 'We would like to call your attention to the following fact: Islam has been in decline ever since men have ceased to draw their lessons directly from the *Qur'ân* and *sunna*, and have instead followed the traditions of other men, those who call themselves Imams. The interpretive works of the four Imams, Shukri argued, were wholly unnecessary. The *Qur'ân* was delivered in Arabic, and the only tool that may be needed for the explaining of the meaning of some of its terms, is a good dictionary' (Kepel 1985: 79).

Shukri goes on to point out that these four Imams closed the door for *ijtihâd* (jurisprudence) so that they alone could stand as the authority for interpretation. They had put themselves as mediators between God and men. Furthermore, Shukri points out that interpretation of the *Qur'ân* continued through the centuries and was monopolized by the puppets of the rulers. These puppet Imams interpreted the verses of the *Qur'ân* in a way that was advantageous to the ruler. This is *jâhiliyya* (barbarianism).

With this thinking he discarded the value of schools of all kinds, whether secular or religious, and started his unique system of education.

4. He attacked the contemporary symbols of popular Islam. Among these symbols were the mosques. In this thinking most of the mosques were not the mosques of God because they were not constructed out of piety. A certain percentage were built by the Ministry of *Awqâf* (Religious Affairs) and therefore, they are manipulated by the government. The Imams of these mosques were paid by the Ministry of *Awqâf* and could say and preach only what the government approved of. The rest of the mosques were *ahli* (private mosques). Only the few mosques out of all the *ahli* mosques that did not adhere to, nor were dominated by, the four legal schools and were not subjected to political or governmental control were the mosques of God.

For Shukri, going to pray in the mosque did not make prayer more appealing. Prayer at the home of any true Muslim was pleasing to God.

5. Another symbol that Shukri attacked was the popular concept of the Friday prayer in the mosque. Shukri believed that this prayer was meant as an open and public declaration of the *umma*. When people rushed on Friday to pray in the mosques, assuming that by doing so they were wiping away the sins of their *jâhiliyya*-type living, they were deceiving themselves. Praying on Friday in the mosque was meaningless to those in *jâhiliyya* and not required of the faithful who were in the stage of *istiḍ'âf* (weakness). Only when the Society of Muslims reached the stage of *tamakkun* would the Friday prayer get its proper meaning and validity.

6. Shukri next criticized the army. In the view of ordinary Muslims, Israel was the police state that was planted in the midst of the Arab World to keep the Arabs under the control of imperialism. On the other hand, Fundamentalists, including the Muslim Brotherhood, viewed Israel as an infi-

del and the occupier of *dâr al-Islâm*. Therefore, Israel was now *dâr al-ḥarb* (the domain of war) which must be attacked under the banner of *Jihâd* (holy war).

In Shukri's view, the Israeli Army was as bad as the Egyptian secret services. He had no sense of loyalty whatsoever to Egypt and its army since it was a *jâhiliyya* nation with a *jâhiliyya* army; therefore, it was the responsibility of his society to withdraw.

When Shukri was asked by the military judges what would the attitude of his society be if Israeli forces invaded Egypt, this was his reply, "If the Jews or anyone else came, our movement ought not to fight in the ranks of the Egyptian Army, but on the contrary ought to flee to a secure position. In general, our line is to flee before the external and internal enemy alike, and not to resist him " (Kepel 1985: 84).

The implications of Shukri's ideology were very revolutionary. His followers did not recognize education, uniforms and fashions, marriage, family loyalties and the whole social and legal systems since they felt no allegiance to the state because it was living in *jâhiliyya* (barbarianism).

So off they went to the caves along with Shukri, later on moving to the furnished apartments to live in communes, completely independent and germ free from the polluted and defiled society.

Shukri and His Society

In 1969, the director of the Egyptian secret services had twelve men from the Abu Za'bal concentration camp stand in front of him and tried to have meaningful dialogue with them. One of the twelve, who seemed to be the leader and who looked a little bit strange, said to the high official, "I refuse any dialogue with you because you are a *kâfir* (blasphemer). Your government and your president as well are blasphemers." This was Shukri (Aḥmad 1987b: 117).

In October 1971, Shukri was released from prison and returned to Asyût, his hometown. In Asyût he began establishing the Society of Muslims by recruiting his first man, who was his nephew. At the same time he was finishing his degree in agriculture at the university. His presence at the university gave him the desired exposure to students in order to continue his call and mission.

With time, his distinct appearance (bearded and wearing a black robe) and his unwavering dedication attracted many around him, and his reputation spread far. Even from Cairo, some young men came all the way to Asyût to meet this unique man.

By 1972, the secret police started watching him, and in early 1973 some handwritten texts of Shukri's ideology that were used in discipling his men were seized and some of the disciples arrested. So off he "emigrated" *(hijra)* with his men to the caves and started a communal lifestyle. With time, women joined them in the caves, and a society with its unique value system and social norms was established. In 1973, after the October war, his disciples who had been arrested were released as a result of a presidential pardon to all political prisoners.

With time, his society grew rapidly, and in a period of five years had grown to about five thousand members. They were of all ages, from fourteen to seventy, and were of both sexes. In some cases whole families were recruited, or part of families, such as a brother and his three sisters, etc. A good percentage of these members were students, others were from all types of small businesses, and some were unemployed (Ḥammûda 1987a: 178).

Before the release of the prisoners in 1973, it was likely that the secret police obtained all the facts they needed regarding the organizational structure of Shukri's society. A year later, the police arrested the members of another Fundamentalist group, and this made Shukri vulnerable. In addition to that, in May 1975 one of the leading daily newspapers wrote an article about Shukri's group, calling them "the people of the caves." These factors convinced Shukri that his society should move to safer places where they could get lost among the masses, and the best places they could find were the "furnished apartments."

In Egypt,

> in theory, anyone can afford to rent a flat, because the law fixed rents at their nominal levels at the time of World War II which inflation had turned into a derisory sum, but the landlords make their profit by demanding that prospective tenants pay 'key money', a practice as universal as it is illegal. The sum paid is more or less what it would cost to buy the property, and since a young man just starting out cannot get credit, the only way to afford 'key money' is to emigrate to the Gulf for some years. That is why most Egyptian men leave the country between the ages of twenty and thirty. During that time the young women wait. However, there is one category of housing which can be rented without paying 'key money'; 'furnished apartments,' which often contain little or no furnishing and whose rents are determined by supply and demand. These furnished apartments are invariably inhabited by foreigners, prostitutes, people living on the margins of society and others who are unable or unwilling to settle in one place on a long-term basis. The furnished flats provide temporary housing. As marginal elements, the members of the Society of Muslims could find lodgings nowhere else. Shukri settled his followers in flats like these, and there they lived communally (Kepel 1985: 88-89).

The areas they chose were the poor suburbs of the cities where rents were relatively lower and where it was easier to get lost among the masses. Because of the lack of sufficient finances, Shukri arranged that there would be more than one couple to a room, protecting their privacy by hanging curtains. Regarding finances, men were required to work in farming and small trade. They were not allowed to have jobs in offices. This brought very little income to the society. The money needed to support all these families and pay for all these furnished apartments came from members who emigrated to the Gulf countries for the sole purpose of making money to support the society. After two or three years of working in the Gulf, the young man would return to Egypt to find a young woman, chosen by Shukri, waiting for him to become his wife.

Two main issues made Shukri and his society once more susceptible to police action. One was the phenomenon of "the disappearance of girls," and the other was the assassinations of dissidents.

In 1975 the newspapers began reporting about several cases where girls left their homes on their way to high school or university and never came back. Parents reported these cases to the police, and the press continued to publish the puzzling stories, causing panic and fear. In time, it started to become clear that weeks or months after the disappearance of a girl, her parents would find out that, with her approval, she was married, and she was living in a furnished apartment along with other members of the Society of Muslims.

The second issue which made Shukri and his society vulnerable came as the result of some rival splinter groups in the Fundamentalist movement who tried to woo members away from Shukri's group. From Shukri's point of view, to leave the group was to become a traitor to Islam, an apostate, and the punishment for that sin was death. Because of this view, Shukri's men assassinated some of the dissidents, which made the police more zealous in going after the Society of Muslims. Many arrests were made, and Shukri himself became a wanted man. The mass media got hold of the story and depicted the Society of Muslims as a gang of fanatics who were taking advantage of lonely girls and naive youth, and started calling them by the name *A-Takfir Wal-Hijra* (excommunication of fellow citizens and withdrawal from the society). Shukri himself was depicted by some newspapers as Rasputin, the Russian priest who had a compelling influence on women, including the wife of the Tsar of Russia.

With all these pressures, Shukri's position and prestige started to weaken in the sight of his followers. So, he needed to do something big to bring back unity to his society and gain back his respect and dignity. The plan he came up with was a daring and suicidal plan; it would make him or break him. The plan was to kidnap a former Minister of *Waqf* (Religious Affairs), Muḥammad al-Dahabi, and demand a ransom. The reason for choosing this particular man as the target was probably because at one time Dahabi wrote a favorable article about the Society of Muslims, pointing out that they were sincere and dedicated youth. So he was considered as a true Muslim, and "one of them." When he later wrote another article criticizing them, he was considered as a *murtadd* (backslider). The punishment for the backslider was death. The kidnapping took place on the third of July 1977 by a squad of Shukri's men dressed as policemen. The abduction took place at dawn. By noon the Society of Muslims made known their demands to the mass media.

Their demands included the release of prisoners, a huge amount of cash, the publication of one of Shukri's books called *Al-Khilâfa* (The Caliphate) in the newspapers, and an apology printed in the newspapers in big red letters for the ridicule and wrong propaganda that was printed about them. Shukri also made an impossible demand for an investigation to be carried out on the activities of the secret services and other governmental offices.

Of course, his demands were not taken seriously, and a few days later the body of the kidnapped Dahabi was found with two bullets in the head. Information that helped the police find the body of Dahabi came from some of Shukri's followers who were arrested. The more arrests that were made, the more secrets were revealed, until finally Shukri himself was arrested on July 8, 1977.

During the court sessions, Shukri presented his views regarding *jâhiliyya*, *takfîr*, the right approach to the interpretation of the *Qur'ân*, the system of education in Egypt, the army and the institution of marriage, all with shocking clarity. The court sentenced him to death. After his execution and the arrest of the leadership, the Society of Muslims disintegrated. Many of the adherents joined other factions of the Fundamentalist movement, and others were "enlightened" to moderate Islam like that of the Neo-Muslim Brotherhood.

In conclusion, the question which we asked at the beginning of this chapter needs to be asked again. Why did Shukri go against the odds with a shortsighted plan when Sâdât was still at the height of his strength, and the probability of the success of Shukri's utopia was very slim? Here are some possible answers:

1. The poverty and the social injustice which Shukri experienced as a child must have left an impression upon him. His mother's divorce and her marriage to another man, and the poor school he attended along with the poor and the deprived, were all factors that contributed to shaping his personality.

2. While at university, the education offered did not satisfy his ambitions. He was always a mediocre student, but Islam was a cause worthy of giving one's life to. He risked being imprisoned by distributing leaflets for the Muslim Brotherhood even before joining them.

3. At the "concentration camp," his convictions about life were formulated. In contrast to the lack of motivation for agriculture at the University of Asyût, he was highly motivated to arrive at solid and concrete conclusions to life's questions in the light of the *Qur'ân*. The combination of the torture and oppression of the government and the books of

Qutb and Mawdûdi was explosive. He not only discovered the answers to the questions that he long sought for, but he also arrived at conclusions and convictions regarding his call and mission in life.

4. He was convinced by what he experienced, whether at the university or in prison, that people are living in *jâhiliyya* (barbarianism). The writings of Mawdûdi and Qutb further confirmed his convictions beyond doubt and he was determined to expose falsehood at every level, whether at the level of the government, the judicial system, education, social institutions, religious practices or goals.

5. Shukri believed himself to be a man of destiny. He knew the world would not be the same without him. He believed that he had a special calling from God to be *al-Imâm al-mahdi*, to lead God's people into true Islam.

6. Shukri, in planning a utopia, was shortsighted. He assumed that his ideas would be accepted solely because he was sure they were right. He did not stop to think about the consequences of his decisions on his followers, their families and the reputation of Islam. He was so narrow-minded that he refused to learn from other Muslims who were as faithful as he was. It seems that his blind spot was large and he refused to have his ideas questioned.

7. He was not able to differentiate between himself and Islam. Criticism or betrayal of him was betrayal to Islam.

8. He craved recognition and respect by the masses. His need to be heard, understood and taken seriously was ignored and even ridiculed. The book he sent to *Al-Ahrâm* newspaper to be published was ignored. The ridicule of calling his society *A-Takfîr Wal-Hijra* was not fair, and calling him Rasputin was degrading. When his reputation started suffering even among his followers, he had to do something big even if it was suicidal. The demands he had for the release of the kidnapped Dahabi included an apology in the newspapers in big red letters. He wanted people to know him as he

believed he really was and not the way he was caricatured. That was why he demanded that his book *The Caliphate* should be published in newspapers, so that it would have the widest exposure possible.

Finally, when that plan failed and he got arrested, he had his opportunity in court. It is sad, though, that the court proceedings were neither open to the public nor televised. His manuscripts were banned and never published. The records of the court proceedings were not published or circulated. With his death, his society collapsed and his vision for the Society of Muslims was condemned as another Kharijite uprising (Ḥasan 1978: 7-13).

Still, militant Fundamentalism continued to grow in strength and numbers. The Fundamentalist associations were making their impact not only in the sphere of the universities but in the nation as they contributed to the sectarian clashes. *Al-Jihâd* (holy war movement) succeeded in being heard and watched by millions as they assassinated Sâdât in 1981.

8

THE FUNDAMENTALISTS' ASSOCIATIONS AND SECTARIANISM (AL-JAMÂ'ÂT AL-ISLÂMIYYA)

The Students' Movement

The 1967 defeat of the Arabs by Israel was the beginning of the collapse of Nâşer as the leader of Arab Nationalism. Before that date, students would have neither dared to demonstrate nor make their voices heard. By February of 1968, workers at factories and students at the universities displayed their dissatisfaction with the sentences resulting from the trials of the men responsible for the defeat suffered by the armed forces in the Six-Day War. The accused among the high ranking officers were either acquitted or sentenced to short prison terms, while the low-ranking officers were given severe sentences.

On February 21, the workers walked out in protest against the leniency of the court sentences. A clash with the police took place, and seventeen workers were wounded. A few days later, the university students took to the streets chanting "death to the traitors," "no socialism without freedom," and "down with the secret trials." The demonstrations turned into riots and the government of Nâşer was shaken by the students' pressure. Egypt was facing sudden and uncontrolled expression of discontent, in contrast to the demonstrations of the past years, which were a display of unconditional support for Nâşer. This new expression pressured Nâşer to promise immediate and long-term reforms, in addition to inflicting more severe sentences on the high-ranking officers responsible for the defeat of 1967.

These street demonstrations turned the students' movements into a political force and freed the students from their chains of fear and intimidation by the regime. With this the student movement began to take shape. The student movement became like the conscience of the nation, demanding reforms, democracy and revenge against Israel.

With this first spark of student demonstrations in February 1968, other demonstrations were ignited. At times the government tried to absorb the anger of the youth by giving in to their demands. At other times violence was used which often resulted in more clashes and more demonstrations. The government did not know how to channel the spontaneity and enthusiasm of the youth to motivate the nation to take constructive steps in the direction of the restoration of lost dignity. The youth felt alienated and deluded, so they began looking for answers to their deep, agonizing questions either by going back to the fundamentals of the faith or to Marxism (Ḥammûda 1987a: 122).

With the death of Nâşer and the beginning of Sâdât's era in 1970, the students' discontentment increased with Sâdât's seeming lack of decisiveness. The Communists and the Nasserists formed the strong left, while the Fundamentalists, who were still in the minority, formed the outnumbered right. In order for Sâdât to have a stronger grip on Egypt, in May 1971 he ordered the arrests of all *marâkiz al-quwwa* (the leading political figures who were Nasserists and were closely associated with the Soviet Union). Furthermore he set all the political prisoners free. These included the Muslim Brotherhood which had suffered torture for years in the prisons and the concentration camps of the Nâşer era. With this move Sâdât started to woo the Fundamentalists. However, the pressure that Sâdât continually faced was the need to fulfill the promises that he had repeatedly made, namely that he would wage a war of revenge against Israel. Sâdât could not throw the army into a battle in the midst of its process of reorganization, yet the students demanded that an offensive should be launched. "To gain time, the president found himself regularly compelled to announce an imminent offensive, but the lack of preparation of the troops led him to postpone it just as regularly" (Kepel 1985: 132). This brought about more discontent by the left in the student movement, and they perceived Sâdât as a weak president and held him in contempt.

The outnumbered Fundamentalists at the universities were marginal and ineffective. In 1972 they found the key to success as they unofficially started an unwritten and an unspoken agreement with Sâdât to collaborate together. He needed them to curb the Nasserists and the Communists, and they needed him to gain strength and stature. So instead of joining demonstrations demanding "democracy at the universities" and "war with Israel," they organized counter-demonstrations of students chanting "*Allâhu akbar*" and "neither East nor West but Islam."

The man whom Sâdât used to strengthen the Fundamentalists at the universities was Muḥammad 'Uthmâm Ismâ'îl, who vehemently hit at the leftists' lawyers, journalists and thinkers and who wholeheartedly cooperated with Sâdât in curbing the leading political figures in the Rectification Revolution[1] of May 1971. In 1973, Sâdât appointed him as the Governor of Asyût, thus he became the godfather of *al-Jamâ'ât al-Islâmiyya* at the universities (Ḥammûda 1987a: 137). This appointment as the governor of the city of Asyût was not only a blow to the leftist students, but also ignited open confrontation with the Christian population of that city. The Fundamentalists, through their strong moral and financial support, became a formidable force, which intimidated the student body and teachers at Asyût University.

Sâdât cooperated with the *Jamâ'ât* (the militant fundamentalists at the universities) and reared them as a lion cub to keep the Nasserists and Communists under control. This lion cub grew and became a huge lion that struck back at Sâdât.

The Jamâ'ât and the University

According to Kepel, it is misleading to think of the Egyptian universities as similar to the institutions of higher learning in the West. It is more accurate to describe them as the "establishments of long-term instruction" along with the term "universities of large numbers." These universities "provide more than half a million students with courses of study rigidly compartmentalized into narrow disciplines, and offering degrees governed by an examination system, that yields little to the Qur'anic schools in its exclusive reliance on the routine memorization of manuals" (Kepel 1985: 135). Once the student graduates and earns his diploma, this gives him the right to a title to his name. The title serves for the purpose of marriage to someone from a good family and in giving the graduate respect and honor in the society.

However, this diploma will help him get a job only as an underpaid state employee that hardly provides money for survival. These doctors, engineers and other graduates have to find other jobs, if not in their fields then as taxi drivers, teachers of private lessons or even amateur plumbers in order to have enough money for a decent living. The universities that Nâṣer's regime created made it possible for any student to enter the university. No matter how long it took, a student could finally graduate with a degree; if not from the respected departments such as the faculties of medicine and engineering, then from faculties such as commerce and liberal arts. In 1970, the number of university students was less than two hundred thousand. By 1977, the number of students reached half a million, and with the years they continued to increase.

The small percentage of the students who could afford the expensive private lessons managed to have some education, and their parents helped them after graduation to get the most lucrative positions. The majority of students could not afford the private lessons, and after graduation they suffered from disguised unemployment. Along with this problem, there were several others that arose as a result of the insurmountable difficulties due to the deficient infrastructure. Lecture halls were too small for the huge numbers of students. Seats could not accommodate half the students. Female students suffered from sexual harassment encountered in the very crowded buses which took them back and forth to the universities. The students had to grudgingly accept these, along with other problems, because there were no other options.

The Fundamentalist students started addressing these issues and spoke to these felt needs. This gave them strength and recognition.

> A mini-bus service was organized by the *Jamâ'ât* along with the student union for the female students, in order to preserve their dignity from the assaults to which they were subjected on public transport.... But since demand exceeded supply, it was first preferable, and later compulsory for the women to dress in Islamic style, (long robe, head-cover and in some cases veil and gloves), if they wanted to use this means of transport.
>
> Their tactic also had the advantage of being supported by more than one university official. It was characteristic of the *Jamâ'ât* to propose a slogan that seemed more or less anodyne, acceptable to the mass of Muslims convinced that this was what Islam was like at its origins, and then suddenly to proclaim, once the masses of students had come out in support of the slogan, that it represented a militant break with *jâhiliyya* (Kepel 1985: 143-144).

One began by encouraging his sister to use the "private" minibus and dress in Islamic style, and then found himself, little by little, fighting for the establishment of the Muslim state.

The *Jamâ'ât* (militant fundamentalists at the universities) addressed a number of issues like the mini-bus service for the female students. Other issues were, segregated seating of the sexes at the university, private lessons at the mosques, manuals summarizing the lectures of the professors sold at reasonable prices. The *Jama'at* also provided clothing, food and lodging for poor students who came from the villages. All these solutions served the purpose of propagating their goals and recruiting more adherents. By the school year 1977-78 the *Jamâ'ât* controlled the students' unions in most of the universities of Egypt, partly because they were aggressive and activists, and partly because the other students withdrew from this unattractive competition and joined the silent majority (Aḥmad 1989a: 118).

With this control, the *Jama'at* became the spokesmen of the student body. Music, drama and fine arts were forbidden at the university. The right to share in decision-making was demanded regarding the syllabi, the system of education and even in some cases the hiring of teachers (Ḥammûda 1987: 143, 161). As the *Jamâ'ât* grew in strength, making full use of the financial and moral support of Sâdât's regime, they started making independent choices even if it aggravated Sâdât and his government. The partnership with Sâdât was dissolved gradually as they embarrassed, irritated and even threatened the regime. Open criticism from both sides was voiced. Financial support for their training camps was stopped and some violence was exercised until the complete divorce took place.

The year 1977 was the year of confrontations. In January it started with the riots following the decision of Sâdât to lift some of the subsidies on certain basic foodstuffs and other essentials. People took to the streets and the *Jamâ'ât*, along with some opposition parties, took advantage of these riots. The army had to curb the riots, making this the first military intervention since the revolution in 1952. Nine hundred were wounded and the number of those arrested was 1,250, most of whom were students. The value of burned buses and destroyed public property was estimated at close to one million dollars.

Another major event in 1977 was the visit of Sâdât to Jerusalem in spite of the sensitivity of Muslims to the issue of Palestine. "Jewry is the ultimate abomination," *Al-Da'wa*, the Muslim Brotherhood magazine, taught.

> The race is corrupt at its roots, full of duplicity and the Muslims have everything to lose in seeking to deal with them.... Because of the essential nature of the Jew, it was futile to seek to establish relations with Israeli progressive forces, as Yâser 'Arafât, the chairman of the PLO, had proposed. In fact all Jews, like Menachem Begin, had spilled the blood of the Arabs and usurped their lands and homes. The inclination to betrayal and belligerence is deeply implanted in the soul of every Jew (Kepel 1985: 112-113).

From the *Jamâ'ât's* perspective, Sâdât was no longer a Muslim. He was identifying with pharaonic and not Islamic Egypt and was behaving like a pharaoh. He lost what it felt like to be a Muslim and now he was seeking peace with those twho usurped part of the Islamic nation, Palestine.

According to one of the leaders of the *Jamâ'ât* at Asyût University,

> Sâdât is giving great attention to the mummy of Ramses II, although Egypt is Islamic and not pharaonic. It is the land of 'Amr Ibnil-'Âṣ (the first Moslem leader in Egypt) and not the land of Ramses II (the most famous pharaoh). The youth of the *Jamâ'ât* are the true representatives of Egypt, and not those who go to night clubs, theaters and cinemas. Egypt is not for the immodest, but for the veiled women and the bearded men that obey the commandments of God. Egypt is the land of Al-Azhar (the center of Islamic theological education in the world) (Ḥammûda 1987a: 165-166).

In fact Egypt is on its way to becoming an Islamic state according to the *Jamâ'ât*, and there are visible signs of that in progress. One is the *muhajjabât* phenomenon (women wearing the head cover). This is an open declaration of resistance to westernization and adherence to Islam. Another visible sign is men wearing the white *gallâbiyya* (robe) and leaving their beards untrimmed. The third sign is early marriage and the fourth is the huge public prayers in open spaces during feast days (in Ḥammûda 1987a: 166).

By the end of the 1970s, the name *al-Jamâ'ât al-Islâmiyya* stood not only for the strong manifestations of Fundamentalism at the university, but it included as well every form of militant Fundamentalism and every splinter group that did not publicize its own specific name.

The Christian Minority and Sectarianism

The Copts (Egyptian Christians, in particular the Orthodox) managed to co-exist as a minority among the Muslims for centuries. At times the relationship between the Christians and the Muslims was tense, and the Copts suffered great persecution. At other times the relationship was good, and the Copts were given key positions of leadership in the country.

In the twentieth century, as the fervor of the western Protestant missionaries grew stronger, the vibrations affected both the Copts and the Muslims. The Coptic Church lost great numbers to the new Protestant churches, which motivated the Copts to go back to the Bible and to start Christian education programs and Sunday schools. The rivalry between Protestants and Orthodox Christians at times was severe, and hatred along with prejudice rather than Christian love were the marks of the relationship.

The Muslims considered the Protestant missionaries as part of a western and foreign type of Christianity that had a desire to convert Copts and Muslims to Protestantism at its core. Muslims were annoyed by the successful social work programs and by the approach of evangelism that attempted to sow seeds of doubt about Islam and the prophethood of Muḥammad in order to convert Muslims to Christianity. The Muslims' stereotype of Protestants was the Crusaders.

Seeds of sectarianism were always in existence, but in the area of our study in this chapter, we want to focus on the relationship of Copts and Muslims from the beginning of the Sâdât era. There were three main factors which contributed to sectarian clashes:

1. During the 1950s, many Copts chose to emigrate to the United States, Canada and Australia. Their choice was based on the desire for success in lands of opportunities and in order to escape the tough measures that Nâṣer imposed upon the rich in Egypt. Through the years these Copts became rich and influential in their new countries, yet they never forgot their people. Their loyalty was not to Egypt, but to the Christians in Egypt and to the church. So money was donated in abundance to the church back home.[2] At the same time, these Copts in the West refused to lose their Coptic identity and traditions. They built Orthodox churches and insisted on raising their children as Copts.

Whenever Sâdât visited the United States, these Copts were available to do whatever the Coptic Pope wished them to do. They were able to communicate to the American public, either that the Christians in Egypt were treated well or were being persecuted (Haykal 1985: 341).

2. Another factor which contributed to producing a great deal of tension between Muslims and Christians is what has been called "*Al-Khaṭ Al-Hamayuni.*" This was a decree that was issued by the Ottoman caliph determining how many churches were allowed to be built by *ahl dhimma* (the Christians) in Egypt. This decree was never challenged because it was based on the conviction that Islam is the last religion and has the final truth. Therefore, Christianity will not expand through the evangelism of Muslims but will continue only through physical descendants. For these descendants, there

will be no need for building new churches, but only maintaining the churches that are in existence and building the new ones that are needed for coping with the increase in the population of the Copts. From a Muslim perspective, it was a fair decree, but from the Copts' point of view, it was unfair and very binding and restrictive. To build a new church, the Ministry of Interior had to figure out whether it was really needed or not, and the final decision could be made only by the president. So, in practice, it was a complicated and prolonged process to obtain permission for building a new church or even repairing an old one. Furthermore, there is an *'urf* (unwritten law) that forbids building churches in the vicinity of a mosque. That is part of the reason why there are so many mosques.

What usually happens in practice is that Christians begin building a church secretly, pretending that it is a garage or a storehouse, and once the walls and the roof are built, a worship service starts. The Muslims in the neighborhood build a small mosque next to that "illegal" church in a hurry. Once the men who are responsible for overseeing churches at the Ministry of Interior discover the illegal church, they send their representative to close the church down and seal the door with red sealing wax. That is when the whole process of negotiations for registration of the church begins. The Copts discovered that practically it is more productive to begin building a church and go through the negotiations later, rather than start with requesting permission that might take years or may never accomplish anything.

Muslims look at these Christians as people twisting the rules and not abiding by the "*Al-Khaṭ Al-Hamayuni*" decree (Haykal 1985: 343).

3. The personality clash between President Sâdât and Pope Shenouda of the Copts was another factor that contributed to sectarianism. According to Haykal, the relationship between Nâşer and Pope Kirollus was very good because of Nâşer's temperament and the humility and piety of the Coptic

Pope. In the late 1960s Nâşer's regime donated money to the Copts to build a big cathedral for Pope Kirollus. Furthermore, when the morale of the Egyptians was at a very low ebb after the 1967 defeat, Pope Kirollus gave his interpretation of the appearances of the Virgin Mary,[3] as God's love for Egypt and his care for this country at its time of humiliation. He encouraged the people to stand around President Nâşer and be loyal to him.

Sâdât succeeded Nâşer in 1970 and Pope Shenouda succeeded Pope Kirollus in 1971. Pope Shenouda was an activist, leading a team of young bishops who followed him with wholehearted loyalty and who were determined to bring forth the church to a life of involvement and impact. Shenouda was young, educated, a good writer and a gifted orator. He was also a man of discipline, for he spent eleven years in a monastery without going out once. His strong personality contributed to making him the sole spokesman of the Orthodox.

He was given additional strength by the Coptic Orthodox churches in the United States, Canada, Europe, Africa and Australia. These churches stood by their pope and supported their mother church financially, morally and politically (Haykal 1985: 355-359).

The conflict started between Sâdât and Shenouda over a church that was being built "illegally." When the police were ordered to destroy it, Shenouda sent bishops and priests to that site to hold a mass, even if the police threatened them with a firing squad. That famous incident is called the *Khanka* incident. The conflict between the two started, but because of the shrewdness of Shenouda and his ability to articulate convincingly, he won Sâdât's admiration. Sâdât soon came to find out that Shenouda was not easy to manipulate and would call on the Egyptians in the United States to demonstrate and influence the American public opinion whenever Shenouda faced pressure in Egypt. The conflict reached a climax when Sâdât, while visiting the United States, was angered by Egyptian demonstrators who were very critical about the persecution of the Christians in Egypt.

Upon his return from the United States, Sâdât was determined to remove Shenouda and blame him along with Islamic Fundamentalists for the sectarian spirit that was threatening the national unity in Egypt.

The Jamâ'ât and Sectarianism

In 1981, after Sâdât's return from his visit to the United States and after his humiliation by the press that the Christians in Egypt were being persecuted, he voiced his anger with the Copts and especially with their Pope. In the meantime, incidents in the city of Minya and its surrounding countryside took place, involving clashes between the Muslims and the Christians where several people were killed. The *Jamâ'ât* distributed a leaflet in Arabic giving their version of the events. Here is its translation as it appears in Kepel's book.

> **Al-Jamâ'ât Al-Islâmiyya**
>
> In the name of God, the Compassionate, the Merciful.
>
> Minya and Asyût caught between the Christians and the Ministry of Interior.
>
> Muslim Brothers.
>
> At a time when Shenouda had announced that the Christians will boycott the celebration of their holiday (Easter), and had refused to go to the airport to greet the president of the Republic, he then sent Bishop Samuel to America and instructed the Egyptian Christians living there to demonstrate and to distribute leaflets against the president. At the same time, Shenouda had ordered the Christians in Egypt to take up arms and attack the Muslims. So it was that a gang of Minya Christians stabbed two Muslims in the back while they were on their way to the mosque. The families of the victims then gathered to make the criminals, who had been acting on the church's instructions, pay the blood

price. But the families never expected that the Christians would come out with unauthorized firearms like machine guns and submachine guns. They fired from the roofs of their houses, killing one Muslim and wounding others, among whom were women and children who now lie in the Minya general hospital.

The police intervened, confronted the Christian militia, seized the arms and arrested the criminals. The next day, the police intercepted a truckload of arms being sent to the Christians. Finally, other Christians were disarmed. And while the Muslims were undergoing this ordeal, the authorities tell us that all these incidents are church provocations designed to strengthen Shenouda's position abroad and to win concessions from the government. Thus did the Minister of Interior ask Brother Ḥilmi al-Jazzâr, *Amîr* (supreme commander) of *al-Jamâ'ât al-Islâmiyya* in Egypt to send the *Jamâ'ât* to calm the families down, in exchange for which the Ministry would release Muslims arrested by the police in the mosques, wherein they had taken refuge to protect themselves against the attacks of the Christians. These arrested Muslims had been atrociously tortured, starved and denied water for two days, their beards ripped out, and so on. Their families then surrounded the police station where they were being held, setting fire to the building. Calm was restored after the mediation of Ḥilmi al-Jazzâr and the local *amîr* of the *al-Jamâ'ât al-Islâmiyya*, Muḥi Dîn, and the first Muslims were released on the night of April 11th. That was the day Sâdât returned from the United States, where we know what kind of welcome he received from the emigré Christians of Egypt. There followed incomprehensible events which God alone can understand. Muḥi Dîn was arrested, the *Jamâ'ât* of Minya and Asyût were persecuted, university courses were suspended and so on. Why all this after the return from the White House? Is it the result of pressure from the American Crusaders to strike at the Islamic movement in Egypt, as indicated in the

> Richard document? How far will they go? The insolent Christians are on the attack, demonstrating and openly procuring arms from the Christian governor of Southern Sinai (the governor in question was then the sole Christian to occupy the post of Provincial Governor and did not last in that position except for a few months), while for the Muslims there is only prison (Kepel 1985: 160-161).

Feuds are typical scenes in upper or middle Egypt where the families of the victims organize vendettas. In this incident the Christians put the Muslims to flight. Furthermore, in this particular incident the Christians broke the rules. Instead of using hunting rifles, they were heavily armed. What could have been no more than a traditional fight about boundary lines in the fields became a conflict that shook the nation, and because the Christians used untraditional arms, *al-Jamâ'ât al-Islâmiyya* intervened. According to Kepel

> the original incident is situated in a context of tension between the government and the church. Shenouda is provoking the state and its chief, not only through the campaign he is waging in the United States, but also through the insurrection of Coptic peasants he has ordered. The assaulted Muslims were 'stabbed in the back' while they were 'on their way to the mosque.' This illustrates the treachery of the Copts and their deliberate intention to attack Muslims as such, for the victims were on their way to their place of worship. This detail is important: its purpose is to prevent the readers of the leaflet from assuming that this was nothing more than a family feud. In fact, the leaflet goes further in the very next sentence, indicating that 'the criminals had been acting on the instructions of the church.'
>
> There is additional evidence that a plot was afoot, for the Christians, according to the leaflet, had procured 'unauthorized weapons' with which they put to flight the 'families of the victims' who had come with full justification to demand the blood money. For any-

> one who knows anything about the villages of the Nile Valley, the argument is hard to believe.... But here again the main point is to reveal that the Muslims through pursuing their vendetta, are on the side of the law, while the Copts are outlaws.
>
> The leaflet concludes by suggesting, in the form of a purely rhetorical question, that Sâdât, having received his orders from the White House, is now applying the instructions of the 'Richard document'[4] and that a top-level functionary, the Christian governor of Southern Sinai, is providing his coreligionists with their automatic weapons (Kepel 1985: 162-163).

According to several writers, the attack on the police station in Minya following that incident was a trial run for planned attacks by the *Jamâ'ât* on police stations in Asyût and other cities. Also, the way the leaflet was written was the *Jamâ'ât*'s way of sowing seeds of discord between Muslims and Christians, between Muslims and Sâdât's regime and between the Christians and Sâdât's regime. Actually, one of the pictures drawn by the *Jamâ'ât* in the magazine of Asyût University showed President Sâdât as a donkey, being pulled by President Carter, with Pope Shenouda riding on the donkey. This picture, along with the leaflet, was an attempt by the *Jamâ'ât* to put the regime in a tight situation, blaming it for not treating the Christians as *ahl dhimma* and allowing them to gain strength through the support of the American government.

The attack on the police station in Minya shows that, in the villages of upper and middle Egypt, the *Jamâ'ât* members are the sons of peasants and these sons can easily use the weapons of their parents. Furthermore, these *Jamâ'ât* can always change the traditional violence of feuds into a political violence against the government.

The *Jamâ'ât* knew well how to fan the flames of sectarian tension in order to place the regime in an awkward position and in order to place themselves as the protectors of Islam and as the genuine representatives of the faithful.

Sâdât's Regime and Sectarianism

Sâdât's position in the summer of 1981 was shaky. The *Jamâ'ât* were pressuring him, and the Christians were critical of him. The opposition newspapers were relentlessly attacking his policies. Among the Arabs, he was considered a traitor of the Arab cause because of the Camp David accords, to the degree that all ties with almost all Arab countries were cut. Furthermore, President Reagan and his government failed him in not pressuring Israel to be more accommodating. In fact, Israel did just the opposite and proclaimed Jerusalem as the capital of Israel, which was an anathema to the Muslims.

Because of Sâdât's success and worldwide fame as a politician, he could no longer tolerate differences in opinion, and so with age he became more and more of a dictator, surrounded by men who would not dare challenge his decisions. The Minister of Interior was at the head of an establishment that was there to protect Sâdât and enforce order.

The *Jamâ'ât* were aware of all these factors and they, along with extremists among the Christians, contributed to the bloody incident of *Zâwya al-Ḥamra* in the hot summer of 1981. In that poor and very crowded part of Cairo, a sectarian clash started between Muslims and Christians.

> Men and women were slaughtered; babies were thrown from windows, their bodies crushed on the pavement below; there was looting, killing and arson. At the same time, leaflets were distributed elsewhere in the city urging each community to take up arms. The neighborhood was finally sealed off by the police, who, according to most witnesses, intervened only after irreparable damage had already been done (Kepel 1985: 166).

These incidents were the excuse needed by the government to hit at the *Jamâ'ât* and all the opposition. The government tried for months to prepare the public opinion for accepting mass arrests of the *Jamâ'ât* leadership and every form of opposition, whether among the Christians, the opposition parties, journalists, analysts or university professors.

One document served as a good illustration of how the government continued to influence the public opinion even after the mass arrests on the third of September. On September 8, a long article in *Al-Ahrâm* newspaper presented the official view of the clash at *Zâwya al-Ḥamra*. On the front page of the *Al-Ahrâm* newspaper, the headline read as follows: "Origin of the Leaflet that Inflamed Confessional Sedition Discovered." It was pointed out that "a Christian faculty member" who had studied in Moscow had taken to sending letters insulting Islam, signed by a pseudonym, to prominent Egyptian personalities. After discovering one of these letters, the *Jamâ'ât* reproduced it in a widely distributed leaflet accompanied by a commentary calling upon Muslims to take action against the Christians. Here, according to the September 8, 1981, edition of *Al-Ahrâm*, is the text of the letter sent to an "Islamic personality" by Dr Fu'âd Jirjis, the arrested Christian university professor of Cairo University.

> The ridiculous Islamic religion, which represses women and sexuality, is murder and destruction through and through...it is the cause of the Middle East's backwardness, and of all the calamities that have occurred there, the cause of the terrible backwardness of the Muslim countries. It is the religion of deafening noise and forced night time wakefulness of loud speakers, (the call to the dawn prayer over the loud-speakers every day at dawn)...the religion of theft, corruption, key money, and violation of frozen prices. Such is Muslim society, and you demand the application of the *Sharî'a*! May you know that your masters, the Copts, view you with contempt and ridicule you every time they see a *Sheikh* striding along in his turban swaying from left to right, as though his head bore an unbearable weight. But will the byproduct of this contemptible religion last much longer? Now that the Camp David accords have been signed, I believe that the extinction

of Islam is near, as is the return of Egypt to Christianity (Kepel 1985: 167-168).

This letter was reproduced in leaflet form by the *Jamâ'ât* of Al-Azhar University and was distributed broadly among the Muslims to fan the flames of sectarian tension. The following commentary was added to the letter in the same leaflet.

> To you my Muslim brother! You who slumber, may you awake! May the negligent pay heed! May the deserters return to the fold! May those who have gone astray all hasten back to us! This is no laughing matter: it is deadly earnest! Shall we abandon our Islam in the tempest? Shall we abandon it to conspiracies? (Kepel 1985: 168).

For several days, *Al-Ahrâm* "uncovered" the causes of the sectarian clashes from the government's point of view. This "uncovering of truth" was for the purpose of influencing the public opinion that Sâdât's decisions, although drastic, were absolutely necessary for the salvation of the nation from civil wars similar to those in Lebanon.

The university professor was blamed for instigating hatred of Muslims, and instead of treating him as an individual case the government considered him as a representative of the fanaticism in Christianity that Shenouda propagated. Therefore, the house arrest imposed on Shenouda was justifiable. The *Jamâ'ât*, in distributing these leaflets with the inflammatory commentary instigating Muslims to hate Christians, was behind the wisdom of Sâdât's daring decision to order the arrest of the known leaders of the *Jamâ'ât*. The same applied to journalists, analysts, opposition parties' leaders and university professors who were all part of the problem, rather than standing next to the president and being part of the solution. These people were self-centered opportunists who deserved their imprisonment.

Early in September 1981 more than 1,500 men were arrested by Sâdât's government. Many of the leaders of the

Jamâ'ât were among them. The arrests of Muḥammad Islambûuli and Nabîl al-Mughrabi were the igniting sparks that brought al-Jihad (the holy war movement) to the surface in perhaps the most spectacular assassination in history.

NOTES:

1 In May 1971, Sâdât brought about a form of democracy, and he called it the Rectification Revolution.

2 After Bishop Samuel died along with Sâdât and many others, it was found that he had the sum of eleven million sterling pounds in a Swiss bank in the name of the Coptic church (Haykal 1985: 347).

3 In 1968 an unusual phenomenon took place in an area of Cairo next to Heliopolis called Zeytûn. For several consecutive nights, many spectators claimed that they saw the Virgin Mary in the sky in the form of a cloud of light. Other spectators could not see what the "devout" saw. However what was significant was that after Pope Kirollus had given that interpretation, the government newspapers gave a large coverage to these appearances. Furthermore, a huge church was built on the site, in spite of the existence of "*Al-Khaṭ Al-Hamayuni*."

4 *Al-Jamâ'ât* refer to Mitchell by his first name Richard, and they claim that he had written a document advising the United States government to fight and crush the Fundamentalists. This was denied both by Mitchell and the American embassy in Cairo.

9

THE HOLY WAR MOVEMENT (AL-JIHÂD)

Immediate Motives for the Assassination of Sâdât

On September 3, 1981, Muḥammad Islambûli, along with 1,535 other men, was arrested. The reason for his arrest was his active involvement with the Fundamentalists at the University of Asyût.

The arrest took place in the early morning hours and he was taken to be interrogated and imprisoned. Khâled, his brother, who was a young officer in the army stationed near Cairo, arrived that day in his hometown of Mallawi, located in the middle of Egypt, for a family reunion. To his shock, he found that Muḥammad had been put into prison and that the family was in a state of tension and rage. Khâled admired his brother, especially for his commitment to God and for his sincerity to the cause of Islamic Fundamentalism. In his fury, Khâled promised and assured his mother that he would avenge Muḥammad's arrest.

On September 23, 1981, Khâled discovered that his yearly leave, which he had asked for from September 25 to October 8, had been cancelled. The reason for the cancellation was the critical illness of the wife of a fellow officer who was supposed to participate in the 6th of October parade. Khâled's leave was cancelled because he was asked to take the place of his fellow officer in the parade, so he returned to his room, and as he lay on his bed the idea struck him. Perhaps this was destiny. It could be that God wanted him to join the parade so that he could use it as an opportunity to assassinate Sâdât, revenging his brother and relieving Egypt from that *ṭâghût* (despot). The idea started becoming more convincing and achievable the more he thought about it.

In the following days as Khâled joined in the practice runs of the parade, he came up with accurate answers to some of his questions, such as the speed of the vehicle that he would be in, the distance of the vehicle from where Sâdât would be sitting, etc. Then he came up with a plan. The main elements of the plan were courage, surprise and suicide. Although he did not know how heavily Sâdât would be guarded, his plan still seemed to be possible, especially since the leader of the regiment entrusted Khâled with the responsibility of assigning new men to his vehicle if any of the appointed men became ill.

On September 25, Khâled was looking for 'Abdul Salâm Faraj, the top leader of al-Jihâd movement. Khâled had met him earlier through the encouragement of his brother, Muḥammad, but now Faraj seemed to have gone into hiding because he knew that the secret police were looking for him and 'Abbûd Zumr, a fellow leader of al-Jihâd.

Khâled finally found Faraj. In the beginning they only talked about the situation in the country and how the true Muslims were suffering, whether inside the prisons or outside. Faraj later confided in Khâled how Zumr had planned to assassinate Sâdât, how that plan had been discovered, and that Zumr was hiding now from the secret police. Furthermore, Faraj confided in Khâled about his deep concern regarding the arrest of Nabîl Mughrabi, one of the top leaders of al-Jihâd. Faraj was quite sure that Mughrabi would soon crack under torture and reveal to the secret police all the names and plans of al-Jihâd movement. His concern was, unless they could do something fast, the whole movement would collapse, and all the members would be arrested.

Khâled then told Faraj about his plan for the 6th of October parade, and Faraj agreed that this was the answer. In less than 24 hours, Faraj provided the guns, ammunition, bombs and men. As Khâled joined Faraj and the three recruited men, Faraj asked them the question, "There is a suicidal mission. Are you ready for it?" Their response was in the affirmative, even before they knew what the mission was (Ḥammûda 1985: 115).

A few days later, almost the whole world watched what happened on October 6, 1981.

Why did it happen? There were many motives, which we will get into later, but there were immediate reasons. The arrest of Khâled's brother on September 3rd, the rage and anger at his home, and the broken heart of the mother motivated Khâled to act and take revenge. The illness of the fellow officer's wife who was supposed to be in the parade forced Khâled to replace him. The irresponsibility of the officer-in-charge who appointed Khâled to be present in the parade, although he had at his disposal a report from the military secret police stating that Khâled should not participate in the parade. Furthermore, the naive trust that this officer-in-charge had in Khâled, in addition to giving him the authority and responsibility of appointing new men in case of sick leaves, was a contributing factor in the success of the plan. Finally, the arrest of Mughrabi and the fear of al-Jihâd leadership that they would soon all be arrested as a result of confessions under torture motivated Faraj to accept the assassination plan and act fast.

The irony was that Mughrabi was interrogated, but the questions he was asked did not force him to say anything that would jeopardize al-Jihâd. The secret police had no clue of how deeply involved Mughrabi was in the al-Jihâd movement.

Other Motives for the Assassination

The immediate motives would not have been sufficient if not for the many other factors that made Faraj, Khâled, and the other team members willing and available to give their lives for such a cause. The following are the most important factors and motives from the Fundamentalists' perspective.

1. The defeat in 1967 was a major factor. As a result of that war, three Arab countries, Egypt, Syria and Jordan, were badly defeated and humiliated. Jerusalem, the third most important city for the Muslims in the world, fell under Israeli occupation. Sinai, which is 61,000 square kilometers, was captured by Israel. Egypt's Air Force lost 95% of its war planes in twelve hours. Eighty-five percent of the military weapons were lost and, on the 11th of October, there were only seven tanks in the city of Cairo (Aḥmad 1987a: 24). God was punishing Egypt because it had forsaken God. Egypt was willing to fight in the name of nationalism, Pan-Arabism or socialism, but not in the name of God.

2. Secularism had penetrated Islam and corrupted it. Since the termination of the caliphate in 1924 through Kamâl Ataturk, the distinctive element of Islam as being inclusive of *dîn wa dawla* (worship and politics) had begun to erode and was continuing to erode through Sâdât's era. He openly declared the slogan of separation between worship and politics (Kepel 1988: 117). That was why Sâdât had to go. He was causing further erosion of Islam.

3. The Iranian revolution was a model that was reproducible. Al-Khumeini influenced not only the Iranian youth, but his impact reached many parts of the world, including Egypt. Out of all of the al-Jihâd leaders, Zumr and Khâled were most receptive to al-Khumeini's ideas because of their military backgrounds. The Iranian revolution convinced the al-Jihâd movement of the need for a political revolution in order to form an Islamic state and the importance of stamina and endurance in resisting and destroying unjust regimes (Aḥmad 1989b: 59-63).

4. Juhainam al-'Uteibi had an indirect influence upon Khâled. 'Uteibi was the military officer who headed the group of Fundamentalists who forcefully entered the big mosque in

Mecca in November 1979. They occupied it as a protest against the Saudi Arabian government until they were arrested. Both Khâled and Zumr were influenced by this event, but especially Khâled, for the following reasons:

a. Muḥammad, Khâled's brother, was in Mecca for the pilgrimage during the time of 'Uteibi's attack on the mosque. In December 1979, one month after the attack, Muḥammad was arrested after weeks of being followed by the police in Egypt on the basis of the assumption that he had been involved in the attack, along with hundreds, under the leadership of 'Uteibi. Khâled must have seen his mother living in anxiety as she worried about her son Muḥammad who was pursued. Furthermore, Khâled must have admired this Saudi officer who led those hundreds of Fundamentalists to enter the large mosque and occupy it for the purpose of starting an Islamic revolution against a corrupt regime (Aḥmad 1989b: 66).

b. The admiration of Khâled was not only on the emotional level, but on the intellectual level as well. This came as a result of Khâled reading two books written by 'Uteibi which his brother had brought from Saudi Arabia. In these two books 'Uteibi declared that the king, the princes and the rulers of Saudi Arabia were living in *jâhiliyya* (Aḥmad 1989b: 67).

c. The way the authorities had dealt with the rebels was by using brute force, with the cooperation of troops from the U.S.A., France, Jordan and Egypt. The death of about 3,000 Fundamentalists from various Muslim nationalities must have left a deep impression on Khâled (Aḥmad 1989b: 68). The reason that Khâled did not mention the name of 'Uteibi in the interrogation and in the court was probably for the purpose of protecting his brother, Muḥammad.

5. Peace with Israel was another factor that stimulated al-Jihâd to plan for Sâdât's assassination. The Egyptian youth, through the influence of Nâṣer, had developed an Arab identity. The sense of belongingness to the Arab world was the mark of Nâṣer's time. Yet there was another identity that

did not conflict with the Arab identity to many of the Egyptian youth, namely the Islamic identity. Somehow the two coexisted because most of the Arabs were Muslims, and the heart of Islam was the Arab world.

After the visit of Sâdât to Jerusalem in 1977 and the signing of the Camp David accords in 1979, the Islamic and Arab identities of the Egyptians started to be shaken. The Egyptians were programmed through the mass media to believe that the other Arab nations were not reliable partners and that the right substitute was the West, even though the West was responsible for planting the state of Israel in the midst of the Arab world. This identity crisis pushed the Fundamentalists to call for the return to Islam, for in this alone one discovers his true identity (Aḥmad 1987a: 39-41).

6. According to the Fundamentalists, the government was never serious in its promises about applying the Islamic law and making Egypt an Islamic state. The arguments which the government used had to do with waiting for the right time for applying the *Sharî'a* and not making drastic changes when the country was not ready for them. The poor needed to reach the stage of financial security so that they would not be tempted to steal in order to eat and thus lose a hand as an Islamic punishment. Once the poor became financially stable, then it would be the right time to begin applying the Islamic law. Everybody knew that the population in Egypt was increasing so rapidly, especially among the poor, that the government would never see what it was waiting for. So the Fundamentalists considered the government's view as a cover up for a promise that Sâdât must have made to the United States for the sake of the Christians in Egypt.

7. The 1973 war gave Sâdât's regime its supreme legitimacy. This legitimacy was used to silence, or try to silence, any criticism of negligence or corruption of the bureaucracy, of monopolization of power by a clique, and of continuing poverty and underdevelopment (Kepel 1985: 191).

Sâdât became so self-confident, as a result of the publicity he had in the West, that he became insensitive to the feelings of his people, especially those who had never travelled outside Egypt and were not acquainted with the culture of the West. Egyptians were shocked when they saw on TV President Carter giving Sâdât's wife a hug as he arrived in Egypt. Furthermore, they were not able to understand how Sâdât could live in such luxury when 70% of the population lived in poverty.

Haykal points out how Sâdât gave himself the freedom to use precious artifacts dating back even to ancient Egypt to give as gifts to presidents, kings and dignitaries. The list of people that Sâdât gave precious gifts to includes, Leonid Bredjnev of the U.S.S.R., Marshal Tito of Yugoslavia, the Empress of Iran, the Shah of Iran, the daughter of the Shah, Dr. Henry Kissinger of the United States, Aristotle Onassis of Greece, Richard Nixon of the United States, Valerie Giscard D'Estaing of France and many others. The list of precious gifts included statues, jewelry and ancient artifacts which were priceless (Haykal 1985: 382-383).

Many of the books at our disposal go into great detail on how Sâdât's lifestyle did not correspond with the image of the devout president who prayed in front of the TV cameras every Friday. The Fundamentalists could see only hypocrisy and corruption in the man they called the "infidel president."

8. The open-door economic policy which Sâdât introduced for the sake of encouraging foreign investments produced not only some positive results but several negative results as well. The rich became richer, and the poor became poorer. Materialism and love of money replaced ethical values that had been esteemed for generations. Self-centeredness and the manipulation of the weak by the strong increased, and in many situations the law that prevailed was the survival of the fittest—whether in having more money or more power.

The Fundamentalists perceived that the only way to be saved from this corruption and manipulation was to follow the standards and principles of the *Qur'ân* in controlling the economy of the country. If Muslims would become true Muslims, then there would be social justice.

9. The situation in the prisons was another factor which convinced al-Jihâd that Sâdât should be assassinated. Torture, to extract confessions, was quite common. Actually, later on after the assassination of Sâdât, the court dropped the case against al-Jihâd because using torture to extract confessions was unacceptable in modern times.

On September 30, 1984, because of the torture in prison, the court gave many defendants sentences that were considered lenient and acquitted more than half of those accused of murder and attempted murder (Youssef 1985: 178).

'Umar 'Abdul Raḥmân, the *Sheikh* who gave the theological legitimacy and justification for the decision to assassinate Sâdât, was imprisoned and later acquitted. While in prison, he wrote a letter that was smuggled outside. In this letter he described in detail what life was like inside the prison cells and what kind of torture prisoners were exposed to ('Abdul Raḥmân 1987: 201-205).

Relatives and friends of prisoners lived in anguish as they knew what prison life was like. Bitterness and resentment against the government was good soil for al-Jihâd to recruit from.

10.When the Shah of Iran came close to his final departure from Tehran, the United States could not take the risk of allowing him to reside in the States, although he was a friend and an ally. Sâdât volunteered and invited the shah to come and live in Egypt. This one-man decision greatly angered many Egyptians, especially the Fundamentalists, who considered al-Khumeini and his desire for an Islamic revolution in Iran as a model to be followed.

The funeral of the shah in Cairo could have easily been arranged as a private family funeral, yet Sâdât insisted on having a royal funeral where he walked in the long procession in the unbearable heat of Cairo. Sâdât was showing all his critics, including the Fundamentalists, that he feared no man.

11.Sâdât, in his final year, in several of his speeches made statements that either insulted Islam or his critics. At one time, he referred to a Fundamentalist *Sheikh* as "the dog who is thrown in prison." In other speeches, he ridiculed the Islamic dress, calling the women who wore veils "moving tents." This greatly offended the Fundamentalists, including his assassin, Khâled.

12.A major factor that motivated al-Jihâd members to think and plan several times for the assassination of Sâdât was the book written by Faraj, leader of al- Jihâd movement. He called his book *Al-Farîḍa Al-Ghâ'iba* (The Missing Precept). According to Faraj, this missing precept is *jihâd* (holy war).

Faraj had 500 copies printed, but Zumr advised him not to distribute them except for a few copies because it was dangerous. About 60 copies were circulated, discussed and studied, while the rest were destroyed.

The Missing Precept is banned in Egypt, but several authors have responded to this book. These responses are available to the public, and it is relatively easy to get most of the book's contents through these responses. Furthermore, Michael Youssef translated *The Missing Precept* into English and included it in his book *Revolt Against Modernity.*

In a later section of this chapter, we will get into Faraj's book, *The Missing Precept*, and its evaluation as well.

The Assassination and its Aftermath

On September 28, 1981, the leadership of al-Jihâd in the South of Egypt met with Faraj and Khâled in Cairo and learned about the details of the plan for the assassination. They discussed the possibility of using the assassination as the spark that would start the fire of the popular Islamic revolution. Zuhdi, the leader of al-Jihâd in Asyût, was to start the revolution in the south and Zumr, along with Faraj, would lead the revolution in Cairo and its suburbs.

The Assassination

By the 5th of October, Faraj had provided four hand grenades and the weapons and ammunitions needed for the assassination.

Khâled issued leaves for the three soldiers who had been assigned to share his vehicle on the day of the parade and through a forged letter had his three companions slip into the barracks on the night of October 5th. Khâled carried the grenades and ammunitions in his bag since officers were not searched. On October 6 the four men took their places in the vehicle along with the driver who was not a member of the assassination team. As soon as the vehicle reached the position in front of Sâdât by the reviewing stand, Khâled pointed the gun at the driver and commanded him to stop the vehicle. Khâled did not need to use the hand brake as was the plan, for the driver stopped immediately.

A few days earlier, Sâdât was informed about Zumr and his desire to assassinate the president. One of Sâdât's bodyguards was stationed in front of the reviewing stand, but Sâdât told him lightly and jokingly to go to the back of the stand, "because Zumr will come from the back." When the military truck stopped with a jerk right in front of Sâdât, the spectators assumed that something had gone wrong with the engine. What helped that assumption was that a motorcycle had broken down in the parade only minutes earlier. As the men got out of the vehicle, Sâdât assumed that the men wanted to show their loyalty to him by saluting, so he stood up to receive them. To the surprise of the world, hand grenades were thrown, shots were fired, and Khâled ran to the reviewing stand and shot more bullets from his machine gun shouting, "I am Khâled al-Islambûli, I have killed the Pharaoh, and I do not fear death." (Kepel 1985: 192). In fact, the one who killed the "pharaoh" was the team member who stood at the top of the vehicle and aimed at the neck of Sâdât, assuming that he would be wearing a bullet-proof shirt. That shot would have been sufficient, but the doctors at the hospital found ten more bullets in the body of Sâdât. Seven other men were also killed, and twenty-eight were wounded in the assault.

The last words that Sâdât spoke before he fell down were, "*Mish ma''ûl*" (it can't be), which might indicate his surprise about the betrayal coming from his "beloved military."

Khâled, along with two others from his team, was shot, wounded and arrested. The fourth managed to get lost among the crowd in the midst of the panic and escaped, only to be arrested a day later. The whole surprise attack took only forty seconds. The team of four expected to be killed and had written farewell letters or communicated their wills. The security guard, along with Sâdât and the Minister of Interior, never expected the attack to come from the parade. Vice President Mubârak and the Minister of Defense were not killed, although they sat on the right and left of Sâdât. Mubârak was told by one of the men during the attack, "I am not after you. We are after the pharaoh" (Ḥammûda 1985: 26).

The most puzzling question was the fourth hand-grenade. Ḥammûda pointed out in his books that Khâled and his team intended to kill only Sâdât, otherwise they would not have told Mubârak and the Minister of the Interior, "move away." A fourth hand grenade was found later in the near proximity of the body of Sâdât. Kepel points out that if that grenade had exploded, it would have wiped out the leadership of Egypt.

Was the goal of the team only to kill Sâdât? Were they aware and convinced of the overall objective of al-Jihâd, namely to spark off a popular Islamic revolution? What could have been more appropriate from that perspective than to have the leadership of Egypt wiped out? What would Egypt have been like if that grenade had exploded? Would the events in Asyût have spread to other cities in the middle and south of Egypt? Would the situation have been any different in the city of Cairo as al-Jihâd tried to paralyze it by attempting to occupy the TV center and the headquarters of the Ministry of Defense? Or, was the fourth grenade thrown inside the reviewing stand by mistake? These are questions which have no satisfying answers.

After the death of Sâdât, Khâled became a famous and popular assassin and was treated with respect and admiration in the prison. Later on he referred to his imprisonment as "good as staying in a hotel," while Sâdât's funeral, which was attended by the world leaders, was met with an openly sullen reaction from the Egyptian people. Those who favoured Sâdât's policy and his political convictions were relieved to know that Mubârak was still alive. Others who were offended by Sâdât's sweeping repression against religious and secular opposition were relieved, knowing that Egypt would no more be run by an old president who had become too inflated with his own self-esteem, making his decisions in light of what would look good in the West's mass media.

The Aftermath of the Assassination

Right after the attack on the presidential stand on October 6, the government acted quickly, silencing the media, including the TV, radio, telephone and telegraph. Because of this, the al-Jihâd leaders in upper Egypt could not communicate with the rest of the leadership in Cairo and assumed that everything was going according to plan.

In Cairo, neither Faraj nor Zumr could do much, partly because of lack of resources, bad planning, and lack of freedom to move around, since both Zumr and Faraj were followed. Al-Jihâd in Cairo was incapable of paralyzing the city's nerve centers in order to spark off an Islamic popular revolution. Cairo was calm apart from a few isolated explosions.

In Asyût, the situation was different. As the leadership of al-Jihâd was watching the parade on the TV, they saw the vehicle stop abruptly. They heard shots, immediately after which the TV screens went blank. Zuhdi and his men received their signal and assumed that the Islamic revolution had started. Their mission was to immobilize the power of the police and political leadership in general. Instead of attacking on October 6, they waited and launched their attack at dawn on October 8, the first day of *'Îd al-Aḍḥa* (the Feast of the Sacrifice). It was the right day for launching an attack since the element of surprise would produce the best results. A group of al-Jihâd members attacked the police headquarters where only a few policemen were on duty because of the holiday. The policemen were massacred without mercy, whether they were Christians or Muslims. Al-Jihâd occupied the headquarters and were not overpowered until the next day when paratroopers were flown in from Cairo and crushed the rebellion. Many arrests were made of al-Jihâd members till prisons became overcrowded. Prisoners who were arrested one month before the assassination of Sâdât were released gradually, while those suspected of membership in al-Jihâd were tried in two separate trials.

The first trial dealt with the assassination of Sâdât. There were twenty-four defendants, five of whom were sentenced to death. Khâled, along with his three partners and Faraj, was put to death on April 15, 1982. Khâled and his partners were sentenced to death because they assassinated the president, while Faraj was sentenced to death for participating in the planning of the assassination and writing the book *Al-Farîḍa Al-Ghâ'iba* (The Missing Precept), which greatly influenced the thinking of al-Jihâd members.

The second trial had 302 defendants, some of whom had fled and were being tried in absentia.

> On September 30, 1984, the court gave many defendants sentences which were considered lenient, and acquitted more than half of those accused of murder,

> attempted murder, and attempting to overthrow the government of Egypt. While the state prosecutors had demanded the death penalty for nearly all the accused, the court sentenced 16 defendants to life imprisonment with hard labour, 89 to terms of between 3 and 15 years with hard labour, and 2 to two year terms. The court acquitted 174. Initially, 302 people were accused in the case, but 2 died before the trial began and 19 were never apprehended (Youssef 1985: 178-179).

According to Aḥmad, it seemed that the judges had already reached their verdicts regarding the first case before the trial began. They were only waiting for the right timing to pass the sentence. Thus, the court proceedings from then on were like a game, with the defense of the accused asking for more time whenever they felt that the judges were getting ready to pass the sentence. The court was trying to give the impression that there was true democracy in Egypt (Aḥmad 1987a: 117).

Ḥammûda showed how the court proceedings were, in reality, not dealing with the assassins of Sâdât, but with Sâdât himself. Sâdât was defendant number one, for he himself, more than his assassins, was on trial. Sâdât was accused of making the peace treaty with Israel, fighting the Muslims in Libya, supporting Kamîl Sham'ûn (the Christian) in Lebanon, and of offering Israel the possibility of extending the Nile water to reach Israel. In short, Sâdât was behaving like a god. The assassins were God's instruments in executing justice. Instead of focusing on those who were accused of murder, attempted murder, and attempting to overthrow the government of Egypt, the focus was more on whether Sâdât deserved this punishment or not. The court proceedings took on a significant and marked contrast to those of 1954 after the attempt on Nâṣer's life (Ḥammûda 1985: 284-285).

'Abdul Raḥmân, who held the highest title in al-Jihâd, was a blind *Sheikh* and a professor at the Al-Azhar University in Asyût. His main responsibility was to provide direction and pronounce the *fatwa* (casuistry), including the *fatwa* that said it was justifiable from an Islamic point of view to kill Sâdât. At the proceedings, he questioned whether the court itself was legal, since it did not follow the Islamic *Sharî'a*. The prosecutors were dragged into argumentation with this man in areas where he was far more advanced, and where, from an Islamic perspective, he questioned their legitimacy and the legitimacy of the court.

Finally, the court was very lenient with most of the defendants, whether in the first or the second court case. "The court accused the security police of incompetence in failing to detect the existence of...al-Jihâd when it was established in 1980. Furthermore, the court accused the nation's security forces of having tortured the Fundamentalists...." According to Youssef the ruling was very significant, because

> it was the first time that the judiciary, or any branch of the government, for that matter, has publicly accused the most powerful segment of the government apparatus of abuse. Furthermore, while the official reason for throwing the case out of court is torture, the most common speculation is that the Islamic extremist group is so powerful and widespread that both the government and the court do not want to jeopardize their safety and what appears to be the government's efforts to establish genuine democracy (Youssef 1985: 178-179).

As the prisoners were released, they, along with their relatives and supporters who were waiting for them outside the prison, immediately started a demonstration. They enthusiastically shouted the slogan, "The Islamic revolution is coming."

Al-Jihâd Organization and Leadership

Al-Jihâd Organization

Al-Jamâ'ât al-Islâmiyya (the Fundamentalists' associations at the universities which were born from the Muslim Brotherhood and were nourished and strengthened by Sâdât in the 1970s) grew stronger and turned against both the Brotherhood and Sâdât. The impact at the universities and outside gave them confidence to declare themselves as underground organized groups with separate identities for the purpose of establishing an Islamic revolution through the use of force.

One of those groups was called al-Jihâd (number one). Seventy of its members were arrested in October 1979 and January 1980. They were accused of attacking churches and stirring religious sectarianism between Copts and Muslims for the purpose of creating a disturbance in the country, paving the way for the establishment of an Islamic revolution.

Al-Jihâd (number two) was led by Sâlem Raḥḥâl. Its strategy was to form cell groups within the military ranks for the purpose of taking over the country and establishing an Islamic revolution. Soon after its formation, members of this group were arrested and al-Jihâd (number two) was dissolved.

Al-Jihâd (number three) was led by Faraj and Zumr. They wanted to follow the Iranian revolution as a model. The Islamic revolution, they believed, would come into existence as a result of mobilizing the masses and stirring them up to get into the streets to demand the regime to resign. From October to December of 1981, all of the leaders and 300 members of al-Jihâd (number three) were arrested and the al-Jihâd of Faraj and Zumr as an organized group was terminated (Ḥammûda 1986: 120, 134).

This third al-Jihâd group was the most famous and most powerful of all the groups that splintered from *al-Jamâ'ât al-Islâmiyya*. The reasons for its strength were their clear-cut ideology, its organizational structure, and its courage to put into action what it believed in.

In his book *Revolt against Modernity*, Youssef covered the organizational structure and operations of al-Jihâd in one of his chapters. He clearly presented the job descriptions and divisions within the organization, such as: the Commander General, the General Consultative Council, the two main branches of Cairo and Upper Egypt, finally ending in the various cell groups where each was led by an *amîr* (prince or a cell leader) (Youssef 1985: 92-98).

Al-Jihâd was the most popular among the groups of *al-Jamâ'ât al-Islâmiyya*. The thirst for more radical action among the militant youth who were disillusioned by the hesitancy of the Muslim Brotherhood and other Fundamentalist groups motivated these young militants to join al-Jihâd in large numbers. Joining al-Jihâd gave hope to the youth because they could see the prospect of rapid and radical changes through violent action. To those militants who were looking for where to place their loyalties, the leaders who were willing to take radical steps through the use of violence were the most attractive.

In Cairo, recruitment of new membership to al-Jihâd organization mostly took place in *ahli* (popular) mosques. Under Nâşer's regime, all mosques were controlled by the government; and therefore, the appointment of preachers was from Al-Azhar graduates which were assigned by the Ministry of Religious Affairs. During Sâdât's time, the privately funded *ahli* (popular) mosques increased rapidly and soon exceeded the number of government mosques. A factor which contributed to this rapid increase was the open door economic policy of Sâdât. Any man who converted the ground floor of his building into a mosque could avoid paying the taxes on that building (Haykal 1985: 303). Thus, popular mosques sprang up everywhere, whether in the rich or poor suburbs of Cairo. Because these mosques were too distant from any governmental control, they were excellent places for recruiting new membership. Furthermore, some of these mosques started having high concentrations of militants attending, which made communication among the members smoother and faster. The poor suburbs of Cairo, with substandard housing, where thousands of rural migrants live packed together, was another area of fertile soil for recruiting new membership.

In Upper Egypt, on the other hand, most of their recruits were from the universities. Statistics show that 64% of al-Jihâd members in Upper Egypt were students. Furthermore, the members of al-Jihâd in upper Egypt tended to have rural backgrounds, thus sharing traditional reflexes, like revenge and vendetta, that were transferred to their new place of belonging, the Jihâd organization.

As for the funding of their operations, al-Jihâd used similar means which other groups used, such as regular membership fees, donations from supporters and sympathizers and money that was sent from the Egyptians working in the Gulf countries. However, al-Jihâd had a new innovation in raising money that no other group dared to practice. This innovation was to tap funds accrued from gold stolen in robberies of Coptic jewelry shops.

There was a marked contrast between the two branches of al-Jihâd in Cairo and in Upper Egypt. In Cairo, the number one target was Sâdât and the destruction of the "infidel state." The problem of the Christians would be dealt with somehow in the future, at the right time. In Upper Egypt, the branch of al-Jihâd led by Zuhdi considered the Christians as infidels and therefore the proper target for al-Jihâd. They were even a more urgent target than the "despot."

Zuhdi later told the examining magistrate,

> The way I see it, Christians are concentrated in Minya and Asyût and take advantage of their numbers to hold demonstrations of strength and superiority. They have arms, and this is what encourages the Muslim youth to react forcibly against missionary prose-

> lytism in order to put an end to the Crusaders' manifestations of superiority.... The Christians have a lot of money...and they use it to buy arms, which they stockpile, as far as we know, in their houses and churches, waiting for the day when they will take them out...so that they can turn Egypt into a Coptic country whose capital would be Asyût (Kepel 1985: 207-208).

With this perspective, they gave themselves a legitimate reason for taking the gold from Christians as *ghanîma* (booty). In one town called Naja' Ḥammâdi, they killed six Christians and came away with five kilos of gold.

Al-Jihâd Leadership

The most outstanding leaders in the al-Jihâd organization were Faraj, Zumr, 'Abdul Raḥmân and Zuhdi. Khâled was not one of the leaders but was the famous assassin.

Faraj

Faraj was an electrical engineer who graduated from Cairo University. In 1978 as he was working in Alexandria, he was recruited to a Fundamentalist group that was called al-Jihâd. A year later, all the leadership of that al-Jihâd were arrested and the group fizzled out. Faraj was not arrested because he was not one of the leaders. He then left Alexandria and moved to work at the University of Cairo. While in Cairo, he thought and dreamed about establishing a new Jihâd organization because he believed that an Islamic state could not be established except by the exercise of *jihâd* (holy combat). He wrote a book which he called *The Missing Precept* and 500 copies were printed. Later, he kept sixty copies and destroyed the rest for the sake of safety.

Faraj succeeded in bringing together his group, another group in Upper Egypt led by Zuhdi, and another group that was led by Raḥḥâl, making the three into one strong al-Jihâd organization.

Faraj as well was the man who made it possible for Khâled to succeed in the assassination of Sâdât. Although he was the top organizer of al-Jihâd group, his greatest accomplishment was the writing of *Al-Farîḍa Al-Ghâ'iba* (The Missing Precept) which we will discuss later.

Zumr

'Abbûd Zumr was an ex-officer in the secret police of the military forces. He was a brother-in-law of one of the active leaders in al-Jihâd who introduced him to Faraj in the summer of 1980. Zumr came to these convictions:

1. The so-called Arab Muslim countries were not Muslim at all, but rather they were a form of twentieth-century barbarianism.

2. The system of government, political parties, the legal system, the system of education, welfare and social work were all forms of *jâhiliyya* (barbarianism), but not the individuals in the society. Therefore, the society and the systems are in *jâhiliyya* but not the individuals in the society.

3. Zumr aimed at establishing an Islamic republic similar to that of Iran. With al-Khumeini as his model, Zumr craved to be perceived like him when al-Khumeini was still in Iraq and Paris. Zumr believed that the greatest barrier to establishing an Islamic republic is the fear of the people. His calling was to break that fear, so the strength of the people would be unleashed and allowed to flow with power (Aḥmad 1989b: 100).

4. The strategy that should be used to bring about the Islamic republic was that of people power—a violent revolution of the masses. A holy combat was the necessary tool to bring about the establishment of the Islamic republic (Aḥmad 1987: 83-84).

When Faraj and Zumr met for the first time and compared their convictions, they decided to work together (Ḥammûda 1986: 39).

Several times Zumr planned to assassinate Sâdât. The Minister of Interior was aware of Zumr and considered him as the greatest threat against Sâdât's life.

Zumr was arrested in 1981 and was sentenced to life imprisonment. He was later able to escape from prison but was caught again. According to some experts, he might be the man who will lead the next Fundamentalist thrust.

'Abdul Raḥmân

Sheikh 'Abdul Raḥmân was born in 1938. In his infancy he lost his sight due to the primitive medical practices of that time. 'Abdul Raḥmân was an eager persevering student who earned a bachelor's degree, then a master's degree in Islamic studies, and later his doctorate and was appointed as a teacher at the Asyût branch of Al-Azhar University. His place of residence was the town of Fayyûm near Cairo.

Zuhdi and the al-Jihâd leadership in upper Egypt got to know 'Abdul Raḥmân, and in due time they introduced the leadership team in Cairo to him.

His relationship with *al-Jamâ'ât al-Islâmiyya* had begun earlier, when he taught in Minya and Bani Sweif and the young militants came to him for counsel and direction.

According to Ḥammûda, 'Abdul Raḥmân, at different times, spent about 30 months in prisons, enduring interrogations and torture. The last imprisonment was for the accusation of being the number one man on the list of the three hundred arrested from al-Jihâd organization. He held the highest title as *al-Amîr al-'Âm* (the chief leader) of the movement. He was not the founder, but Zuhdi convinced Faraj and Zumr to invite Dr. 'Abdul Raḥmân to assume the leadership of the movement for three main reasons: One was because of his education and recognition as a respected Islamic scholar.

Another was his valuable contribution of pronouncing *fatâwa* (casuistries). The third was his ability to give general direction to the movement.

The leadership team visited him at his home in Fayyûm and persistently asked him to be their leader. To start with, he refused the offer because of his blindness, but as they insisted he gave no more reasons and sat quietly. From his silence the team understood that he accepted the responsibility. (This worked for his advantage during the court sessions, because his silence could have more than one interpretation.)

His most important *fatwa* (casuistry) had to do with the legitimacy of the assassination of the unbelieving president and the legitimacy of taking the gold from jewelry shops owned by Christians (Ḥammûda 1986: 199-209).

In the court sessions, Dr. 'Abdul Raḥmân proved to be a powerful foe, so that the court finally had to declare him innocent, although to start with he was number one on their list and considered to be the most dangerous man in the al-Jihâd organization.

When he was accused of leading a Neo-Kharijite movement, he responded saying,

> *Al-Khawârij* were those who refused to obey the true caliph and rebelled against him. Who is, and where is the true caliph today? Where is Caliph 'Ali today? If we are *al-Khawârij*, then what are you? Are you representing 'Ali? Did 'Ali make an alliance with the Jews and call the terrorist Begin of Israel, 'my dear friend' (Ḥammûda 1986: 211-213)?

During that court session, the man who in reality was behind the bars was Sâdât rather than 'Abdul Raḥmân.

Zuhdi

Karam Zuhdi had links with *Sheikh* 'Abdul Raḥmân from 1974, when Zuhdi was a member of *al-Jamâ'ât al-Islâmiyya*, where 'Abdul Raḥmân was regularly invited to speak at meetings and answer the questions of the militants in both Minya and Asyût.

Karam Zuhdi was a student in Asyût, and he was known to be a man who was openly and boldly critical of Sâdât, especially after inviting the Shah of Iran to come and live in Egypt. Furthermore, the visit of Sâdât to Jerusalem was another reason for Zuhdi's open attack on the president.

To start with, Zuhdi was leading a group of militants in Upper Egypt. After meeting Faraj for the first time they discussed their strategy and decided to work together in one group called al-Jihâd (Ḥammûda 1986: 39-41).

Zuhdi's uniqueness came as a result of his conviction that Christian proselytism was the major obstacle for the propagation of Islam. He then legislated the following:

> If a Christian aids the church financially with the aim of causing injury to the Muslims and takes up arms against them, then it is licit to deprive him of his life and property. If he only takes up arms, then it is licit to take only his life, and if he only aids the church financially, it is enough to take up his property (Kepel 1985: 208).

These were the four men, in addition to Khâled, who shaped the al-Jihâd movement of 1981. The banned book of Faraj is still circulating among the militant youth. Although the original copies are not available, several critics have responded to this book. The militant youth can get these books, pluck out the quotations of Faraj and ignore the rest.

The following section in this chapter will deal with *The Missing Precept.*

The Missing Precept and its Criticism

The Ideas of Faraj in *The Missing Precept*

Faraj wrote a little book, about 100 pages long, during the summer of 1980, where he accumulated the teachings of earlier Islamic scholars, especially Ibn Taimiyya, on the subject of *jihâd* (holy combat). In spite of the Islamic expansion taking place during Sâdât's regime, Faraj indicated that radical solutions were still necessary. Although "mosques were being constructed everywhere, the codification of the *Sharî'a* was under discussion in the People's Assembly (the Parliament), and veiled women and bearded young men had become common features of the Egyptian landscape" (Kepel 1985: 193), Faraj was not satisfied, all of this amounted to nothing.

Unless Muslims returned to *jihâd* and made it their cutting edge once more, they were living in disillusion like the days of the Mamluks. Faraj felt that Egypt now is similar to the time of Ibn Taimiyya and the Tartars.

Ibn Taimiyya and His Time

Faraj, in his book, quoted heavily from the writings of Ibn Taimiyya, and perceived himself as a "prophet" in this twentieth century, like Ibn Taimiyya had been a "prophet" in his own time.

Ibn Taimiyya (1263-1328) was born to a family of jurists and grew up during the time of the Mamluks. During that period, injustice was widespread and instead of correcting the situation through radical solutions, Muslims were satisfied to live in the delusion of a life of prayer, fasting and giving alms.

The Mamluk rulers, who were Arabized Turkish ex-slaves, sought legitimacy through declarations made by the *'ulamâ'* (religious scholars), justifying whatever these rulers chose to do as "right from a Qur'anic point of view." These "justifications" were conceived by Ibn Taimiyya as hypocrisy because these *fatâwa* brought the *'ulamâ'* financial gain and secure positions in the palaces of the ruler.

Another manifestation of the Mamluks' era was the ineffective social revolts that were not motivated nor sustained by theology and ideology. Instead of leading these social revolts against the despots, the *'ulamâ'* (religious scholars) defended the ruler and were a hindrance to change.

The *'ulamâ'* cemented this class of military dictators over the devout Muslim masses. Furthermore, the judicial system was not based on the *Sharî'a* but on a legal code that had a variety of sources, which enhanced secularism as a virtue. The pious masses groaned under the heavy weight of the injustice and corruption of the rulers and their administrative staff, finding their escape in a type of religiosity called *darwasha* (escapism into piety)

Comparison between Egypt and the Tartars

The Tartars were Mongols who ruled the city of Mardin on the Syrian/Turkish border. Their legal system was called the "yasa" and was an amalgam of rules taken from different law codes, including Judaism, Christianity, Islam and rules that were the personal contribution of Genghis Khan, the prince of the Tartars. To start with, Mardin was ruled by the laws of Islam but later fell into the hands of the Tartars who established an infidel government and introduced the "yasa." When Ibn Taimiyya was asked about the people of Mardin whether they were *dâr al-ḥarb* (house of war) or *dâr al-Islâm* (house of Islam), he answered:

> It is a composite that has elements of both, it is neither the house of Islam, where the laws of Islam hold sway nor the house of war—whose population are infidels—but lies in a third zone.... Peace then, for he who is worthy of it, and war on he who merits war. The state is governed by infidel laws even though the majority of its population is Muslim (Kepel 1985: 195-196).

Faraj then compared Egypt to the Tartars saying,

> The laws that rule the Muslims today have been infidel laws...since the definitive disappearance of the caliphate in 1924, the eradication of all the laws of Islam and their replacement by laws imposed by the

> infidels.... What was true during the time of the Tartars is true today as well.... Today, rulers are apostates from Islam, nourished at the table of colonialism, be it crusader, communist, or Zionist. All they have preserved of Islam is its name. It is imperative then to combat the infidel until he is brought to govern in accordance with the injunctions of God and his pophet (Kepel 1985: 196-197).

Faraj assumed that the Egypt of today is similar to the situation of the Tartars in the thirteenth century; therefore, the analysis of Ibn Taimiyya on the Tartars is applicable to the Egyptians of today. The hidden Muslim tradition or the forgotten precept should be brought to the focus once more, that is the only hope for Egypt. *Jihâd*, according to Faraj, is better than pilgrimage, prayer and fasting. It was restoring *jihâd* that God put on Faraj as a responsibility and task because it was the only effective way to fight for the establishment of an Islamic state.

Faraj's Evaluation of Islamic Groups and Emphasis

Faraj started by criticizing Muslim charitable associations. Those who believed in these charity causes showed that their contribution was not only on the social welfare level, but it also encouraged people to pray, give alms, etc. Faraj questioned the value of these efforts saying, of course we must not ignore those commands, "but one may well wonder whether these acts of charity and this devotion will establish the Islamic state. The immediate answer, without the slightest hesitation, must be negative. Not to mention the fact that these associations are subject to state control, registered and directed by it" (Kepel 1985: 200).

To those who were convinced of the importance of creating an Islamic party similar to the existing political parties, Faraj said, "This would only achieve the opposite of its objective, namely the destruction of the infidel state, for it would lend comfort to the state by participating in political life, by sitting in the legislative assemblies that legislate without God" (Kepel 1985: 200).

Others said that Muslims should penetrate and infiltrate the society in order to control the posts of responsibility so that one day the infidel regime will collapse and the Islamic state will fall in the palm of the hand like ripe fruit. To these people, Faraj said, "One need only hear this argument once to realize that it is pure fantasy" (Kepel 1985: 200).

To those who believed in the importance of *da'wa* (proclamation) as the proper basis for broadening the base of recruits, Faraj asked, "How can the proclamation score any great success when all the media are controlled by the infidel regime which makes war on the religion of God?" (Kepel 1985: 201).

To those who asked, "What must be done now is to apply ourselves to study, or how can we wage the sacred struggle if we are not educated?" Faraj responded by saying,

> To wage the sacred struggle, it is not enough to be aware of the imperative of *jihâd*, and let he who is ignorant of its rules...be aware that they may be learned easily and in very little time!...To delay the *jihâd* on the pretext of lack of education is shallow reasoning.... Since the dawn of Islam, there have been combatants of *jihâd*...who were not scholars. (Kepel 1985: 201)

To those who said that the primary goal of *jihâd* is the liberation of Jerusalem and Palestine, Faraj replied,

> Of course this is a legal obligation and a duty for all Muslims. But:
>
> First: ...the fight against the enemy at home, takes priority over the fight against the enemy abroad.
>
> Second: ...who benefits from this victory? Was it the Islamic state, or the infidel regime, whose foundations were only consolidated by this victory? The entire fight must be waged exclusively under Muslim command.

> Third: ...the responsibility for the existence of colonialism or imperialism in our Muslim countries lies with these infidel governments. To launch a struggle against imperialism is therefore useless and inglorious, a waste of time. We must concentrate on our Islamic problem, namely the establishment of God's law in our own countries. (Kepel 1985: 203).

Kepel concludes this section by saying,

> Reading these lines, we recognize now familiar features of the various tendencies of the Egyptian Islamicist movement. Faraj reminds the Neo-Muslim Brethren, who loudly demanded the creation of an Islamic party, that one cannot participate with impunity in a system controlled and manipulated by infidels.... To *al-Jamâ'ât al-Islâmiyya*, who were unable to move beyond the campuses and some of whose members dreamed of infiltrating the state apparatus in an effort to undermine it from within, he replies that knowledge must not enfeeble determination, and that participation in the state strengthens the state. Faraj perceived with remarkable acuity the common factor in his predecessors' lack of success: the inability to pose the problem of the seizure of power (Kepel 1985: 201-202).

The Solution According to Faraj

According to Faraj, the ultimate goal of the Muslims around the world is the caliphate, which will bring the Muslims into one *umma*. The nuclei of the caliphate are the Islamic states that practice the *Sharî'a*.

The longer Muslims are deprived of the caliphate, the more it becomes urgent and compelling. Actually, the prophetic gospel is the hope for the caliphate, that will spread to the uttermost parts of the world ('Amâra 1983: 25). The ultimate goal then is the caliphate, and the long-range goal of establishing Muslim states. The best and most effective means to reach these goals is *jihâd* (holy combat).

Muslims are all in agreement that if the enemy attacks and occupies a part of the Muslim land, it is the compelling duty of Muslims to fight that enemy and liberate that land. The enemy now is inside the Muslim countries; in fact, the enemy is now controlling these Muslim countries. The despots who run these Muslim countries under the disguise of Islam are the real enemy. Therefore, fighting holy war against these despots is a precept and a command of God, as important as fasting and prayer. Obedience to this command does not need permission from parents since God commands it ('Amâra 1983: 27-30).

Faraj goes on in his argument to say,

> In spite of its gravity and its extreme importance for the future of Islam, the *jihâd* (holy combat) in the path of God has been neglected by contemporary *'ulamâ.'* They claim to know nothing about *jihâd*, although actually they know very well that if the greatness of this religion is to be reestablished there is only one path to follow; each and every Muslim must adopt exclusively the ideas and systems of thought which God has inspired in him, for His greatest power.
>
> Now, there is no doubt whatsoever that the *ṭawâghît* (false gods) and despots of this earth will only disappear at swordpoint. This is why the prophet said, 'I was sent sword in hand, that they might worship only God—He has no associate...' The prophet proclaimed the construction of the Islamic state and the establishment of the caliphate. This was God's order, and it is the duty of every Muslim to spare no effort to execute that order.... Nevertheless, certain Muslims claim to know nothing of this, although God's book offers striking proof of it 'Govern them according to what God has revealed' (Sûra 5:48). Today a question must be asked, 'Do we live in an Islamic state?' This would be true only if the laws of Islam held sway (Kepel 1985: 194-195).

According to Faraj, the distinct mark of the Islamic *umma* is *jihâd*. "In previous nations, God brought down His torture upon infidels and enemies of His religion through nature's own rule—earthquakes, floods, and strong winds. This differs from Muḥammad's *umma*, for God spoke to them saying, 'Fight them.' God will torment them at your hands" (in Youssef 1985: 160). To those who emphasized worship and discipline, Faraj said,

> Anyone who thinks that this wisdom has cancelled the duty of *jihâd* is causing himself to perish and causing others who obey him to perish. Anyone who truly seeks the highest form of obedience and wants to reach the height of worship must begin *jihâd* in the way of God and must not ignore the other pillars of Islam. The apostle of God described *jihâd* as the highest glory of Islam (Youssef 1985: 156).

Thus, Faraj yearned for the caliphate to return and unite Muslims around the world. This would only happen when the so-called Muslim countries become truly Muslim. Since the problem is at the head, because the head controls the whole state, then the head, whether a king or a president, must be removed. The only sure way of removing these idols that manipulate and use the masses is to use force. That is why *jihâd* is defined as "spilling of blood" and not mere discipline and self-control.

Faraj concludes his book by illuminating the importance of having pure motives as the Muslims fight the holy war.

An Evaluation and Critique of Faraj's Ideas

Faraj did not reject the four schools of Islamic thought like Shukri did; instead, he tried to go back to the fundamentals of Islam and early scholars to reach certain conclusions regarding the issues that were facing Egypt and the world. The following are his strengths and weakness:

1. He had a clear perspective of the ultimate and long range goals and the means to reach these goals. He was a clear thinker.

2. He evaluated the various groups with courage and boldness, challenging each Islamic group, whether their goals were shortsighted, unrealistic or even contrary to the real goals of Islam.

3. He was aware of the injustices and oppression that the masses were living under as they attempted to live in piety, having been brainwashed by the mass media that the rulers are good Muslims and that it is the duty of Muslims to obey and be loyal to their rulers.

4. He was able to boldly present the role of *jihâd* in giving new life and a sharp edge to Islam. When a Muslim goes far enough to be willing to risk his life for the spread of Islam, then this Muslim will be liberated from halfheartedness, intimidation, disillusions and short-range goals. The small number of militants who are willing to live such a lifestyle will make a difference no matter how small their numbers are.

5. Faraj translated his convictions into action. He was not an armchair ideologist who was writing a theoretical ideology for the people, but instead he was writing a syllabus for discipling militants in a life oriented towards clear goals.

6. Faraj did not look at the Muslims with a black-and-white perspective. He learned from the mistakes of his predecessors and did not declare all the population to be infidels. Instead, he followed Ibn Taimiyya's classification and wrote about the third option.

7. Faraj did not reject the schools of Islam nor the history of Islam. He did not need to go right back to the Meccan stage and start as Muḥammad started. Instead, he only went back to 1924 when the caliphate ceased to exist.

8. With groups like al-Jihâd it is easy for the leader to make all the decisions alone. Instead, we saw Faraj making the decisions together with his leadership team.

9. Faraj claimed that the "yasa" of Genghis Khan, which was an amalgam of rules taken from different law codes including Judaism, Christianity, Islam, etc., is even better

than the infidel laws of today. 'Amâra questions whether Faraj had read the "yasa" before making such a blunt judgement ('Amâra 1983: 58).

10.Faraj had a narrow interpretation of *jihâd* (holy combat). The purpose of *jihâd* was to fight for the cause of God and liberate the oppressed, facing the false gods and despots who are unbelievers. The Qur'anic "sword verse" was directed to the idolators who broke the covenant, bewitched the Muslims from following Islam, and attacked the Muslims, pushing them away from the lands.

Spilling blood should not be associated with propagating the faith because *lâ ikrâha fi dîn* (no compulsion in religion) ('Amâra 1983: 70).

11.Whose responsibility is it to remove the ruler? Is it the *umma*, or the small groups of young militants who might be swayed and influenced by youthful enthusiasm? What is a revolution, and how can it be distinguished from rebellion? A good test is whether the people and the masses respond to the revolution. That is what failed to happen after the assassination of Sâdât.

12.The main thesis of the book *The Missing Precept* is based on the *fatwa* of Ibn Taimiyya of the Tartars who were living in Mardin. Faraj assumed that the rulers of today were like the Tartars, therefore they deserved death.

The Tartars, although Muslims, had treaties with the enemies of Islam and fought Muslim countries, killing men, kidnapping the women and defiling holy places. Their wars had nothing to do with the cause of Islam. Their loyalty to Genghis Khan was greater than their loyalty to the prophet. The Tartars claimed to have adhered to Islam, yet they were against Muslims. Ibn Taimiyya was right in declaring them as infidels.

In contrast, the Mamluks who were in Egypt and Syria were different from the Tartars. Although they followed the "yasa" as their legal code, they were the defendants of Islam and fought the invaders of the Muslim countries. Ibn Taimiyya did not call the Mamluks infidels just because they followed the "yasa", but he called them *al-ṭâ' ifa al-manṣûra* (the victorious people). It would be fair to compare Sâdât's regime to the Mamluks' rather than to the Tartars ('Amâra 1983: 80-90).

13.Faraj did not discredit early scholars, but instead quoted them to prove his points. Furthermore, he recognized the caliphate till 1924 in spite of all the corruption and disintegration of the Islamic *umma* for centuries. Yet, he could not tolerate the Islamic nations of today and declared their kings and rulers as infidels. In what ways were the caliphs better than the existing rulers? Would Faraj have been satisfied if the caliphate was restored, like it was early in the twentieth century, if the caliph was corrupt?

There are "missing links" in his ideology, and it lacks coherence.

14.Faraj lacks the depth and consistency of Sayyid Qutb. Although Faraj's ideology is motivating and alive, it remains one dimensional and flat.

Qutb, in contrast, has a more coherent, rich and deep theology, rendering his ideology a multidimensional quality.

Faraj could have stood on solid ground if he had built his ideology on his predecessors', especially al-Banna and Qutb, and then added his own emphasis.

15.Faraj fell into the same trap that the Kharijites fell into when they could not see and judge the political issues from a political perspective, but instead confused them with theology ('Amâra 1983: 90).

16.Faraj lacked the wisdom to wait patiently aspiring to accumulate strength. He wanted quick results. Because of this, he had to move fast in a race imposed on him by the government. He had to act before he was arrested. There was "success" in assassinating the "infidel pharaoh," but how much did that accomplish of his ultimate goal?

In conclusion, as we look at the twentieth century, we see an escalation and progression in the direction of militancy.

Al-Banna laid a solid foundation, and in the 1940s he was accused of going too far in his involvement in politics. Qutb came after him, and in his imprisonment Mawdûdi furnished him with the needed push and boldness to perceive the whole society as infidel—both rulers and masses. Shukri then practiced, in his unique way, that which Qutb's ideology concluded, but Shukri's experiment finally ended in disaster. 'Uteibi went a step further in Saudi Arabia by attempting to occupy the holiest shrine in the Islamic world. Faraj, finally, along with Khâled's plan, succeeded in killing Sâdât, yet that success was far short of the desired goal to which any of these men aspired. All these men were either assassinated or executed and are all *shuhadâ' abṭâl* (martyrs and heroes) in the sight of their admirers. As the saying goes, "Islam is a tree that is nourished with the blood of its martyrs." There is a "success" story that remains a model to all aspirers—Iran.

Who will come next after Faraj, and how far will he go? That is what we will attempt to answer in the concluding chapter. Before we go into that, we need to turn to the underlying factors, whether religious, political, economic, social or psychological, which create the environment in which this escalation will continue.

PART FOUR

FACTORS CONTRIBUTING TO THE DEVELOPMENT OF FUNDAMENTALISM

10

POLITICAL AND RELIGIOUS FACTORS

A hypothesis which is believed as a fact in Egypt is the longer it takes to reach a peaceful solution for the Palestinian problem, the stronger the Fundamentalists will become. Furthermore, the more it is known that Christian Zionism plays an influential role in giving Israel financial, moral, political and theological support, the deeper the conviction of the Fundamentalists will become. That conviction is that the alliance between Zionism and the "modern crusaders" is still continuing and will reflect on how the Arab Christians in the Middle East will be treated by Muslims.

Another dimension of this hypothesis is when the moderates like 'Arafât, King Ḥusein and Mubarâk among the Arabs, and Ezra Wiseman and Perez among the Israelis, fail to lead the Arabs and Israel to negotiate for peace, there is more likelihood that extremists in Israel, like Shamir of theLikkud party and the Islamic Fundamentalists like *Ḥamâs* group in the West Bank, and other Fundamentalist groups all over the Middle East, including Egypt, will take the upper hand in the struggle for power.

What is it that motivates people to join the Fundamentalist groups? In this chapter we will deal with the dimensions of the political and religious arena.

Islamic Resurgence

According to the Fundamentalists, Islam is in a state of resurgence because resurgence starts in the depth of the conscience and is later manifested in life and doctrine. Furthermore, Islam is in a constant state of change and progression and demands Muslims be committed to a continual revolution and change in the midst of changing circumstances. Therefore, from within Islam itself the resurgence emerges because of its dynamism, comprehensiveness, and relevance to man's basic needs (Aḥmad 1989a: 42).

The evidence of this Islamic resurgence is seen in the following points:

1. The speed of its expansion. Islam is not limited to national or racial boundaries, nor to certain political, cultural or economic environments. The proclamation of Islam has not only spread in the Arab World, but in Nigeria, Turkey, Pakistan, Iran and Indonesia as well. Its expansion, furthermore, was not limited to Muslim countries, but also in countries like India, the Philippines, the Soviet Union and some Western countries.

2. Diversity of its centers. Islam, in its resurgence, went beyond the national and denominational boundaries. The spiritual dimension gave unity to this resurgence. In the 1970s, resurgence was seen mostly in Egypt, Iran, Saudi Arabia and Turkey. These are countries that have a diversity of languages, denominations and cultural backgrounds. Iran's revolution, in spite of its being Shiite and Iranian in culture and language, made an impact on many countries of the world.

3. Continuity. In Egypt there has been a series of ebbs and flows between secular waves and Islamic resurgence. The first wave started at the end of the nineteenth century, when Afghâni, followed later by Muḥammad 'Abdu, responded to the westernization process which came as a result of the strong colonialism of the nineteenth century.

The second wave came between the two wars through Ḥasan al-Banna and the Muslim Brotherhood. This was in response to the westernization process, which came with colonialism and manifested itself in openness to the western culture and education.

The third wave came in response to the secularization brought about by Nâṣer's revolution, resulting in the humiliating defeat of the 1967 war with Israel. This third wave started right after the 1967 war and is continuing into the 1990s in response to the successive failures of socialism and capitalism, and in response to man's basic needs of which most Egyptians have been deprived. According to Aḥmad, these repeated waves are sure evidence of the continuity of the Islamic resurgence (1989a: 43-44).

4. Comprehensiveness of Islam. At certain times in the history of Islam, resurgence was seen in attempts made to defend the faith and attack heresies. At other times, it was seen in conquests of new lands and spreading Islam through the power of the sword.

However, in this century, whether in the Islamic League of Afghâni, the Muslim Brotherhood of al-Banna and Qutb, or others who came in the 1970s, 1980s and continuing into the 1990s, the distinct characteristic of this resurgence is the comprehensiveness of Islam. Islam is *dîn wa dawla* (doctrine, life, and politics) and it includes all the various aspects of the life of the individual and of the nation. Economics, politics, theology as well as the judiciary system, are part of this all-inclusive and comprehensive Islam (Qutb 1987: 36).

5. The impact of this resurgence on the various classes of the society. In Egypt, the Fundamentalists are recruited mostly from active youth in their twenties and thirties. They are university students and graduates who tend to be conscientious and ambitious. Furthermore, most of these recruits spent their childhood in villages and little towns.

Aḥmad agrees that Fundamentalism in Egypt is most appealing to these groups, yet states that in later stages of its development the resurgence will penetrate the various strata of the society. Iran, in its Islamic revolution, was not limited to the students and the young graduates, but appealed to a wide spectrum of society (Aḥmad 1989a: 45).

Resurgence is attractive and appealing. It gives the recruit a sense that he belongs to an attractive and powerful solidarity and gives him a conviction that his faith is the only true faith because it is alive and is in a state of resurgence.

Political Pressure and Maneuvers

Throughout this century, whenever the Fundamentalists were arrested and tortured they became more committed and dedicated to Islam (Ḥammûda 1986: 171). Al-Banna, because of his assassination, became *al-Imâm al-shahîd* (the martyred *Imâm*). The same with Qutb, Khâled and others. Shukri graduated from the prisons of Nâṣer to start working on his utopia from the first day after his release from imprisonment. The torture of the Muslim Brotherhood in the 1960s motivated Qutb to write his syllabus for Islamic discipleship, *Ma'âlem Fi Ṭarîq*.

Imprisonment, torture and execution produced a push for the expansion of Fundamentalism and an increase to its appeal. Political maneuvers brought similar results as well. Sâdât, for instance, needed the Fundamentalists to strike at the Nasserites and the leftists in order to curb his opposition at the universities. Through Muḥammad 'Uthmân Isma'il, the governor of Asyût and the godfather of the *Jamâ'ât* at the universities, the Fundamentalists became strong and bold. They demanded that lectures come to a halt during the time of prayer. They used all means, whether incentives or threats, to recruit fellow students or to control the university professors. Whenever political maneuvers served their cause, they took good advantage of it, and thus Fundamentalism grew and motivated the undecided to join on the side of the winner (Ḥammûda 1986: 24).

The Dynamic of Momentum

In the late 1970s, the Fundamentalists gained momentum and spread their control outside the universities as well. They went into the streets and controlled some small towns. Some popular mosques became their platforms for recruiting, teaching and discipling. In 1980, the momentum of the Fundamentalists continued to build, as they united together all over Egypt, forming one central organization to govern and coordinate. As a result of the confidence they gained, they no longer needed the help or the encouragement of Sâdât or his regime. They began to openly be critical of his hospitality to the Shah, the peace with Israel and his economic open-door policy. Their strength gave courage to other groups to plan on the use of violence to achieve what they considered as their legitimate goals. What one group achieved became the starting point for another group, to build on to higher and further goals, until they finally succeeded in assassinating Sâdât (Aḥmad 1989b: 69).

The *fatâwa* (formal legal opinions) which were made in the late 1970s made it theologically legitimate for the Fundamentalists to attack Christian jewelry shops and "take" gold in order to buy weapons. These gave momentum for more *fatâwa* to be made in the 1980s. The escalation of violence was the spontaneous next step in the dynamic of this continuing momentum. Even in the beginning of the 1990s, we see the momentum continuing and gaining strength.

The Failure of the Establishment to Curb the Fundamentalist Momentum

Throughout the past forty years in Egypt, the government has vacillated between two extremes in its dealings with the Fundamentalists. At times, arrests, imprisonment and torture were the chosen path. At other times, the government, along with Al-Azhar, competed to look as religious and devout as the Fundamentalists. Television programs, official newspapers and radio had large coverage of Islamic teaching. In its attempt to look religious, the government created an atmosphere where the whole nation was constantly exposed to Qur'anic preaching and teaching. This prepared the soil for Fundamentalists to recruit youth who were saturated with theoretical teaching about Islam but had no practical models to look to nor a definite promise of the establishment of the Islamic *umma*. The Fundamentalists, on the other hand, pointed out the hypocrisy of the national and religious leaders and invited the youth to dedicate themselves to an organization where they could put what they believed into practice.

Faraj Foda in his book *Al-Nadhîr*, criticized the government for its failure of not seeing more than these two options. He stated that confrontation does not necessarily only mean arrests, imprisonment and tortures. Confrontation could take various other forms.

1. Increasing the lines of defense, where the press, political parties, and the public form front lines of defense, leaving the final line of defense to the government.

2. The mass media could be a form of confrontation to uncover the weaknesses of the Fundamentalists, exposing them so the public would have greater awareness of their danger.

3. Another form of confrontation is to deprive and deny the Fundamentalists publicity, at least in the official sectors of the mass media.

4. Confrontation could take place by strictly enforcing the existing laws and constantly curbing the Fundamentalists, so that they would not be allowed to grow and flourish.

5. A final form of confrontation could be exchanging some laws with better ones that would give the government tighter control and more flexibility (Foda 1989: 45-46).

The Dream of the Return of the Caliphate

Since 1924, when Ṣultân 'Abdul Majîd II in Turkey died, the caliphate has been in a state of vacancy. The caliph, like the pope, was a symbol of unity and solidarity. Under the caliph, the Islamic *umma* spread from Morocco in the west to Indonesia in the east, reaching as far as parts of the Soviet Union in the north and some black African countries in the south—a grand *umma*.

As Muslims look back in their history, they see not only the model of the prophet in Medîna, but also the models at the time of 'Umar Ibnil Khaṭṭâb and 'Umar Ibn 'Abdul 'Azîz, where justice reigned.

The dream of the return to the caliphate, where all the Muslims unite together and live with dignity and social justice following the precepts of the *Qur'ân*, is a utopia which appeals to the emotions of most Muslims ('Amâra 1985a: 47-49).

In 1952, the Muslim Brotherhood bought a piece of land on Muqattam mountain in the suburbs of Cairo and intended to have an Islamic utopia with 30,000 families living there. Their plan was foiled when Nâṣer took the land in 1954.

Shukri took his people to the desert to live the utopian Muslim society, and he was able to make an appeal to the youth to join him, in spite of how absurd it must have looked.

The dream of the return to the caliphate and the establishment of the Islamic *umma* is an impossibility when perceived rationally. Yet, when perceived with the eyes of faith, supported by yearning emotions, it is possible. Who would have ever thought that the banished *Imâm* would return one day to Iran, shaking the foundations of a throne? If it succeeded in Iran, it could succeed in other countries, and perhaps one day Muslims around the world will forget their differences and agree on a caliph.

The Impact of the Gulf Countries

Waves of Egyptians returned from the Gulf countries to Egypt in the 1970s, carrying with them new convictions. While in the Gulf they saw how the petro-dollar that "God blessed the Muslims with" was used for the propagation of Islam. They became aware of how Saudi money was well spent in printing and distributing the *Qur'ân*, building mosques all over the world, and training and sending Muslim missionaries. No wonder God is blessing these countries with oil. Unlike Egypt, which is geographically located between Saudi Arabia on the one side and Libya on the other side, both countries have an abundance of oil. Egypt is hardly self-sufficient. Why is it that the western desert in Egypt, which is the continuation of the Libyan desert, has no oil, while Libya "floats" on oil? Is this a coincidence, or is God punishing Egypt? Not only that, but Sâdât's efforts to take back the oil wells of Sinai as a result of the peace treaty with Israel was not blessed by God. By the time the oil wells returned to Egypt, the price of oil had dropped dramatically. God is punishing Egypt because it has not been faithful to Him. Al-Azhar, which was supposed to be the lighthouse of Islam, has become the loudspeaker of the socialist (Nâşer) and capitalist (Sâdât) regimes. If Egypt returns to its God, He will then remove the shame and dishonor that has befallen her. If Muslims repent and apply the *Sharî'a*, then God will have mercy.

The other impact that came from the Gulf was Iran's model. Al-Khumeini, who dared to look at the "truth" and dared to call hypocrisy by its name, was endowed with courage similar to that of the prophet, who challenged corruption and unbelief and dared to stand against the stream. Al-Khumeini, who lived by the precepts of Islam and established an Islamic country over the ruins of the Shah's empire, had the courage to stand alone against the superpowers, the world, and even against the leaders of Muslim countries and their hired Imâms who were living in hypocrisy ('Amâra 1985b: 230). Al-Khumeini was able to wage an expensive war for eight years against Iraq, in spite of the limited resources caused by the United States' blockage of the Iranian capital in American banks, the low prices of oil, and the damage which occurred to the oil industry as a result of the war. Al-Khumeini, who stood alone with the courage that springs from the faithful adherence to Islam, was able to bring Islam to the front pages of the newspapers of the world. With one sentence he forced self-imposed imprisonment preceding the "day of the execution" on the famous author of the book *Satanic Verses* that was published in England which criticized Khumeini in one of its chapters.

The Impact of Israel and Christian Zionism

The dominance and strength of Israel in the Middle East for so many years is a persistent thorn in the side of the Muslim Arab. Israel's ability to win the loyalty and support of the West and portray the Muslim Arab as backward and untrustworthy has served Israel and frustrated the Muslim Arab. How is it that the United Nations, the non-aligned countries, the Muslim nations of the world, the Arab oil and its impact, and the friends of Arabs around the world were unable for decades "to twist the arm of Israel" and bring it to serious peace talks?

Various reasons have been given by Muslim analysts and substantiated by western writers.

1. For some Muslims, the reason was the continuing alliance between the Zionistic aim and the "western imperialistic attitude." The West needed a police state that would keep the Muslim Arabs in check and Israel was willing and eager to play that role (Sherîf 1985: 110-112).

2. To other Muslims, the reason for Israel's power was the control of Zionism in the West, especially the United States, over financial and business centers, decision-makers

and mass media, using them all for its aims and ambitions (Findley 1987: 53).

3. To some others, as it appears in the introduction by the Muslim publishers of the Arabic translation of Halsell's book, the alliance between Israel and the Christian West is motivated by their animosity, hatred and fear of Islam. Christians and Jews are afraid of the Islamic resurgence (Halsell 1990: 5-6).

4. Another group interpreted the cause of this alliance to have had its roots in the guilty conscience of the Christian West because of the Holocaust and the persecutions that the Jews experienced in Europe, especially in the twentieth century (Chapman 1989: 63-64).

5. A new interpretation and awareness is coming to the surface now. To some Muslims, the reason for this powerful alliance between Israel and the Christian West is not only because of the preceding reasons, but primarily because of the subtle and dangerous root cause—namely, the right-wing Christian Fundamentalists in the West who call themselves Christian Zionists. The translation of Grace Halsell's book called *Prophecy and Politics* into Arabic, and its vast distribution in Egypt, is confirming in the minds of Muslim intellectuals that the theology of Christian Zionism is behind the "biased foreign policy" of the United States government. Fahmi Huwaidi wrote in the *Al-Ahrâm* newspaper in 1989 and in 1990, drawing the analogy between Islamic Fundamentalists in Egypt and Christian Fundamentalists in the United States. His 1990 article was totally based on the Arabic translation of Halsell's book.

The quotes and figures about television evangelists and Christian Zionists' activities, which Halsell's book is saturated with, fuels the fanaticism of the Muslim Fundamentalists to become more anti-West and anti-Christian (Halsell 1990: 30).

These are the waves of impact that have influenced the Egyptians. These are scenarios and conclusions the Egyptians themselves have perceived and interpreted from current events.

These waves, along with other elements such as the resurgence of Islam, the growth of the Fundamentalist movement in Egypt, the dynamic momentum of Fundamentalism which is continuing into the 1990s, the corruption in the political and official religious spheres, the dream of the establishment of an Islamic *umma*, and the danger coming from the collaboration of Zionism and "modern crusaders," form political and religious factors which have enhanced the growth and spread of Fundamentalism.

There are other factors, which are as important, that have to do with economic, social and psychological motivations. These factors will be covered in the following chapter.

11

ECONOMIC, SOCIAL AND PSYCHOLOGICAL FACTORS

According to the prophet and Muslims throughout the centuries, Islam is the best economic, social, religious, legal and political system on earth, *khayru 'ummaten 'unzilat linnâs*. Yet as Muslims look around them, they find a large gap between what Islam is in the world today and what it should be. Efforts have been made to bridge this gap by charismatic leaders like al-Banna and al-Khumeini, by ideologists like Qutb and Mawdûdi, and by influential Islamic writers like 'Amâra and al-Ghazzâli.

The youth of Egypt are being assured that they belong to the greatest *umma* on earth and that corruption, hypocrisy and lack of dedication are the causes of the "catastrophe" which Islam is experiencing. Furthermore, the models of al-Banna, Qutb, Khâled and Faraj are presented as the martyrs and models who paved the way for others to follow in their footsteps. Teaching, training and dedication are available to equip future generations. The places for teaching are available in popular mosques and apartments of members, scattered beyond the reach of the secret police. The syllabi for teaching are available in the books of Ibn Taimiyya, al-Banna, Qutb, Faraj and others. All that is needed is for youth to respond to this challenge and become committed and available for the process of teaching and equipping.

Afghâni, late in the nineteenth century, presented this call to the elite and educated, and the Islamic League was formed. Ḥasan al-Banna, in the 1930s and the 1940s, presented the same call to the masses, and the Muslim Brotherhood was formed (‘Amâra 1985a: 55). The *Jamâ‘ât*, in the 1970s, presented this call to university students and young graduates, and *al-Jamâ‘ât al-Islâmiyya* along with al-Jihâd were the results. Today, the same call is presented to broader sectors of society, and the response to the call is increasing with the years.

On the front page of *Al-Ahrâm* newspaper on May 6, 1990, the Minister of Interior declared that al-Jihâd organization members are recruiting and training boys and teenagers to attack police stations with Molotov cocktails. Why is it that even the young are so motivated to join the Fundamentalist movement? We have considered in the previous chapters the political and religious factors. In this chapter we will consider other causes, such as economic, social and psychological factors, as independently as possible, and as they interrelate with one another.

Economics and Poverty

From the beginning of the revolution in 1952, attempts have been made to give a blow to the feudal lords and to give members of the lower classes an opportunity to improve their economic and social status through upward mobility. University education was open and within reach of every person who could graduate from high school. University fees were minimal, almost non-existent. Furthermore, promises of secure jobs within the government and public sectors gave hope and motivation to the new generation to seek to have a university degree, which would be the ultimate solution to all problems. Later it was discovered that neither the degree nor the job were the ultimate solution. Kepel described the disguised unemployment with the following words.

> By law, every graduate in Egypt has the right to state employment. This measure, a powerful weapon against non-employment, is actually the purveyor of

massive disguised unemployment in the offices of a swollen administration in which productivity is as low as the employees are badly paid. If a state employee lacks an additional source of income, he can still manage to feed himself by buying the state subsidized products on sale in the cooperatives,[1] but he is unlikely to rise above this level of bare subsistence. The price of anything determined by the market would be beyond his reach. Almost every state employee has a second or even third job (Kepel 1985: 85).

During Nâşer's time, the people were forced to live under these difficult conditions because there was a war to be waged for the liberation of Palestine. Sacrifice was needed, and people were in general willing to sacrifice because Nâşer gave them dignity and honor by making Egypt one of the leading countries in the Third World.

Then the defeat in the 1967 war with Israel came, followed by stricter measures of tightening the belts. The slogan that the mass media propagated was "*lâ ya'lu şawt 'ala şawt al-ma'raka*" (no priority is higher than that of getting ready for the war of revenge). Streets were unpaved for years; cars were scarce; telephone lines were a commodity which only very few "enjoyed"[2]; there was a shortage of food varieties, and even football or soccer matches were stopped so that people would not be side-tracked from the priority of the war of revenge, which would restore to the Arabs and the Egyptians their lost dignity.

In 1971, Sâdât inherited a heavy mantle from his predecessor. It was a struggle for him to prove himself in the shadow of Nâşer. Conditions were going from bad to worse, especially when the promises of Sâdât were proven wrong as he had to delay the long-awaited battle of revenge. Not only was there poverty, but there was also a sense of despair and self-ridicule among the Egyptians. The 1973 war with Israel was a surprise to many, but finally Sâdât was able to do what he and Nâşer promised to do.

After the war, Sâdât, through the mass media, offered an attractive promise to the masses, through the "open-door economic policy," of radical solutions to the problems of poverty. He even used the term *rafâhiyya* (living in luxury) to describe the future. This luxury became reality for the few who were able to take advantage of the open-door policy. These few became rich quickly, very often through corruption and theft. A new class of millionaires emerged. They were not the aristocratic and sophisticated of Farûq's time, but they were the merchants, the import and export agents, and even some butchers. The market was open to the import of all sorts of luxury items, from soft drinks, such as Seven Up, to the Mercedes. Because Egyptians had been deprived of these luxuries for decades, they either bought and hoarded, if they could afford it, or only looked, envied and felt frustrated and resentful as they desired to have, but could not afford it.

Marriage almost became an impossibility for the majority of people because of the difficulty of owning an apartment. Kepel described the situation with the following words.

> In theory, anyone can afford to rent a flat, because the law fixes rents at their nominal levels. But the landlords make their profit by demanding that the prospective tenants pay 'key money,' a practice as universal as it is illegal. The sum paid is more or less what it would cost to buy the property, and since a young man just starting out cannot get credit, the only way to afford key money is to emigrate to the Gulf for some years. But there is one category of housing that can be owned without paying key money: 'furnished apartments,' which often contain little or no furnishing and whose rents are determined by supply and demand. These 'furnished' apartments or rooms are invariably inhabited by foreigners, prostitutes and people living on the margins of the society.... The furnished flat provides temporary housing (Kepel 1985: 88-89).

During Sâdât's tenure, finding a job in the Gulf was a possibility, but in the 1980s, the Gulf countries began tightening their grip on Egyptians and others coming from abroad. Only a select few were able to find jobs. The situation in Egypt went from bad to worse. The debts of Egypt were in the billions, and foreign investors did not trust the Egyptian economy because the Egyptian pound had one rate at the bank and another rate in the black market. In 1977, Sâdât tried to remove the subsidy from many items, including bread, so the masses took to the streets, burning government buses and destroying whatever they could reach. Sâdât had to pull back and continue with his ailing economy, knowing that what the West demanded as conditions of economic support were too difficult for the people to accept.

The university degree which had offered hope now gave only a title of an engineer, a doctor or a teacher. Housing became an impossibility for the majority of the population, unless the young couple were willing to be satisfied living in one room of the parents' small apartment. Some went to live in buildings housing tombs; others had to live temporarily in expensive "furnished" rooms or apartments.

Socialism failed during the time of Nâşer, and capitalism failed during Sâdât's period. Both are failing at the time of Mubârak. The new slogan propagates "Islam as the solution." By returning to Islam there will be no injustice; the rich will not abuse and manipulate the poor and basic needs will be met. In this environment the message of the Fundamentalists is very appealing because it offers housing possibilities, marriage at a young age, and hope for a job with a salary that is sufficient for survival. The Fundamentalists, through the gifts from rich Egyptians and establishments outside Egypt, were able to provide the youth with hope. Egyptian companies like al-Sherîf, Sa'd and others, which are controlled by Muslim Brethren who made their fortunes in Saudi Arabia after 1954 and had invested heavily in Egypt upon returning in 1975, are now providing jobs and housing for the youth who are committed to the Fundamentalist cause. At one time in the 1980s, these rich Fundamentalists appeared strong enough to control the whole Egyptian economy. Through their pressure, banks have opened special Islamic branches which do not accept the principle of banking interest, but instead follow the principle of *murâbaḥa* (genuine gain and loss),[3] which is what the prophet modeled.

With these Islamic firms, the youth have fresh hopes for justice and prosperity in the shadow of Islam.

Social Factors

The people who are attracted to the Fundamentalist movement are the lower middle class and the students. The reasons for their attraction to Fundamentalism lie in their social and religious sense of despair and in their being a class of the society that has no future. They see themselves as marginal in their impact on the history of the nation.

The lower-middle-class people do not see a place of significance, either in the religious sphere, or in the social ladder; therefore, they have a pessimistic perspective on life. Since the impact on the history of a nation is made through individuals, and since the individuals belonging to the lower middle class are deprived of their rights and the qualities which give the person a platform, they find that the only way they can enter history is through the door of Fundamentalism. Fundamentalism promises to radically change this unjust social system and give these marginal people the opportunity to enter the heart of the history of the nation. These groups end up playing not only the normal roles which they were deprived of, but they even play a much bigger role, rejecting the values and the foundations of the social system (Ḥabîb 1989: 130).

The other group of people who go through a similar experience are the university students.

When education is compulsory and a long span of years is required to graduate from the university in an educational system which offers no motivation, except to the few who enter the faculties of medicine and engineering, students become marginal as well. University students are a class of society made up of people in the middle. They are neither children nor adults who are involved in meaningful and gratifying work and production. They are forced to be marginal as students and look to the future with anxiety and despair because they know that what is waiting for them is disguised unemployment. The students become an ethnic group in the society with their distinct cultural values. They, along with the young graduates who find no hope for upward mobility, become open and eager to respond to a Fundamentalist invitation which promises involvement, significance and a role to play in making history.

Because the revolution of 1952 made education free and available to all, lower-class people were given the hope that they could join the upward movement of social mobility and reach the middle class. As a result, the universities grew, producing about half a million young men and women annually who were supposed to have become middle-class people because of their education. The middle class became the huge tail on a disproportionate creature, with a small head and body.

People belonging to the tail are basically the lower middle class. Some of these people came from the villages and small towns to the big cities to live in the suburbs, bringing along with them their rural culture. Most of these people arrive to a sort of self-actualization through jobs where both the husband and wife are working, but many find it hard to make it in this difficult battle for survival. These are the ones who become good candidates for Fundamentalism. If this group of deprived people in the lower middle class becomes big, then revolution becomes inevitable (Ḥabîb 1989: 133).

By comparing these poor suburbs in Cairo with the rest of the city, we see a tremendous contrast. Not only are the streets narrow and dirty, but the water supply, sewage system, telephones, electricity and all other necessities are under tremendous pressure because of the over-crowded situation. It is very common to see sewage water covering the streets, which are more like alleys. Water does not reach higher floors, due to low pressure, except in the very few hours of the early morning. Telephones are a luxury which very few can afford, and power failures are frequent.

Those families who remained in the villages and small towns, when compared with the suburbs of the big cities, are better off. Village and small-town people are not ambitious beyond their means. They have the space and the culture which corresponds with their living situation. Because some of them have worked in the Gulf countries, they have the means to buy not only a color television, but a video-cassette recorder as well.

Therefore, in the suburbs of Cairo with its population of over sixteen million, the message of Fundamentalism is most attractive and appealing to the youth. In these poor suburbs of Cairo, the young, the ambitious and the conscientious, yet marginal, have nothing to lose and everything to gain by joining al-Jihâd or other Fundamentalist organizations. The white robe, beard and veil demand fear or respect in the eyes of those around them. These people become leaders and men of influence. As they preach their slogan that Islam is the solution, they begin having followers and their impact starts to be felt among their families and friends. Because they are young and idealistic, they tend to see issues from a black-and-white perspective. The solution for everything can be found in Islam and the application of the *Sharî'a.* Although their families are not fully convinced of these idealistic views, in time they at least become sympathizers with the cause of Fundamentalism.

Life at the University

According to *Al-Ahrâm* newspaper, the percentage of the unemployed in Egypt has reached twenty-eight percent, a figure which does not include the disguised unemployment that we talked about in the previous section. A high percentage of the population of the small Gulf countries is made up of foreigners. The goal in the coming years for these Gulf countries is to get rid of most of the foreigners. This reflects the difficulty which the Egyptian faces in finding a job nowadays.

A student graduating with a degree which is worthless unless he has a rich and influential family backing him results in a sense of despair, lack of motivation and lack of purpose.

Kepel describes the university educational system with the following words.

> Universities provide more than half a million students with courses of study rigidly compartmentalized into narrow disciplines and offer degrees governed by an examination system that yields little to the Qur'anic schools in its exclusive reliance on the routine memorization of manuals. It is not unusual for two or even three students to share a seat in the packed lecture halls and laboratories. Considerable prowess is required even to hear the teachers' voices, especially when the microphone is broken or when there are power failures. Success in exams depends not only on buying the manual sold by the professor, but also on industrious attendance of the special tutorials given by teachers during the two months preceding the end-of-year examinations (Kepel 1985: 135-136).

The rigid system that is used for the selection of disciplines at the universities divides the choices into compartments. The highest scores are required by the faculties of medicine and engineering. Down the ladder comes the faculties of pharmacology, computer sciences and political science. Other fields of knowledge, such as social sciences and commerce, are called "garbage faculties" by the Egyptians themselves.

The university students also suffer from the transportation system back and forth to the university. The situation of the students who live in overcrowded dormitories or rented rooms in apartments surrounding the universities is even worse.

Another problem which the university students face is indecent behavior, which threatens the female students' modesty. This is due to lecture halls which are packed and have limited seating and jam-packed buses which carry the students on the daily journey to campus. "In a society in which relations between the sexes occur late and are strictly circumscribed by marriage, the jostling bus, in which bodies are pressed one against the other becomes a site of furtive eroticism in which the female students feel themselves the victims" (Kepel 1985: 136).

Why all the effort, when after graduation there is no guarantee of work except for jobs which are not more than disguised unemployment? Boredom, despair and lack of motivation to struggle against a system which will reach only a dead end are the experiences of many students.

No wonder then, that in one of the leading plays in Cairo in 1989 called "*Inqilâb*," the theme of the play pointed out that there are two outlets open for the bored youth in Egypt, drugs or Islamic Fundamentalism.

Al-Ahrâm newspaper, in an interview with the Minister of Interior which appeared on the first page on May 6, 1990, stated that the two greatest dangers facing the youth today are drugs and Fundamentalism. Egypt passed a new law in 1989 that the penalty for dealing drugs is capital punishment. This shows the magnitude of the problem. Hashish, which for decades was the "drug of choice" for illiterate Egyptians, has been supplemented with cocaine and heroin for a new class of people, which includes university students, who obtain the money through stealing. The other major outlet for bored university students is Fundamentalism.

In an environment where jobs of "disguised unemployment" give no sense of dignity, when the future is not certain, and where the identity of the youth is lost, Fundamentalism offers a bright answer and a sure solution.

Jobs are available in companies belonging to Islamic millionaires. It is better still to be committed to working full-time in the ministry of recruiting, teaching, training and equipping new generations of Fundamentalists. For these people, apartments are available at a reduced price, donated by rich Islamists; therefore, early marriage is a possibility. Furthermore, the ideology built on the conviction that Islam is the solution to all problems has a strong appeal to any conscientious young man who wants his life to count.

Having purpose, a sense of belonging to a strong solidarity, and available financial resources make Fundamentalism an excellent choice.

Psychological Factors

We have seen earlier that economic, social and even psychological factors interrelated to form the environment in which the candidate of Fundamentalism lives. The economic open-door policy at the time of Sâdât, which was accompanied by manifestations of western life styles, resulted in estrangement. The young people who belonged to the lower middle class, because of their university degree and because they could not find a way to work at the small companies of the private sector which pay good salaries, looked at those "estranged and westernized" young people who got the jobs and money with resentment and envy. That kind of perception made them consider themselves inferior to those who become westernized, thus they withdrew from the society to marginalization ('Abdul-Fâḍil 1982: 108).

This state of marginalization needed to be justified, and the justification came through the condemnation of the evil, injustice and corruption in the society. To stay pure, one must adhere to God and separate oneself from this polluted society (Ḥusein 1982: 207). The gap between the rich and the poor was greatly widened as a result of the open-door policy. The new class of millionaires, who owned the very expensive and latest models of Mercedes, existed in the same city next to the multitudes of poor.

The poor are not only the lower-middle-class people, but rather the lower classes who live at times below the subsistence level. It is quite common nowadays to hear of apartments which serve as a residence to more than twenty persons. Each family, of about eight members, takes one bedroom in a three-bedroom apartment which has one bathroom. The father and the mother sleep on the one bed, the teenage girls sleep under the bed for the sake of privacy, and the rest of the family are spread on the floor of the room. In the morning a queue of more than twenty are waiting to use the bathroom. The battle for survival is not only finding a place on the floor to sleep, but having enough to eat and riding the crowded buses to school. The battle for survival is in operation every hour of the day. For instance, teenage girls who sleep under the bed listen to the sounds of the bed creaking as their parents have their sexual intercourse. Brothers are worried about protecting their sisters from boys belonging to the families living in the neighboring bedrooms in the same apartment. The battle for survival goes on, and with it there is the growing conviction that life is a jungle. Survival is for the strongest and the most violent. It is no wonder that sayings such as "*Ma'ak irsh bitsâwi irsh*" (Your value is by how much money you have) and "*Tghadda bî abl ma yit'ashsha bîk*" (Eat the other person for lunch before he eats you for supper) are becoming the convictions of the new generation who are fighting for survival.

In this jungle, the persistent question is, "Where is God, and where is the justice of Islam?" According to Allport, progression to violence might follow this path:

1. Long period of categorical pre-judgements on the rich, the government, and the puppet Imams who serve as the mouthpiece of the government.
2. Long period of verbal complaint.
3. Growing discrimination. (e.g., the rich, through their connections and bribes, can get anything with the least effort, while the poor are treated like the scum of the earth).
4. The existence of strain that results from economic privation, a sense of low status or fear of unemployment.
5. People have grown tired of their own inhibitions and are reaching a state of explosion. They no longer feel that they can or should put up with rising prices, humiliation and bewilderment. Irrationalism comes to have a strong appeal.
6. Organized movements such as al-Jihâd and other Fundamentalist groups attract the discontented individuals.
7. From such formal or informal social organization, the individual derives courage and support. He sees that his irritation and wrath are socially and even theologically sanctioned. His impulses to violence are thus justified by the standards and the *fatâwa* (casuistries) of his groups or organization.
8. Some precipitating incident occurs. What previously might have been passed over as a trivial provocation now causes an explosion. The incident may be wholly imaginary, or it may be exaggerated through rumor. A story goes around that a Christian man raped a Muslim teenager, so leaflets are distributed to that wholly imaginary incident, and the spark ignites the fire of violence.
9. When violence actually breaks out, it is likely to happen when two opposing groups are thrown into close contact, such as Christians and Muslims living in the same neighborhood, or university students in the same campus. At

such meeting points, the precipitating incident is most likely to occur (Allport 1958: 56-58).

The factors which help produce the type of environment where the youth become good candidates for Fundamentalism could be political, religious, economic, social or psychological. More specifically, according to the Egyptian psychiatrist Yaḥya Rakhâwi, the most important motivating factors for becoming a Fundamentalist are the following:

1. A method of education in Egypt that trains the mind on passive reception without critical evaluation. It is a system which puts emphasis on memorization, rather than research and understanding. It is the blind acceptance of "truth" delivered to the obedient recipients. Most certain and absolute truths are the religious precepts which are received with obedience and awe.

2. Reception of data on two parallel and many times contradictory channels. When young people receive this contradictory data, they attempt to escape confusion through resorting to black-and-white answers and simplistic solutions.

We see these double channels as the young people are daily exposed to the "necessity of applying the *Sharî'a*," expounded and preached over the screen of the colored television. Or, they hear the promises for hope of solving all of life's problems, yet live in a miserable reality.

Therefore, resorting to the escapism to a life of absolute purity in a polluted and corrupt environment is a natural solution to the problems of life.

3. The absence of identity and weakness of the sense of belonging. At the time of British colonialism, the identity of the Egyptians was seen in nationalism. At the time of Nâṣer, it was socialism against capitalism. At the time of Sâdât, it was independence and liberation against old forms of authority such as the police and government.

Because of peace with Israel, who the enemy is has become confused and less clear-cut.

In this vacuum, the youth look for an identity, a place of belonging and an enemy to channel his hatred against. In resorting to Fundamentalism, the youngsters find their identity in following God, their place of belonging in becoming dedicated members in the various Fundamentalist groups, and their enemy in Satan and the hypocrisy of the so-called "Muslim society."

4. The collapse of big dreams and ideas. Several dreams and ideas collapsed over the past fifty years in Egypt. For instance, modern technology failed to bring about radical solutions to daily problems. Social justice was not brought about as it was promised by socialism and communism. To avoid more failures, the only option that has not failed so far, because it has not been "thoroughly tested," is Islam.

5. The failures of "official" Islam in providing the proper solutions to man's problems. Because "official" Islam is not the right model, the youth rebel against the hypocrisy of the existing model and surrender wholeheartedly to the dream that Fundamentalism offers (Rakhâwi 1982: 144-146).

Perhaps if the Egyptian society, government and "official" Islam listens, attempts to understand and take the young Fundamentalist seriously, they might hear him say the following:

> I am afraid and lonely, and you are all liars.
>
> I am sad and resigned, and you are failures and hypocrites.
>
> I am committed to God, and I must have the opportunity and the right to live, but I am incapacitated and chained because of you.
>
> Any initiative or creative approach which I might take is going to be condemned by you as heresy and thwarted by you. Therefore, I will resort to the already certain and proven, which is the inspired *Qur'ân*.
>
> Since my place of belonging is with those who believe in absolute purity and divine idealism, I am going to force this purity upon you in order to protect myself from you and your secret police.

> Since I came to the conviction that my deliverance is in my commitment to a solidarity of like-minded dedicated followers of God, my vengeance and anger is going to be directed against you hypocrites. You are idol worshippers and liars; you preach and do not practice what you preach, and you govern without honest adherence to God's precepts.
>
> Even if I do not succeed, that is not the issue. I might become a martyr and a model to be followed. After all, what is ahead of me is paradise, but as for you, the fires of hell are waiting to receive you.

In this scenario, we see concepts and emotions such as loneliness, fear, despair, idealism, purity, absolutism, dependency, martyrdom spirit, the dream, the revolution, surrender to God, aggression and suicide (Rakhâwi 1982: 146-147).

Fundamentalist numbers are growing rapidly because the environment is ripe for recruiting, discipling and equipping men who are willing to be commandos for Islam. After all, is it not true that "Islam is a tree which is nourished by the blood of its martyrs"?

NOTES

1 Cooperatives are stores where food items are sold at cheap rates because of government subsidy. It is a sad sight at times. Long queues of people waiting for an item, like sugar or rice or chicken, which are not found in the market for some days. Fights take place among frustrated multitudes waiting in the queues, and the treatment of these people by the man behind the counter, as if they are beggars, is humiliating. It is a humiliating, time-consuming and exhausting experience.

2 Telephone lines were unavailable, and at times people had to wait more than ten years for their turn to come. Calling

other cities from Cairo, until 1980, had to be done through the central telephone stations and calls outside the country sometimes demanded waiting for hours.

3 The prophet was against "interest, gambling and wine," but he lent his money to a Jew who did not promise him a fixed interest, but a genuine gain or loss. This was called *murâbaḥa*.

PART FIVE

IMPACT OF FUNDAMENTALISM

12

CONTEMPORARY IMPACT

As we look back briefly at the history of Fundamentalism, we see the following:

The Kharijites considered themselves the ones who "withdrew" from immoral, unjust and weak leadership. Their withdrawal was not from Islam but unto Islam, and unto the holy war *(jihâd)*. The Kharijites' identity had to do with the element of rejecting wrong leadership and resorting to *jihâd*.

In chapter four, al-Khumeini stood out as a man who courageously and honestly looked at the Muslim world and directed his attention to its state of deprivation and hypocrisy. Although al-Khumeini was a Shiite, he pointed out that the "quietism principle" should not be used as a cover-up for cowardice, but Muslims should give themselves totally to God in a spirit of *jihâd*.

Ḥasan al-Banna looked at the situation in Egypt and was moved with grief. The caliphate no longer existed; the westernization process which was occurring was leading the Muslims away from authenticity and deep faith; colonialism was choking the country, and the politicians were immersed in self-serving politics. Although he did not use the term *jâhiliyya*, either for the society or for the leadership of the country, it was implied since proclamation of the message was the most urgent need. He started a new brand of Muslims which he considered "the real Muslims," unlike the Muslims of the ignorant masses and the hypocritical Al-Azhar community. Furthermore, al-Banna formed the "special apparatus," which was a *jihâd* task force.

Sayyid Qutb, in *Signposts on the Road*, declared that not only were the rulers living in *jâhiliyya*, but the whole society as well. Qutb did not emphasize the transcendence of God but emphasized His lordship *(ḥâkimiyyat Allâh)*. Because He is one Lord, He should be the only Lord to be obeyed, feared and respected. Muslim commandos should have an attitude of *jihâd* in order to grow in discipleship. The *jihâd* was the task before them when the time came for the society to be confronted with force.

Shukri, the *Jamâ'ât* and Faraj all agreed that the rulers were living in *jâhiliyya*, and that *jihâd* by the "spilling of blood" was an absolute necessity for bringing about an Islamic society. Yet, they varied in how much the society was living in *jâhiliyya*. Shukri went to the extreme of completely separating his people from Egyptian society which was living in barbarism and ignorance.

The following set of questions can help us evaluate the degree of Fundamentalism al-Banna, Qutb, Shukri, the *Jamâ'ât*, Faraj and other Fundamentalists reached:

1. What is the attitude towards "popular" religious practices? Is the society living in *jâhiliyya*?
2. What is the attitude towards ideas and techniques developed by non-Muslims?
3. What is the attitude towards Islamic traditions which have accumulated over the centuries? In other words, are the *Qur'ân* and the *sunna* sufficient, or do they need to be supplemented by the teachings of the Muslim scholars through the years?
4. What is the attitude of the Fundamentalists towards the rulers and "official" Islam, and vice versa?
5. What is the attitude towards *jihâd* and the lordship of God? (power and sanctity).

Attitude towards Popular Religiosity and Jâhiliyya

Popular religion is defined as "that kind of religiosity which found expression in certain religious practices which enjoyed great popularity among the common people.... That religiosity is the continuation of ancient pagan usages" (Vrijhof 1979: 12).

All of the men who have led the Fundamentalist movements in the twentieth century, to various degrees, criticized "popular" Islam. Activities which embody "popular" Islam, such as visiting the tombs, celebrating the prophet's birthday, celebrating the spring day of *Shamm Nasîm* which has a pharaonic origin, and festive television programs during the month of Ramadân are manifestations of paganism. Fundamentalist leaders looked at the masses with grief and considered them to be puppets indoctrinated by the mass media, swayed by ignorant or mystic leaders, or the final product of a deteriorating Islam, especially since the time of the Fatimids. The masses need to hear the "pure" message, respond to it, and have the opportunity to follow godly rulers, who lead them in the right direction. Qutb, Shukri and Faraj went further by identifying the need of the masses to be delivered from despotic ungodly rulers, so that it would become possible for them to hear, comprehend and fully understand the "pure" message of Islam, otherwise they would continue in *jâhiliyya*.

Attitude Towards Non-Muslim Ideas

Afghâni was critical of the modernization and the westernization process penetrating the class of intellectuals towards the end of the nineteenth century. Al-Banna was critical of the same movement propagated by 'Abdul Râzeq and Ṭâha Ḥusein in the 1920s. Both Afghâni and al-Banna believed that the ideas which come from the West undermine Islam, both as a religion and as a culture. Egyptians who considered themselves "westernized" lost their Islamic identity and authenticity. In fact, those "westernized" Egyptians considered Islam inferior to Christianity and the Islamic culture inferior to the western culture. The biggest threat to Islam, according to Afghâni and al-Banna, is not colonialism or Protestant evangelism, but the attack which comes from within, from the Egyptians themselves, when their minds are polluted and their authenticity is washed out.

Qutb, after his visit to the United States, vehemently attacked the lack of spirituality and depth among the Americans. He advocated that Muslims should learn nothing but western technology from the United States. He considered everything else inferior and a cause of destruction.

The *Jamâ'ât*, along with al-Jihâd organization, despised Sâdât for his peace talks with Israel, the open-door policy and the close ties with the United States. They considered him the tool used to bring about another wave of the western Christian modernization process, which was aimed against Islam.

Therefore, on this second evaluation question of the attitude towards non-Muslim ideas, the twentieth-century Fundamentalists in Egypt rank high.

Attitude Regarding Tradition

Al-Banna considered the teachers of Al-Azhar to be spiritually impotent because they were bogged down by the tradition of Islamic scholarship through the centuries. Al-Azhar Imams did not teach or preach with power because the message of Islam was no longer pure but was diluted and watered down by tradition and a life without dedication and sanctity.

Qutb discarded the scholarship of the past and wrote a new commentary on the *Qur'ân*. Muslims today need to go back to the time of Muḥammad in Mecca and face the *jâhiliyya* of today as the prophet faced the *jâhiliyya* of his day.

Shukri was satisfied only with the *Qur'ân* and *sunna*. He tried to establish a Muslim society based upon his interpretation of the *Qur'ân*, disregarding tradition, commentaries, education, Al-Azhar, mosques and Imams. As Shukri reflected on the whole system of education in Egypt, whether secular or religious, during his school and university days, he was not satisfied.

> Since there is no science or knowledge except in God...the Muslim is obligated to seek his path and knowledge before God alone, and the so called knowledge, which is actually no knowledge at all because it is not founded in the Lord, is forbidden. Indeed the *Qur'ân* teaches (Sûra 2:216, 232) that God knows and you know not. This means, according to Shukri, that everything which came after the Book and the accounts of the traditions of the prophet *(sunna)*, is excluded from the domain of legitimate knowledge. The four great legal schools of the Sunni Imams Abu Ḥanîfa, Ibn Ḥanbal, Mâlik and Shâfi'i are null and void. Shukri told the court, 'We would like to call your attention to the following fact: Islam has been in decline ever since men have ceased to draw their lessons directly from the *Qur'ân* and the *sunna*, and have instead followed the traditions of other men, those who call themselves Imams. The interpretive works of the four Imams,' Shukri argued, 'were wholly unnecessary. The *Qur'ân* was delivered in Arabic, and the only tool that may be needed for the explaining of the meaning of some of its terms, is a good dictionary' (Kepel 1985: 79).

Faraj did not discard tradition but only learned from men in the past who agreed with his perspective of Islam. Ibn Taimiyya was his favorite scholar.

In this evaluation question as well, we see that twentieth century Fundamentalists of Egypt tended to have a fresh and new interpretation of the *Qur'ân* and *sunna* in order to come up with a dynamic and relevant message, pertinent to the needs of the day.

Attitude of Fundamentalists towards the Rulers and "Official" Islam and Vice Versa

According to Waardenburg

> in Islamic thought, the term 'official' is applied to what is lawful and what, consequently, enjoys divine sanction. Its contents are held to go back to revelation as contained in the *Qur'ân* and *sunna*, or phrased differently, all that goes back to something religiously authoritative like revelation, that is expressed in its turn in an authoritative way, and for the faithful transmission of which man is responsible can be called 'official' in Islam. In Muslim terms, revelation is the true official religion, and whenever man fails to transmit this revelation faithfully...ignorance and error prevail (Waardenburg 1979: 353).

The difficulty with this presentation of what "official" Islam is lies in putting the authority in "the revelation" as the true official religion. Revelation can have various interpretations, and each interpreter can claim that his is the proper, and therefore authoritative, interpretation. With this background *Sheikh* Al-Azhar can claim to have the authoritative interpretation because of his scholarship and official position. The ruler, whether king or president, can claim to have the authoritative interpretation of revelation because he has the best religious counselors and advisors. The Fundamentalists as well can claim to have the authoritative interpretation of revelation because of their pure motives and deep commitment to God. Their having no fear of the authorities and their economic independence from the regime gives them the assurance that their understanding of the *Qur'ân* and *sunna* is the proper one; therefore, their interpretation is the authoritative one.

Furthermore, making *fatâwa* (casuistries) is not limited solely to *Sheikh* Al-Azhar. *Sheikh* 'Abdul Raḥmân, the advisor of al-Jihâd organization made *fatâwa* too, one of which was the legitimization of "taking" the gold from Christian jewelry shops and using it to buy weapons.

In Waardenburg's definition of "official" Islam, we see the difficulty of the situation. The Islam of Egypt is unlike the Catholic church where "official" Christianity is represented by the ecclesiastical authorities, the bishops (Van Den Broek 1979: 12). Perhaps Islam in Egypt is becoming more and more like Protestantism, which has allowed a variety of interpretations of revelation and therefore a multiplicity of centers of authority.

In this study, we have used the term "official" Islam to mean the Islam of the recognized Al-Azhar, which usually has the approval and the blessing of the government. It has been a simplistic definition and a theoretical assumption. The materials that we have seen in the chapters of Part Three prove the truth of Waardenburg's definition and the inadequacy of the definition of "official" Islam as being that of Al-Azhar and the government.

We see one of the most powerful proofs of the truth of Waardenburg's definition in the contrast between the trials of the Muslim Brotherhood in 1954 and the trials of al-Jihâd organization in 1981. In 1954, "official" Islam was the Islam of Al-Azhar and the government. In 1981, the situation changed dramatically. Dr. 'Abdul Raḥmân, the advisor of al-Jihâd organization and the number one man on the list of the accused after the assassination of Sâdât, proved to be a powerful foe in the court sessions.

As he was accused of leading a Neo-Kharijite movement, he responded saying, "*Al-Khawârij* were those who refused to obey the true caliph and rebelled against him. Who is, and where is the true caliph today? Where is Caliph Ali today? If we are *al-Khawârij*, then what are you? Are you representing Ali? Did Ali make an alliance with the Jews and call the terrorist Begin of Israel, 'My dear friend'?" (Ḥammûda 1986: 211-213). Van Den Brock's definition of "official" religion as the view of the religious authorities and the Imams is recognized neither by the Fundamentalists nor by a great sector of the masses who have been sympathetic with the Fundamentalists' cause since the late 1970s.

Another illustration we see is in the evaluation of *Sheikh* Al-Azhar of Sayyid Qutb and the response of the Fundamentalists to that evaluation. *Sheikh* Al-Azhar indicated that Qutb, like his ancestors the Kharijites, used the concept of *jihâd* in a wrong way. Qutb interpreted *jihâd* to mean a fight against all those who disagree with his interpretation. His books are dangerous because they mix truth and falsehood, and they delude the simple-minded and turn them into fanatics.

The Fundamentalists on the other hand considered *Sheikh* Al-Azhar as the puppet of the rulers. He merely says what his gods *(ṭawâghît)* want him to say.

Another important distinction that needs to be made has to do with the terms Fundamentalism, radicalism and moderation. Confusion among these three terms often results in problems and long range dangers.

According to Lazarus-Yafeh, "'Fundamentalist' (according to Egyptian authorities) is applied to all those who are radical in their demand for an Islamic state and the full application of the *Sharî'a* in every realm of life, where all others are wrongly considered 'moderate'" (Lazarus-Yafeh 1983: 290). While according to Shamir,

> Radicalism may be described as a state of mind that negates the present and wishes to change its very foundations, seeks to impose on reality a set of rules that is usually driven to its logical extreme, and adheres to a vision of a basically different order—always seen as an end that justifies the means. It is manifested not only in politics, but also in the various fields of intellectual life. Thus, radicalism in modern Egypt, in all of its major forms—nationalist, Islamic and leftist—finds expression not only in political actions, but also in such intellectual endeavors as historical writing (Shamir 1983: 215).

Therefore, radicalism does not necessarily mean Fundamentalism, and not all Fundamentalists are radical. Fundamentalism means going back to the sources and the fundamentals, and accepting their literal inerrancy, thus desiring and demanding a new and changed society which is ruled by *Sharî'a*. This brand of Fundamentalism is conservative, but not necessarily radical. Therefore, the government mistakenly considers it as moderate, which is a drastic mistake that could have dangerous and far-reaching effects.

The government considers those who are radical in their demands for an Islamic state as the only Fundamentalists. Therefore, it imprisons and confronts them, while the rest of the "moderate" Fundamentalists are at large, spreading their influence among the masses. There are famous journalists who write daily or weekly in pro-government newspapers, like *Al-Ahrâm* and *Al-Akhbâr*, who are "moderate Fundamentalists" because they are not radical. The government is not aware of the danger of these writers. Another illustration of this phenomenon is *Sheikh* Sha'râwi, who is the most famous Muslim television preacher in Egypt and the Arab world as well. The government gives him time and position to speak and teach on the government-sponsored television, assuming that he is serving its purposes. In reality, he is a Fundamentalist, perhaps one of the most effective ones, although he is considered moderate by the government. It may well be that through his religious Fundamentalist approach, he is paving, perhaps unconsciously, the way for the radical Fundamentalists. In his subtle preaching he leads the masses into a sure conclusion without being radical. As he speaks about the need to apply the *Sharî'a*, and the road towards its implementation, he expresses himself in the following words:"Were every Muslim to try living according to Islam in these spheres of life which do not belong to the state's affairs, then Islam would become implemented almost automatically in the state as well, mainly because the rulers would be convinced that the people really wish it..." Here is where the real danger of

Sha'râwi's "moderate" approach lies; he offers no real alternative to the radicals' demand for a Muslim state. He only hopes to achieve it peacefully. He, along with others, are

> helping to develop among the masses some kind of tolerance and sympathetic understanding for religious terrorism which is extremely important for the success of the violent activities of the radical groups. Thus, although they may be truly loyal to the regime and opposed to any violent measures—their basic Fundamentalist approach to religious problems make them very dangerous.

Lazarus-Yafeh concludes, "This seems to prove the simple fact that an *'âlim* considered moderate in politics like Sha'râwi, may nevertheless be more 'Fundamentalist' than a radical activist belonging to the Muslim Brotherhood, like Sayyid Qutb" (Lazarus-Yafeh 1983: 282, 287).

The implications of these distinctions and definitions are very important. We saw in chapter nine how Sâdât ordered the arrests of about 1,500 Muslims and 120 Christians one month before his assassination. He and his government thought that they were giving a radical blow to Fundamentalism. Their confusion of Fundamentalism with radicalism resulted in the continuation of the growing danger of Fundamentalism, rather than its eradication. Because the government supports and elevates men like Sha'râwi, it becomes easy for people living in Egypt to assume that Sha'râwi is not a Fundamentalist. Of all the books that I have read on Islamic Fundamentalism, whether in English or in Arabic, only one book, *Islam, Nationalism and Radicalism* (Warburg and Kupferschmidt), has a chapter on Sha'râwi as a Fundamentalist. Either because of a lack of courage, or the subtlety of the issue, men like Sha'râwi and many journalists of the same convictions continue to influence the masses with their Fundamentalistic thinking and remain unnoticed by the critics.

Attitude toward Power and Sanctity

Patricaa Crone, along with P.J. Vatikiotis, has argued that Muḥammad was a militant preacher. He performed the marriage between a universal religious truth and a tribal community which believed in this truth, held to it and fought for it.

> As conquerors, the early Muslim Arabs broke out everywhere with a common identity, but without the structures for a state. Whatever instruments they took over (e.g. bureaucracies and courts) mercenary and slave professional armies served to keep them in power. Once they lost their own military power to the new groups of mercenary and slave armies recruited by the caliphs to fight their wars, the very nature of their state was transformed beyond all recognition (Vatikiotis 1983: 55-56).

This analysis would be in total agreement with Fundamentalists such as Qutb, Shukri and especially Faraj. Instead of speaking about power, those men spoke about *jihâd*. Faraj called it the "missing precept." It was at the heart of what Muḥammad did in establishing the *umma*, and it was what gave the successors of Muḥammad (the first four caliphs) strength, expansion and respect. Islam with no *jihâd* (power) is weak, deformed, impotent and transformed beyond recognition.

This power was given to the Muslims by God. They possess the truth and power—a dynamic combination. "Power belongs to God, His apostle and the believers," the *Qur'ân* says. Possessing the "ultimate truth," and being given the assurance that it is the "only truth," motivated the early Muslims to expand and conquer the Byzantines and the Persians. As long as the message was kept pure and the believers lived in sanctity, there was power. "Power in Islam had to be intrinsically sacred: it was only when power and sanctity no longer could be kept together that the Muslims had to make do with an illusion" (in Vatikiotis 1983: 56).

According to Qutb, *jihâd* is a means to an end, and not an end in itself. It is characterized by the following:

1. A holy combat *(jihâd)* is against the devil within one's heart to free oneself from the pollution of the world. Furthermore, it requires the discipline of relying on one source which is the *Qur'ân*. Otherwise, the purification process will not occur.

2. A holy combat *(jihâd)* is against the rulers who make themselves gods, and give themselves the right of sovereignty. This holy combat is not against the society, but against the rulers who enslaved the society.

3. Once the holy combat *(jihâd)* has set the society free from the tyranny of the rulers, then, and only then, the proclamation of the message to the society can be useful. (In this, Qutb departed from the teaching of Ḥasan al-Banna.)

4. The holy combat *(jihâd)* should spearhead the proclamation to the uttermost parts of the world. There will always be confrontation with cultures and religions, and Islam should not compromise. These societies should either come to Islam, or surrender to Islam by paying the taxes. Then the individuals in these societies are really free to respond to the proclamation of the message of Islam, one way or the other. No force is needed to compel people to become Muslims *(lâ ikrâha fi-dîn)*.

5. When people are set free from the tyranny of their rulers then their nature *(fiṭra)* which was created by God, will be set free to respond to God by the exercise of the will.

6. No political program is needed in advance. This is a trick that people will use as they ask the vanguards, 'What is your political program?' *Jihâd* (holy combat) is the starting point and once the *umma* is being formed, the program will emerge as it occurred with the prophet in Medina (Qutb 1987: 66-91).

So *jihâd*, the spearhead of the proclamation to the uttermost parts of the world, is what gives Islam cohesion and strength.

The Kharijites, along with the Shiites, came out of the main body of Islam because they could not tolerate halfheartedness, compromise and injustice. Ḥasan al-Banna realized that through dedication to God as Lord the result would be a life of sanctity. Sanctity, along with passivity, would result in Sufism. He had his experiences in that realm and admired the devotion and dedication of the Sufis and their love for God, but still there was something missing in Sufism. That was why he started his new organization, where he combined sanctity with power.

The Neo-Muslim Brotherhood was not militant enough, according to the eager youth who wanted to go back and relive what Muḥammad experienced on the Arab Peninsula. Qutb and Faraj, along with Mawdûdi, provided them with fuel and a model.

Because "*lâ ilâha illa Lâh*" (there is no God but God), any attempt of some men to become gods for others is a transference of sovereignty. Only God is *Rabb* (Lord). Only He has the right to rule and be sovereign. Thus, *ḥâkimiyyat Allâh* (sovereignty of God) was the cornerstone of Qutb's theology.

> The necessary and sufficient criterion for determining whether a given society is Muslim, or belongs to *jâhiliyya* therefore, lies in the sort of *'ubûdiyya* (worship) and *ḥakimiyya* (sovereignty) that may be observed with it. In Muslim society God alone is worshipped and holds sovereignty, while in *jâhiliyya* societies, the status is held by someone or something other than the one true God (Kepel 1985: 51).

Sanctity, according to Qutb, is the natural fruit of *ḥâkimiyyat Allâh* and our *'ubûdiyya* (worship).

Instead of talking about power, twentieth-century Fundamentalists spoke about *jihâd*. Also, instead of talking merely about sanctity, they talked about the lordship of God and the authority He should have over the lives of the believers. When believers live in obedience to God, who is the one Lord, who alone has the right to be worshipped and obeyed, then lives will be sanctified and cowardice will disappear. Even the fear of authorities and fear of death will vanish. According to the Fundamentalists, this is the wonder of the life of obedience to God side by side with *jihâd.*

Some Additional Definitions and Remarks

According to Waardenburg,

> Official religion implies that people in certain offices can perform specific actions which are religiously binding and juridically valid. For example, the *'ulamâ'* establish the conditions for a *jihâd* and the caliph carries it out, the *mufti* gives responses to legal questions *(fatâwa)*, and the *qâḍi* administers justice. In other words, to carry out certain actions, a certain office or status is required and it is through religious law that man can know what 'official' status is needed in these cases and what the nature of the prescription is (Waardenburg 1979: 353).

This is the ideal way of looking at "official" Islam. But in practice, "official" Islam means that which has legal validation or the stamp "Islamic." In Egypt, the *'ulamâ'* or the Imams of Al-Azhar have an "official" character supposedly because of their religious scholarship, their conviction of the *Sharî'a* as the absolute norm and ideal, and the fact that their opinions could be accepted by *ijmâ'* (consensus). In addition to these factors, there is a fourth factor, which is the support the Imams receive from government authorities.

According to Fundamentalists, the Al-Azhar *'ulamâ'* have an "official" character only, or mostly, because they are close to the government and they are financially supported by the Ministry of Religious Affairs.

The Fundamentalists, on the other hand, perceive themselves as *muhyii al-din* (revivers of religion), whose authority must be recognized. The reason it is not recognized is because the body of Islam has been diverted from the path of truth.

When Sunnis perceive themselves as the embodiment of Islam, Shiites, Fundamentalists and others are considered as "alternative" groups. On the other hand, when the Fundamentalists perceive themselves as the embodiment of Islam, then Sunnis are considered as "alternative" groups.

Waardenburg suggests the use of an alternate concept other than the concept of "official" Islam, namely "normative" Islam, which is more suitable and applicable to the religion of Islam.

> The difference between 'official' and 'normative' is mainly in wording, but the term 'normative' is better suited to the data and structure of Islam. If one of the characteristics of Islam is the constant search for clear norms for human life on the basis of well defined revelation, 'normative' Islam is that form of Islam through which man has access to these ultimate norms for life, action and thought (Waardenburg 1979: 357).

Muḥammad was the person par excellence who was in a position to determine what would be "normative" Islam. This privilege was given to religious scholars after the death of Muḥammad, specifically the jurist-theologians. The Fundamentalists feel that it should have been given, instead, to those that represent *iḥyâ' al-dîn* (the revival of religion), the Fundamentalists. Al-Banna, Qutb, Shukri, Faraj, Zumr, 'Abdul Raḥmân and others perceived themselves as the men who faithfully walked in the footsteps of the prophet, and who persistently demanded the application of *Sharî'a.* Therefore, from their own perspective, they are the embodiment of "normative" Islam.

Hermeneutics and Phenomenology

Hermeneutic thinking and phenomenology are interrelated and come from the same philosophical background.

Hermeneutic Approach

Hermeneutics is not limited to the interpretation of old literary or religious texts but is inclusive of the interpretation of more recent or even current works, such as Picasso's paintings, or a "strange" piece of music, and so on. "Hermeneutic thinking is rooted in the experience of the 'strangeness' of some cultural products, whether they are far removed from us today in time, or whether they are expressed by people who belong to a different culture from our own" (Krüger 1982: 20-21).

Islamic Fundamentalism in Egypt is a "strange" phenomenon to many Egyptian Muslims. Fundamentalists are condemned as people following an Islamic heresy or are perceived as young people who are suffering from an inferiority complex, or uneducated narrow-minded fanatics who want to control the country at any cost. Egyptian Christians are even more distant because of the fear they have of these "blood-thirsty fanatics." Non-Arabs have a hard time understanding and respecting Islam, let alone Islamic Fundamentalism.

"Respect" is a prerequisite condition for the success of the hermeneutic process. "To do science of religion in this spirit, is to respect the dignity of whatever I am trying to understand, and to allow it to speak for itself. I become an attentive, humble listener to the human spirit reaching out to me across the barriers of time and cultural differences" (Krüger 1982: 21).

As I began to study the phenomenon of Islamic Fundamentalism, I was drawn to its world and got involved with its message. The Kharijites, the Shiites, even al-Khumeini began to appear in a new light. Ḥasan al-Banna, when he was led into the arena of politics at the age of forty in the late 1940s, was surrounded by old and highly experienced politicians who taunted him like a cat does a mouse. It became clear that the Muslim studying the life of al-Banna must be stricken with grief to see this great man manipulated, cheated, humiliated and finally assassinated. The obvious love this man had for God challenges us.

A spark of communication occurred between me and Qutb the philosopher, Shukri the "strange" young man, Khâled, 'Abdul Raḥmân, Faraj and others. Our two worlds met, and I got involved with the message, discovering that it has a dynamic vitality of its own.

My goal is to communicate to non-Arab readers as much of that spark as possible, aspiring that their understanding of Islamic Fundamentalism would grow.

Phenomenology

Islamic Fundamentalism should be rediscovered and re-experienced as a phenomenon. It should be allowed to speak for itself and affect the reader because of its dynamic vitality as a "raw material." "The intentionality of phenomenology is intended toward the world" of Fundamentalism, as it is experienced by the Fundamentalists themselves, who form that world. The reader should not describe what he observes from his point of view, but rather he should attempt to understand the world of religion from the adherents' point of view (Krüger 1982: 18).

Looking at the difference between the two branches of the al-Jihâd movement shows how Zuhdi's group, which is usually seen as a sectarian, sadistic group, can be perceived differently when looked at from the adherents' point of view.

The Cairo branch and the Upper Egypt branch differed in their primary target. The priority for the Cairo branch was the assassination of Sâdât, while dealing with the Christians was not as pressing. The primary target for Zuhdi and his group in Upper Egypt was the Christians. The reason for this was the atmosphere which existed in Upper Egypt, especially in Minya and Asyût where Christians formed a strong minority and became a challenge to Islamic Fundamentalism. The daily frictions and confrontations between Muslims and Christians in Upper Egypt made the Christians look like a formidable force that needed to be reckoned with and deserved immediate attention. In fact, the phenomenon of the Christian presence became the lens through which issues were perceived and interpreted. For Zuhdi's group, in contrast to the al-Jihâd Cairo branch, Lebanon, not Iran, was the more forceful model that demanded attention.

Ḥasan al-Banna, who might have been perceived by the British as dogmatic, stubborn and fanatic, can be seen differently when he is observed as a phenomenon.

For al-Banna, the existence of the British in Egypt as a colonialist power was the disturbing factor. The strong British presence in Ismâ'îliyya, where the Muslim Brotherhood started, along with the existence of Protestant evangelism in many of the towns where al-Banna had his Muslim Brotherhood branches, affected his perspective and vision. Al-Banna linked the two together. He viewed colonialism as an umbrella of protection for western Christians who were proselytizing the crushed and intimidated Egyptian Muslims. Britain, the way al-Banna perceived it, not only controlled the Egyptian government, but indirectly controlled the minds of the Egyptians. This control was manifested in the way it presented itself as the superior, civilized and educated nation coming to bring civilization and education to those with an inferior religion and culture. British colonialism created the environment for protestant evangelism.

Furthermore, according to Muslims like Afghâni and al-Banna, colonialism in the world was preceded by preparing the soil through Christian missions. Schools, hospitals, and universities constructed by western missionaries influenced the minds of the elite to perceive the West as a superior culture and Egypt an inferior culture with an inferior religion. The Muslim student who attended a school or university established by the western missionaries could not help but compare the education he was receiving with the education that other students receive. Due to the backwardness of education at Al-Azhar which existed at that time, the student came to a sure conclusion of which was the superior culture. Cultures are the outcome of religion. Therefore, if western education is superior, it must be because of Christianity, and if Egyptian culture is inferior, it must be because of Islam. When these Muslim students who graduated from Protestant schools and western universities gained powerful positions in the nation, it was already determined how they would make their decisions. These men were mentally programmed to become tools to open the door for the West and keep it open. Afghâni perceived the enemy not only as an external force, but internal also, in the form of Egyptians who had been corrupted and polluted to view their culture and religion as inferior and believe that progress comes as a result of westernization.

Manifestations of the Impact of Fundamentalism

In his book *Al-Nadîr* (The Warner), Faraj Foda[1] blew the trumpet of warning that the Fundamentalists were growing very rapidly. His outline and arguments were very convincing, but his conclusion was to the contrary. The evidence he gave for the manifestations of the impact of Fundamentalism included some of the following main points.

Fast Growth of Islamic Finances

Since the mid 1970s, huge economic establishments have been formed which include *sharikât tawzîf al-amwâl* (companies for the investment of money), as well as Islamic banks.[2] These establishments have had involvement in a wide variety of economic projects. The capital that the *sharikât tawzîf al-amwâl* have amassed is immense.

Strangely enough, these establishments grew within the context of the Egyptian legal system, in spite of the illegal activities carried on by some of these companies. One example is the famous Rayyân scandal (Rayyân is a multi-millionaire who is currently serving a prison sentence). The *sharikât tawzîf al-amwâl* competed with the government and were able to attract the investments of Egyptians living and working abroad. Furthermore, they competed over the value of the Egyptian pound in its relation to the dollar, thus contributing in the eighties to making a large gap between the value of the dollar in the bank and its value in the black market.

The impact of *sharikât tawzîf al-amwâl* has expanded to reach influential men in the mass media, business and ex-government ministers and governors. These men are given big salaries for being on the boards of these establishments.

In the 1987 Parliament elections, the Islamic millionaires heavily supported and financed the coalition of Islamicists, contributing to the great success of the Fundamentalists in those elections.

Furthermore, they either attempted to or actually bought some banks and turned them into Islamic banks, but their greatest impact has been the huge numbers of their investors (Foda 1989: 10-11).

Increase in Numbers and Diversity of Revolutionary Islam

At the end of the 1970s, the number of known Fundamentalist groups was twenty-two, and by the end of the 1980s, they had reached forty-four (Foda 1989: 12).

These organizations and groups are forming a threat to public figures, video-renting shops, churches, Christian owned jewelry shops and pharmacies, and are trying to impose their standards and ideas on the society as a whole. Some of these groups specialize in sowing seeds of sectarianism by burning churches and attacking Christians, while others specialize in assassinating public figures, such as ex-Ministers of Interior. It seems that there is an increase in diversity, specialization and numbers of these Fundamentalist groups.

Muslim Brotherhood Back on the Stage

The Muslim Brotherhood has been legally banned since the 1950s, because it was not merely a political organization, but religious as well. Through coalitions with sympathetic political parties, they have been able to increase the number of their representatives in the Egyptian Parliament from twelve members in the 1984 elections, to thirty in the 1987 elections. It is expected that by November 1992 their numbers will increase even more.

Their influence was fully exercised through their newspapers and magazines such as *Liwâ' al-Islâm*, *Al-Mukhtâr Al-Islâmi*, and *Al-I'tiṣâm*. They also have access to use other newspapers and magazines of sympathizers.

The publishing houses which print their books and ideas, especially books of al-Banna, Qutb, and Mawdudi, along with writings of more recent figures such as Talmasâni and 'Abdul Rahmân, can compete with many other publishing houses by the sheer number of books printed and the subsidized prices at which these books are sold (Foda 1989: 13).

Cooperation and Coordination

In the past the rich Muslim *al-Islâm al-tharwi* failed to cooperate fully with the militant Muslim *al-Islâm al-thawri*, but in the last Parliament elections, which took place in 1987, good cooperation and coordination was witnessed. The Fundamentalist millionaires fully financed the expenses of the election campaigns of Fundamentalists all over Egypt. The cooperation and coordination was seen in the wide spread publicity of the slogan, "Islam is the solution." The Muslim Brotherhood laid aside some of their differences with the other Fundamentalist groups and a declaration by the various leaders communicated that the Fundamentalists were united together in the campaign. The significance of this election experience is that it was an object lesson of "strength and unity" for Islamist groups. Therefore, it is very likely that, in future elections, unity among the groups and the support of the rich will produce the desired results for the Fundamentalists.

The issues and goals these groups united around were: substituting the existing regime with an Islamic one, rejection of the Camp David Peace Treaty with Israel, rejection of the emphasis on Arab unity because it dilutes the Islamic cause, rejection and refusal of the presentation of a political program except the application of the *Sharî'a*, veneration of recent leaders and martyrs such as Khâled, and criticism of the government for permitting the use of alcohol, nightclubs and immoral films and video tapes.

In spite of the major differences which still exist between the Muslim Brotherhood and Fundamentalist groups, they managed to agree, at least for a certain span of time, for the sake of the elections.

The Role of Official Islam

Al-Azhar, which is considered to have expounded official Islam since Nâşer's time, has lost a great deal of ground to the new Fundamentalist leadership. It appears that the Al-Azhar Imams lost their credibility as a result of being seen as cowards and puppets of the government. During the elections of 1987, declarations were made and articles were written by important and public Al-Azhar figures supporting the coalition of the Fundamentalists in order to prove the contrary. In these articles and declarations, statements were made, such as "whoever stands against the application of the

Sharî'a is an unbeliever," and "Muslims should boycott national banks and deal only with Islamic banks." Official Islam's temporary shift from being the defender of the government to the supporter of a Fundamentalist coalition was influenced partly by the invitation to some of the important and famous official Islam figures to be board directors and members of Islamic banks. This new recognition, expressed in monthly salaries and in organized trips to other Muslim countries for teaching and preaching, proved to be a worthwhile public relations task carried by Islamic millionaires (Foda 1989: 20-21).

Penetration of Associations, Clubs and Unions

There are towns and villages over which the government has no influence. The mayors in these remote places, along with the police, have come to the conclusion that the real power lies in the hands of the Fundamentalists.

Since the late 1970s, associations, clubs and unions have been penetrated by Fundamentalists. In spite of the relatively great cooperation between Christian doctors who competed against the Fundamentalists in the election of the Doctors Association in April 1990 and moderate Muslims, the Christian doctors were still defeated by the Fundamentalists.

In addition to the large amount of representation Fundamentalists have in the Union of Engineers, Lawyers and Dentists, the Muslim Brotherhood has even attempted to have representatives in each political party.

The Fundamentalists came to the conclusion that "if we cannot alter the system through revolution, then we should penetrate it and change the system from within." It looks like they are succeeding.

Penetration of the Mass Media

The Fundamentalists succeeded in penetrating the mass media in the 1980s. The reason the government lost this ground was because it did not know how to use the newspapers and television for its goals and objectives.

Pro-government newspapers, such as *Al-Ahrâm* and *Al-Akhbâr*, started giving journalists the opportunity and space to write on Islam. Several of these journalists have used the opportunity to propagate the Fundamentalist views. Fahmy Howayadi, for instance, criticized Egypt for following a legal system "imported from Europe," rather than following the Islamic *Sharî'a*. Aḥmad Bahjat defended "Islamic long shorts" which Fundamentalist athletes wear for the sake of decency. Furthermore, Bahjat wrote a famous article on the day of the execution of Khâled and his partners, which he entitled "The Martyrs."

Preceding the elections of 1987, a whole page in *Al-Akhbâr* was written under the title, "In the Memory of Ḥasan al-Banna." According to Foda, this served as a powerful propaganda tool for the coalition of the Fundamentalists (Foda 1989: 25).

In addition to this, Islamic millionaires have used their money well by paying for advertisements in these supposedly pro-government newspapers. In *Al-Ahrâm* for instance, the whole of the last page has been given, more than once, to advertising of the multimillionaires Rayyân, Sherîf and Sa'd, showing blown-up pictures of them wearing white robes and black beards.

The television as well was used for Islamic purposes, whether in terms of time or contents. Whenever the time of prayer comes, the program is stopped for the call of prayer. This was started duṛing Sâdât's era. Furthermore, gifted Imams like Sha'râwi are given the time, opportunity and freedom to teach and interpret Islam and Christianity. They are permitted to do this in whatever way they find appropriate, whether or not their teaching is contributing to sectarian strife.[3]

Mistakes Committed by the Government

Fundamentalists in Egypt are becoming a nation within the nation. They have finances, military power, ideology, availability of mass media, and unions. What they do not have is unified and continuous leadership.

The government, so far, has assumed that there is a possibility of reconciliation for mutual benefit. This assumption is incorrect because there is a total disagreement on the basics. One area where there is disagreement is in the Islamists' desire for a return to the caliphate and the application of *Sharî'a*, while the regime wants a continuity of the present system which is working on a combination of factors such as Pan-Arabism, secularism and Islam.

In the realm of economics, the Fundamentalists do not recognize the legitimacy of the national banks. They only recognize the Islamic system for banking that the prophet followed and taught.[4] Furthermore, their concepts of Pan-Arabism and Islamic world vision are quite contradictory.

The government's assumption regarding reconciliation and cooperation is incorrect. Where did the government go wrong?

Failing to Put the Law into Practice

With the failure of the government to put the law into practice, the government has lost respect. People go against the law to accomplish their goals. For instance, the Muslim Brotherhood entered the Parliament, although legally they are nonexistent.

Other illustrations are: popular mosques are built on government property without receiving prior permission; loudspeakers positioned on minarets are used five times a day, including the dawn prayer; Fundamentalist students intimidate teachers and students and sometimes force the segregation of male and female seating in lecture halls; work in government establishments stops for the sake of prayer (Foda 1989: 41).

These are illustrations of where Fundamentalists take more freedom, while the government stands in chains, fearing that if it intervenes and puts the law into practice, it will be interpreted as anti-Islamic.

The Government Is the First Line of Defense

In any battle, the armies involved should build several lines of defense, rather than only one line. Otherwise, it will not be possible to keep the enemy from reaching the heart of the nation.

The government has not seen the importance of having several lines of defense. Instead, it has relied on its police and army to defend its policies against Fundamentalism. Because of this strategy, the Fundamentalists are creeping in, step by step, and the government will not be able to stop their advance, unless the Fundamentalists make big mistakes, like the assassination of *Sheikh* Dahabi by Shukri's group in 1977.

Some of the lines of defense could include the following:

1. The full use of the mass media, whether television or newspapers, which are supposed to be spokesmen for the government.

2. Sâdât founded a political party called the National Democratic Party. It is the party of the government, yet it is not serving as a line of defense. The reason for this is that it has fallen into the trap of trying to prove that it is pro-Islamic, thus losing its authority to confront and lead.

Reconciliation Rather than Confrontation

The government goes back and forth between two extremes, either arrests, torture and imprisonment, or attempts at reconciliation and cooperation. The government has failed to recognize that there are various degrees of confrontation, such as:

1. Having several lines of defense.
2. Using mass media to educate the public about Fundamentalist weaknesses.
3. Denying the Fundamentalists the use of the government's mass media for the propagation of their goals.
4. The strict and strong adherence to the law.
5. Changing laws which can be twisted and turned around by the Fundamentalists, and making these laws as free of loopholes as possible (Foda 1989: 42-44).

Failure of the Government to Cooperate and Coordinate

According to Foda, the government of Egypt is sick with "Parkinson's disease." This is because it does not have control over its organs. Some examples are:

1. Minister of Interior Badr was at times criticized rather than supported by pro-government newspapers.
2. Some government representatives have praised and supported the establishment of Islamic banks.
3. Uncoordinated actions take place in the same city. For example, when an attack by Fundamentalists for the purpose of intimidating students and professors takes place, the police might violently confront the Fundamentalists, the governor may give in to the Fundamentalists and forbid the use of alcohol, the University President could negotiate with the leader of the Fundamentalists, and there may be confusion and lack of a clear trumpet call in the pro-government newspapers (Foda 1989: 49-50).

Failing to Learn the Lesson from the Iranian Revolution

The regime tends to communicate to the public that everything is under control and there is nothing to worry about.

On May 6, 1990, on the front page of *Al-Ahrâm*, the new Minister of Interior declared that,

> because of democracy, more time is needed to arrest and deal with the al-Jihâd organization. In 1954, at the time of Nâşer, it took the government forty-eight hours to round up all the leaders of the Muslim Brotherhood. Therefore, there is nothing to worry about because al-Jihâd organization is quite small in comparison with the Muslim Brotherhood of the 1950s.

Are the Fundamentalists taking good advantage of this democracy, using it for their continued growth?

It is quite possible that the reports which reach President Mubârak tend to minimize the danger and make it appear that the government is in full control. The Shah of Iran was shocked when he saw the magnitude and strength of the Fundamentalists firsthand.

The following are comparisons between the situation in Iran and the situation in Egypt:

1. Tehran and Cairo are the centers of the Shiites and the Sunnis, although their holy places are in Iraq and in Saudi Arabia respectively.

2. The Iranian clergy were strongly supported with finances by their followers. In Egypt, the rich Islamist *al-Islâm al-tharwi* are strongly supporting the militant Islamist *al-Islâm al-thawri*.

3. Both Tehran and Cairo are surrounded by poor suburbs. Poverty, frustration and deprivation in poor suburbs were the marks of Tehran before the revolution and are the marks of Cairo in the last decades of this century.

4. The foreign policy of the United States seems "to stand with and support the strong man," or situations advantageous to them.

When the Shah lost his grip on the situation in Iran, the United States abandoned him. They did not even allow him to retire in the States.

The United States fully supports the regime of President Mubârak. What will happen if he loses his grip on the situation in Egypt?

5. The Revolutionary Guard in Iran was composed of daring and ambitious youth. In Egypt, membership in the Fundamentalist organizations is mostly made of youth.

6. Use of Friday sermons and circulation of al-Khumeini's cassette tapes were quite effective for preparing for the revolution in Iran.

Tapes of *Sheikh* Kishk and *Sheikh* Sha'râwi are very popular and inflammatory in Egypt.

7. In Iran, the army turned against the regime because the soldiers could not stand for the shah against the crowds which consisted of relatives and friends.

If the crowds are mobilized in Egypt, would the army fight against them? This is highly questionable.

8. The shah was enemy number one in Iran, not the communists or the Christians. Once the revolution succeeded, they started dealing with the communists and the Christians (Foda 1989: 63-73).

The primary issue in Egypt today is to overthrow the government, seize power and turn Egypt into an Islamic state. After the success of the revolution, the time will come for working out the political program and dealing with the Christians.

Since 1952, as a result of Nâşer and the power of Egypt as a nation, several countries have regained their independence. The fever of independence spread like wildfire in the Arab world, the Muslim world and Africa. If Egypt turns to Fundamentalism, its influence will spread as well, especially in the Muslim world and Africa. How long, for instance, can other Arab countries survive if they are bombarded with Fundamentalism from Iran and Egypt?

Prospects of what might happen in the future will be the topic of the concluding chapter.

NOTES

1 Faraj Foda was assasinated by the Fundamentalists in 1992 because of his boldness in confronting them.

2 Rayyân attempted to and almost succeeded in buying the American Egyptian Bank, while Sherîf succeeded in buying another.

3 *Sheikh* Sha'râwi, in one of his messages, declared that Jesus had ten wives. Matthew 25:1-13

4 Secularism and Islam might sound contradictory and it is contradictory to the minds of the Fundamentalists. But from the government's perspective, it is possible to have a legal system made up of a combination of Islamic principles side by side with secular principles.

13

PROSPECTS

We have looked at the history of Islam in Egypt, considering the historical roots of Fundamentalism. Then we looked at the more recent and current manifestations of it, and considered the various factors which motivate the youth to join the Fundamentalist movement. Now we want to look at the future. What are the prospects?

1. We have seen the escalation of ideology and practice of violence during this century. Al-Banna focused on the proclamation of the message to the masses, but he also had the "special apparatus" whose members were receiving training in military tactics. Al-Banna negotiated with the government, related to those he did not agree with, and was even critical of the violent behavior of his own men. That was in the 1930s and 1940s, but the escalation continued. After tortures in prisons in the 1950s and 1960s, Qutb reached the conviction that

> the entire world lives in a state of *jâhiliyya* as far as the source from which it draws the rules of its mode of existence is concerned, a *jâhiliyya* that is not changed one whit, by material comfort and scientific invention, no matter how remarkable.... A vanguard must resolve to set in motion, in the midst of the *jâhiliyya* that God reigns over the entire earth. That vanguard must be able to decide when to withdraw from, and when to seek contact with the *jâhiliyya* that surrounds it (Kepel 1985: 44-45).

Qutb was finally hanged in 1966 after and because he wrote down his convictions in the famous and popular "syllabus for discipleship" among the Fundamentalists, *Ma'âlem*

Fi Tarîq. What Qutb reached for in the 1960s, al-Banna did not dare to reach for in the 1940s. The escalation continued and Shukri saw himself as the "chosen" leader of a group of committed people, a vanguard, and "decided to withdraw from the *jâhiliyya*" that surrounded him and formed his own Muslim society. In the 1970s Shukri practiced what Qutb wrote about.

The escalation continued in the 1970s and 1980s as al-Jihâd members assassinated Sâdât, attacked Christians, and intimidated university students and professors.

According to Aḥmad,

> Ibn Taimiyya passed the helm on to Mawdûdi, and Mawdûdi passed it on to Qutb, Qutb to Sariyya and Sariyya to Shukri, all passed it on to 'Uteibi of Saudi Arabia. 'Uteibi formed a link that connected to the link of al-Khumeini. Al-Khumeini passed the helm to Faraj, Khâled and Zumr. Are these men the end of the chain (Aḥmad 1989b: 69)?

The most likely answer is that they are not the end of the chain, and those who have and will come after them will start where their predecessors have finished.

Therefore, I believe that the escalation will continue and *fatâwa* (casuistries) that would have sounded as sheer madness early in this century will sound like the only proper option available in a world that lives in a state of *jâhiliyya* at the latter part of this century.

2. We have seen that the Fundamentalists have altered their tactics over the years, but the strategy continued with persistence and stamina. Wave after wave of Fundamentalists went into prisons, then came out, and some went in again. But whether inside the prison or outside it, they did not give up. The core of Fundamentalists is continuing and persisting and in their persistence they have the key of success.

By 1990, the Fundamentalists started training boys to throw Molotov cocktails at police stations. The arrests of young teenagers is not satisfying to the police and a cause of embarrassment to the government. Will the time come when the police will get fed up with the situation of being in a state of alert for years in a battle that does not seem to have an end? The Fundamentalists are counting on this factor of limited stamina in their war with the system, and there are signs that time is on the side of the Fundamentalists. This long war on all fronts with the regime is giving the Fundamentalists more confidence, strength and support.

3. We saw earlier that there is a significant similarity between the cities of Cairo and Tehran, especially the existence of several poor suburbs in which Fundamentalists grow and multiply. Although the Fundamentalists do not have a strong presence in the rich and sophisticated districts of Cairo, from their strategic presence in the suburbs they can control the whole of the city. Their strategy includes gaining control over the suburbs where they have a strong presence. The illustration of what happened in 'Ain Shams in 1988 and 1989 (refer to chapter two) proves this point.

When the day comes, and the spark for igniting the revolution is fired, these suburbs will be the bottlenecks that could choke Cairo and other major cities, forcing them to surrender. Flour, petrol, food and other essentials could be cut off and the cities would then be forced to accept the new status quo.

4. We have seen how the Fundamentalists have come to the conviction that they need to work on all fronts, including the use of violence. In fact, their strategy of penetrating the system is proving to be a great success. The Parliament has thirty Fundamentalists in it, and the number increases with every election. Unions and associations are mostly under their control; in addition, several distant towns are completely under their control. Talmasani always believed that the Islamic revolution in Egypt is like a fruit which is maturing with time. If you leave it on the tree and work on watering and nourishing the tree, sooner or later, the fruit will drop down right into your hand.

There are signs that, with even better cooperation among the various Fundamentalist groups and with continued support by the rich Islamists *al-Islâm al-tharwi*, the Fundamentalists will have more seats in Parliament in the next elections. In time, they will have more to say about who should be the next president, prime minister, etc. Furthermore, the time of applying the *Sharî'a* will come as they gain more strength by penetrating the active cells of the Egyptian nation.

5. A major question mark still remains regarding the role of the army. It is believed that the army is the final weapon which the government can use to fight Fundamentalism. So far it has been used only once in a similar situation, to quell the riots and burning of hotels by frustrated army members in 1987.

"A revolution will never succeed in Egypt unless the army intervenes," is the view of several leading Egyptians, but the army is made up of a cross section of the population. Since the population is moving towards sympathy with the cause and supports the Fundamentalists, we can then assume that the army is moving in the same direction. After all, irrespective of the indoctrination that could be carried out, the army is still made up of individuals who belong to families where family members could be Fundamentalists. Khâled's tie with his brother Muḥammad was the main motivating factor for creating the plan for assassinating Sâdât. How many Khâleds are there in the army now who have brothers, relatives, and friends suffering imprisonment and torture, or who are basically dedicated to the cause of Fundamentalism?

Foda says that an indicator, although it is not very reliable, is to look at the percentage of women who go to the Officers Club wearing the *hijâb* (headdress). The percentage is quite high, and although the motives for some could be social pressure, it is still a good indication of the resurgence of Islam taking place within the ranks. "The veil over the head could become a veil over the mind" (Foda 1989: 38).

If the whole society is slowly moving towards Fundamentalism, then we can assume that the army is keeping the same pace. As the Iranian Army proved to be useless in standing against the masses in the Iranian revolution, the same could happen in Egypt. If the regime decides to use the army when it is too late, the army could turn against the regime and become the major weapon of the Fundamentalist movement.

6. Where is the strong charismatic leader, like al-Khumeini, who could lead the new Islamic state? This is a question of great importance. Some people think that "without that type of leader there can be no success to the new Islamic revolution."

This could be true, and the question before us is, "Where is the leader?" There are usually three possible answers given in response to this question.

- The leader is there underground and is one among several possible leaders. As he gains strength with time, he will come up to the surface and will gain the recognition he needs.
- The leader is born and not discovered yet. Circumstances and the progression of Fundamentalism will reveal him at the right time.
- There is a leader, or a leadership team, which is actually leading the whole movement now, but is unknown or out of reach of the secret police. The arrests that are made are merely the firecrackers which are used to camouflage the real leadership.

Any one of these three options could prove to be true, although option number two is the most likely one. Given time, the leadership will emerge.

7. An Egyptian Catholic Bishop, who has close ties with the Vatican, stated that both the United States Government and the Vatican believe that by the year 2025, Christianity will cease to exist in the Middle East. What will happen to the Christians in Egypt where they form a sizeable commu-

nity? It is true emigrations to the West will increase with the years, and many Christians are turning to Islam for economic and social reasons, and more of that will take place. But will Christianity cease to exist in Egypt?

There are signs that what happened in China could happen in Egypt. The missionaries left China at the beginning of the communist revolution, leaving behind about one million Christians, worn out, fearful and forced to go underground. However, to the amazement of the world, when China finally opened up its doors to the West again, they discovered a powerful underground church numbering more than forty million Christians.

There are signs that, with persecution, the underground church will grow and will learn to cope and adjust to the new situation. The result could be a church that is strong and established although it is underground.

8. Population increase is the number one problem for President Mubârak according to a front page article in *Al-Ahrâm* on May 10, 1990. The population increases annually by about one million people. Every sixteen seconds a new baby is born in Egypt. Every year about half a million new graduates wait on the government for disguised unemployment, which is costing the government about nine million Egyptian pounds yearly.[1] These graduates seek marriage and produce more babies and the vicious cycle continues.

There are signs that, as long as there is uncontrolled population increase, poverty, unemployment and social injustice, the youth will be ripe for the Fundamentalist message. The debts of Egypt are increasing over the years. The rich are still getting richer; and therefore, social injustice will continue, and even increase with the increase of poverty and unemployment.

Islam has not been tried in Egypt in recent history. Both socialism and capitalism have been tried and failed. Perhaps, to the doubting spectator, "Islam could be the Solution." The spectator considers accepting an Islamic state that puts the *Sharî'a* into practice.

9. There are signs that Egypt is becoming ripe for an Islamic revolution. Some people think that Mubârak will be the last "secular" president. This could be true, or it could take longer, but it could be coming. The Islamic state might one day become the future of Egypt.

According to Vatikiotis,

> as long as Egypt has no political order that is clearly based on a secular consensus, it will remain afflicted by religious and communal antagonisms. Depending on the ability of the state to satisfy the economic and other needs of its public, these antagonisms, though usually muted or subterranean, will surface periodically. Until a secular formula of identity and social cohesiveness is found that is acceptable, the religious, or traditional one will dominate the social order. And to this extent, the question of religion and state will remain unresolved. But that will require a commitment on the part of the leadership to remove religion from the public realm altogether, and relegate it to the realm of private belief (Vatikiotis 1983: 69).

To remove religion from the public realm altogether and relegate it to the realm of private belief is an impossibility in Egypt. Unless something very unusual such as a major war, military coup, a complete and satisfactory reconciliation with Israel, or AIDS epidemic takes place, the signs point to the coming of an Islamic state.

Perhaps, after a few decades of Fundamentalist autocratic rule, the people may finally revolt. After trying Islam and finding out that it is not the solution they dreamed of, their revolt will be against despotism and for freedom. What happened in Eastern Europe in 1989 could happen in Egypt and the Arab world in the future.

- The manuscript for this book was finished just before the Gulf Crisis erupted. Now as we look back in 1993 at Egypt, we see Islamic Fundamentalism still growing and flourishing. Kuwait stopped donating money to the Fundamentalists; new sources of finance are being tapped. The government still follows the policy of honey and vinegar in dealing with the Fundamentalists.

In 1992, the Fundamentalists sharpened their challenge to the state by declaring war on tourism—Egypt's chief source of revenue. They condemn the stately pharaonic statues and monuments as pagan shrines that generate dirty money. They perceive that the earthquake in October 1992 was God's punishment of Egypt's leadership for their mediocracy and hypocracy. The Fundamentalists are urging their followers to become more militant against a government that in their black-and-white perspective has strayed from God's path.

The government, meanwhile, attempts to look tough and measured. Every day there are new arrests, and suspects can be detained indefinitely under the emergency laws, yet most are released after a few weeks. As in the past, the government still appeases the outwardly respectable elements, such as Shi'râwi and the Muslim Brotherhood, but cracks down hard on the violent fringe. The volcano is rumbling, and the eruption is inevitable unless a "miracle" happens, and miracles do happen.

NOTES

1 In 1975 the US dollar was less than one Egyptian pound. By 1992 the US dollar was worth 3.30 Egyptian pounds.

A

TRANSLITERATION

Several Arabic words appear in this book, whether names or terms. The Arabic terms are written in italics. In Appendix B there is a glossary of the important Arabic terms and in Appendix C there is a glossary of the important names.

A standard form of transliteration is chosen to make it easy for the reader.

Transliteration and pronunciation of Arabic alphabet

ARABIC NAME	SIGN USED	ENGLISH PRONUNCIATION WHERE UNCLEAR
hamza	'	glottal stop, as 'a' in 'apple'
alif	a	
bâ'	b	
tâ'	t	
thâ'	th	as in 'think'
jîm	j	
ḥâ'	ḥ	(aspirated)
khâ'	kh	as in German 'nacht'
dâl	d	

ARABIC NAME	SIGN USED	ENGLISH PRONUNCIATION WHERE UNCLEAR
dhâl	dh	as in 'this'
râ'	r	
zâ'	z	
sîn	s	
shîn	sh	as in 'shoe'
ṣâd	ṣ	(velarised)
ḍâd	ḍ	(velarised)
ṭâ'	ṭ	(velarised)
zâ'	z	(velarised)
'ayn	'	voiced counterpart of ha'
ghayn	gh	similar to throaty French 'r'
fâ'	f	
qâf	q	(uvular) as 'k', not 'kw'
kâf	k	(palatal)
lâm	l	
mîm	m	
nûn	n	
hâ'	h	
wâw	w	
yâ'	y	
âlif yâ	ay	(diphthong)
âlif wâw	aw	(diphthong)

ARABIC NAME	SIGN USED	ENGLISH PRONUNCIATION WHERE UNCLEAR
tâ' marbûṭa	a	
unmarked (short) vowels are:		
	a	as in 'had'
	i	as in 'sit'
	u	as in 'fruit'
vowels with a circumflex above are long:		
	â	as in 'aah'
	î	as in 'eee'
	û	as in 'ooo'

B

GLOSSARY OF NAMES

The following are names of important persons that were mentioned in the text several times.

The word "Al" is placed in front of several family names, and it means "the," for example Ḥasan Al-Bana. In the text this name could appear as Al-Banna, or Ḥasan Al-Banna.

In the glossary, names will appear under the first letter of the famous name, whether the first name or family name or under both. Ḥasan Al-Banna will appear under Banna, and Khâled Islambûli will appear under Khâled, and 'Abdul Salâm Faraj appear under both first and family name.

'Abbûd Zumr: One of the leaders of Al-Jihâd organization.

'Abdul Salâm Faraj: Top leader of Al-Jihâd organization.

Afghâni: A Muslim leader who originally came from Afghanistan and lived in Egypt. He propogated an Islamic state based on Islamic principles.

Aḥmad Sukkari: The co-founder of the Muslim Brotherhood organization.

'Ali: The fourth Caliph.

'Ali 'Abdul Râzaq: He gave theological legitimacy to abolishing the caliphate.

'Ali Mâher: One of the politicians that Ḥasan Al-Banna had to deal with.

Al-Mukhtâr: see Mukhtâr

'Amr Ibnil 'Aṣ: The Muslim general that conquered Egypt and established Islam within it.

Banna: Founder of the Society of Muslim Brotherhood.

Farûq: The last king in Egypt who was deposed in 1952.
Faraj: Top leader of Al-Jihâd organization.
Ḥasan: Son of 'Ali who sold out his right to the caliphate.
Ḥasan Al-Banna: see Banna.
Ḥusein: Son of 'Ali who took up the cause of succession to the caliphate and was brutally killed. His death started the Shiite sect.
Imâm Ṣadr: A Lebanese Shiite leader who founded the Amal movement in Lebanon.
Jamâl Dîn Al-Afghâni: see Afghâni.
Juhainam Al-'Uteibi: The military officer who headed the attack on the big mosque in Mecca, Saudi Arabia, in 1979.
Khâled Islambûli: The assassin of Sâdât.
Khumeini: Founder of the Islamic state in Iran.
Mu'âwiya: Competitor of 'Ali for the caliphate.
Mawdûdi: A Pakistani Muslim philosopher whose writings greatly influenced the resurgence of Islamic Fundamentalism.
Muḥammad 'Abdu: Encouraged a revolt against the British.
Muḥammad 'Ali: An Ottoman who started ruling Egypt in 1805. During his reign, Egypt's rule expanded all over the Middle East.
Muḥammad Islambûli: Brother of Khâled, the assassin of Sâdât.
Mukhtâr: He mobilized the clients and the second-class citizens to fight the mainstream Muslims.
Mughrabi: One of the leaders of Al-Jihâd organization.
Muṣtatfa Kamel: An Egyptian modernist who propagated nationalism.
Nabîl Al-Mughrabi: One of the leaders of Al-Jihâd organization.
Nâṣer: The president of Egypt in the 1950s and 1960s.
Sa'd Zaghlûl: One of the great Egyptian national leaders at the time of the British occupation.

Sâdât: President of Egypt in the 1970s who was assassinated in 1981.

Ṣalâḥ Dîn al-Ayyûbi: A powerful ruler of Egypt who fought against the crusaders.

Ṣâleḥ 'Ishmâwi: A member of the Muslim Brotherhood who maintained a link with Nâṣer's regime, and his name was associated with *Al-Da'wa* magazine.

Ṣâleḥ Sariyya: A Palestinean who attempted to establish a Muslim state in Egypt in 1974.

Sayyid Qutb: An author, philosopher and leader whose writings form the foundation of militant fundamentalism in Egypt. He was hanged in 1966.

Sheikh Sha'râwi: A very popular television preacher who is endorsed by the government and whose preaching paves the way for Islamic Fundamentalism.

Ṣûfi Abu Ṭâleb: A head of the Egyptian parliament.

Sukkari: The co-founder of the Muslim Brotherhood organization.

Ṭâha Ḥusein: A blind scholar who challenged the legitimacy of the caliphate.

Talmasâni: One of the leaders of the Muslim Brotherhood organization.

'Umar 'Abdul Raḥmân: The Sheikh that gave theological legitimacy and justification to the assassination of Sâdât.

'Umar Ibnil Khaṭṭâb: The second caliph.

'Urâbi: An Egyptian officer who lead a revolt against the British who were colonizing Egypt.

'Uteibi: The militant Saudi officer who lead the attack on the big mosque in Mecca, Saudi Arabia, in 1979.

'Uthmân: The third caliph.

Yazîd: Son of Mu'âwiya and his successor to the Ommayad caliphate. It was during his time that Ḥusein was brutally killed.

Zuhdi: Leader of Al-Jihâd organization in the city of Asyûṭ.

'Abbûd Zumr: One of the leaders of Al-Jihâd organization.

C

IMPORTANT WORDS AND TERMS

Adîb: Man of letters.

Ahl Dhimma: The protected people. Minorities of Jews and Christians that live in Muslim nations.

Ahl Kitâb: People of the book. (Jews and Christians that believe in monotheism.)

Ahli mosques: Private in contrast to government mosques.

Al-Ahrâm: The pyramids. It is the name of the largest daily newspaper in the Middle East. In its recent history it has played the role of spokesman many times for the Egyptian government.

Allâhu Akbar: God is great. It is the opening statement in the call of the minaret, and it is one of the Muslim Fundamentalists' slogans.

'Âlim: An expert in religious matters.

Amal movement: A Shiite religious and political party in Lebanon.

Al-Amr bil ma'arûf wa-nahy 'anil munkar: Bringing about a change in behavior according to Muslim principles either by teaching or by enforcing obedience.

Al-Aqṣa mosque: The mosque in Jerusalem which is highly esteemed by Muslims.

'Ashîra: A clan or four cell groups in the Muslim Brotherhood organization.

Awqâf: Ministry of religious affairs.

Al-Azhar: The largest and oldest Muslim seminary in the world. It is situated in Cairo, Egypt, and is the center of Islamic theology.

Dâr al-Awqâf: The ministry of religious affairs under the Egyptian government.

Dâr al-Ḥarb: The domain of war.

Dâr al-Islam: The household or domain of Islam.

Dâr al-'Ulûm: Teachers' training institute in Cairo.

Darwasha: Escapism into piety.

Da'wa: Proclamation. It is also the name of a Muslim Brotherhood magazine.

Dîn wa dunya: Religion and life.

Al-Farîḍa Al-Ghâ'iba: The missing precept, namely, holy war. It is the name of the book written by Faraj, leader of Al-Jihâd organization.

Faqîh: The Imam's representative.

Fatwa: Casuistry. A theological justification.

Fiṭra: Nature.

Fî Zilâl Al-Qur'ân: Commentary on the Qur'ân written by Qutb.

Gallâbiyya: Robe.

Ghayba: A state of temporary inactivity.

Ḥadîth: Tradition or the sayings of Muḥammad outside the Qur'ân.

Ḥâkimiyya: Sovereignty of God and His right to govern.

Ḥamâs: A Palestinian Fundamentalist group in the West Bank and Gaza (Israel).

Ḥaraka: Movement

Ḥijâb: Head cover for women.

Hijra: Emigration of Muḥammad to Medina. Detachment from society.

Hizbullâh: A militant religious and political party of Shiites in Lebanon.

Ihyâ' al-din: The revival of religion.

Ijmâ': Consensus.

Ijtihâd: Jurisprudence. Interpretations of the Qur'ân. Thinking through difficult religious issues.

Imâm: Religious leader.

Imâma: The line of leadership of the Islamic nation through history. It is similar to what Catholics believe about the popes.

Imâm al-Waṣi: The trustee.

Al-Islâm Al-Tharwi: The Muslim "rich."

Al-Islâm Al-Thawri: The "revolutionary or militant" Muslims.

Ismâ'iliyya: A city in Egypt where Ḥasan Al-Banna started the Muslim Brotherhood organization.

Iniqiḍâḍ: Attack and conquest stage. It is the third stage, according to Qutb, that follows being underground and then gaining strength.

Istiḍ'âf: Stage of weakness. Underground. This is the first stage, according to Qutb, which is followed by gaining strength and then attack.

Jâhiliyya: Days of ignorance or barbarianism before the time of Muḥammad.

Jamâ'ât al-Islâmiyya: The Fundamentalist groups at the universities.

Jawwâla: The rovers in the Muslim Brotherhood organization.

Jihâd: Holy war or holy combat.

Al-Jihâz al-sirri: Secret apparatus of the Muslim Brotherhood organization.

Ka'ba: The black stone in Mecca where the pilgrimage takes place.

Kâfir: Blasphemer

Katîba: A battalion or one hundred cell groups in the Muslim Brotherhood organization.

Al-Khaṭṭ al-hamayoni: The decree issued by the Ottoman caliph determining how Christians, as a minority in Muslim states, should be treated and the laws governing building churches.

Khawârij: The Kharijites. Those who withdrew. A sect of Islâm which is considered heretical.

Kûfa: City in Iraq.

Kufr: The grave sin of unbelief or pride against God.

Kuttâb: The Quranic school for children where the Qur'ân was memorized.

Lâ Ḥukma illa lilâh: God is the only ruler and judge.

Lâ ikrâha fi-dîn: No force should be used to compel people to become Muslims.

Lâ ilâha illa Lâh: There is no god but God. God is one. The slogan of monotheism.

Ma'âlem Fi Ṭarîq: Signposts on the road. A famous book written by Qutb, and it is used in discipling Muslim Fundamentalists.

Mahdi: A messianic concept, where the hidden Imâm will come back to earth to rule with justice.

Marâqiz al-quwwa: Power centers.

Al-Mawâli: The clients who entered voluntarily into a covenant with an Arab patron. They are associated with Al-Mukhtâr.

Al-Miḥna al-'ula: The first calamity in the history of the Muslim Brotherhood organization.

Muḥajjabât: Women that cover their heads.

Muḥyi al-dîn: Reviver of religion.

Murâbaḥa: Islamic economic law of genuine gain and loss.

Murtad: Backslider.

Al-Naṣṣ wal-waṣiyya: Appointment and deligation.

Qur'ân: The holy book of the Muslims.

Qurrâ': Those who have memorized the Qur'an.

Rabb: Lord.

Rafâhiyya: Living in luxury.

Rahṭ: Twenty cell groups in the language of the Muslim Brotherhood organization.

Ramadân: The month of fasting for the Muslims.

Shahîd: Martyr.

Sham nasîm: Spring day celebration in Egypt.

Sharî'a: The legislative code derived from the Qur'ân and the sunna.

Sharikât tawzîf al-amwâl: Companies for the investment of money.

Sheikh: Muslim religious leader.

Shî'a: Party, or those who believed that the caliphate is for 'Ali and his descendents.

Shirk: Polytheism.

Shuhâda' abṭâl: Martyrs and heroes.

Shûra: Agreement by majority.

Ṣiffîn: Battle in Iraq between Mu'awiya and 'Ali in 657 A.D.

Sûra: A chapter or section in the Qur'ân ranging from a few verses to hundreds of verses.

Takfîr: Declaring the society as living in barbarianism.

Takfîr wal-hîjra: Excommunication of fellow citizens and withdrawal from the society. Name of the Society of Muslims under Shukri.

Ṭâghût: Despot.

Tamakkun: Gaining strength. Discipleship.

Taqiyya: Quietism principle. Appearing to be satisfied, but in reality surviving on the hope that God's deliverance will come one day.

Tawḥîḍ: Perfect unity of God.

'Ubûdiyya: Worship and submission to God.

'Ulamâ': Religious scholars.

'Umarâ' al-jamâ'ât: Group leaders.

Umma: The Muslim nation.

'Urf: Unwritten or conventional law.

Usar: Literally it means families. The name of cell groups in the Muslim Brotherhood organization.

Ustâdh: Master.

'Uzla: Withdrawal from society.

Wafd: Delegation. It is also the name of a political party in Egypt.

Al-Wathîqa al-'umariyya: The pact of 'Umar. A pact describing how Christians and Jews, as minority groups, should be treated by the governing Muslims.

BIBLIOGRAPHY

'Abdul Râzeq, A

[sa]. *Al-Islâm Wa 'Uṣûl Ḥukm*. Beirut: Dâr Maktabat Al-Ḥayât

'Abdul Fâḍil, M

1982. Zâhirat aṭṭa ṭarruf Al-Islâmi. *Anadwa Al-Râbi'a Libaḥth Al-Ḥarakât. Al-Dîniyya Al-Mutaṭarrifa*. Cairo

'Abdul Raḥmân, U

1987. *Kalimat Ḥaq*. Cairo: Dâr Al-''Itiṣâm.

Aḥmad, RS

1986. *Al-Yaqza Al-'Arabiyya* (December) 83-103. Namûdhaj Ṣâliḥ Sariyya.

1987a. *Al-Islambûli*. Cairo: Maktabat Madbûli.

1987b. *Al-Yaqza Al-'Arabiyya* (January) 117-129. Namûdhaj Shukri Aḥmad Muṣṭafa.

1989a. *Al-Ḥarakât Al-Islâmiyya*. Cairo: Sîna Linashr.

1989b. *Limâdha Qatalu Sâdât*. Cairo: Al-Dâr Al-Sharqiyya

'Ajamy, F

1983. *The Arab Predicament*. Cambridge: Cambridge University Press.

Allport, G

1958. *The Nature of Prejudice*. New York: Double Day Anchor Book.

'Amâra, M

1983. *Al-Farîḍa Al-Ghâ'iba*. Beirut: Dâr Al-Wiḥda.

1985a. *Aṣaḥwa Al-Islâmiyya Wa Taḥaddi Al-Haḍâri*. Cairo: Dâr Al-Mustaqbal Al-'Arabi.

1985b. *Tayyarât Al-Fikr Al-Islâmi*. Beirut: Dâr Al-Wiḥda Liṭṭibâ'a Wa-Nashr.

'Amîn, A

1986. *Al-Firaq Wal-Madhâhib Al-Qadîma Wal-Mu'âṣira*. Beirut: Dâr Al-Ḥaqîqa.

Banna, H

[sa]. *Majmû'ât Rasâ'il Al-Banna*. Cairo: Dâr Shihâb.

1966. *Mudhakkarât Ada'wa Wa Dâ'iya*. Cairo: Dâr Al-''Itiṣâm.

Bayumi, ZS

1979. *Al-Ikhwân Al-Muslimûm*. Cairo: Maktabat Wahba.

Ben-dor, G

1983. "Stateness and Ideology in Contemporary Egyptian Politics." In Warburg and Kupferschmidt, *Islam, Nationalism and Radicalism*. New York: Praeger Publishers.

Chapman, C

1989. *Whose Promised Land*. Sydney: A Lion International Paperback.

Cragg, K

1985. *The Pen And The Faith*. London: Allan and Unwin.

Foda, F

1989. *Al-Nadhîr*. Cairo: Dâr Miṣr Al-Jadîda Linashr Watawzî'.

Findley, P

1987. *Man Yajru' 'Ala Al-Kalâm.* Beirut: Sharikat al-Matbu'at Litawzi' Wanashr.

Ḥabîb, R
1989. *Al-Iḥtijâj Al-Dînî Wal-Ṣirâ' Al-Ṭabaqi.* Cairo: Sîna Linashr

Halsell, G
1990. *Al-Nubuwa Wa Siyâsa.* Tripoli: Jam'iyat Al-Da'wa Al-Islâmiyya Al-'Âlamiyya.

Ḥammûda, A
1985. *Ightiyâl Ra'îs.* Cairo: Sîna Linashr.
1986. *Qanâbil Wa Maṣâḥif.* Cairo: Sîna Linashr.
1987a. *Al-Hijra 'Ila 'Unf.* Cairo: Sîna Linashr.
1987b. *Sayyid Qutb.* Cairo: Sîna Linashr.

Ḥanafi, H
1988. *Al-Ḥarakât Addîniyya Al-Mu'âṣira.* Cairo: Maktabat Madbûli.

Ḥasan, H
1987. *Muwajahat Al-Fikr Al-Muṭatarrif Fil-Islâm.* Cairo: Matba'at Al-Jabalâwi.

Haykal, MH
1985. *Kharîf Al-Ghaḍab.* Beirut: Sharikat Al-Maṭbu'ât Litawzî' Wanashr.

Ḥusein, A
1982. Waraqat Mawâqef. *Anadwa Al-Râbi'a Libahth Al-Ḥarakât Al-Dinîyya Al-Mutaṭarrifa.* Cairo

Kepel, G
1985. *The Prophet and Pharaoh.* London: Al-Saqi Books.

1988. *Al-Nabi Wal-Fir'aun.* Cairo: Maktabat Madbûli (Translation).

Krüger, JS
1982. *Studying Religion.* Pretoria: University of South Africa.

Kupferschmidt, UM
1983. In Warburg and Kupferschmidt, Introduction. *Islam, Nationalism and Radicalism.* New York: Praeger Publishers.

Lazarus-Yafeh, H
1983. Muhammad Mutawalli al-Sharawi. In Warburg and Kupferschmidt, *Islam, Nationalism and Radicalism.* New York: Praeger Publishers.

Mitchell, RP
1969. *The Society of Muslim Brothers.* London: Oxford University Press.
1977. *Al-'Ikhwân Al-Muslimûm.* Cairo: Maktabat Madbûli (Translation).

Najrâmi, MY
1987. *Ashî'a Fil Mizân.* Jadda: Dâr Al-Madani.

Qâsem, AQ
1979. *Ahl Dhimma.* Cairo: Dâr Al-Ma'ârif.

Qutb, S
1987. *Ma'âlem Fi Ṭarîq.* Cairo: Dâr Shurûq.

Rakhâwi, Y
1982. Waraqat Amal. *Anadwa Al-Râbi'a Libaḥth Al-Ḥarakât Al-Dîniyya Al-Mutaṭarrifa.* Cairo

Shah, N
1987. *Al-'Aqâ'ed Ashî'iyya.* Cairo

Ṣâdeq, H
1988. *Judhûr Al-Fitna Fil Firaq Al-Islâmiyya*. Cairo: Maktabat Madbûli.

Sa'îd, R
1977. *Ḥasan Al-Banna*. Cairo: Dâr Al-Thaqâfa Al-Jadîda

Sa'îd, EW
1979. *Orientalism*. New York: Vintage Books Edition.

Ṣayrafi, YM
1985. *Ṣuwar Min Ṭarîq Maṣr Al-Islâmiyya*. Cairo: Al-Hay'a Al-'Âma Lishu'ûn Al-Islâmiyya.

Sherîf, R
1985. *Al-Ṣahyûniyya Ghair Al-Yahûdiyya*. Kuwait: 'Âlam Al-Ma'rifa.

Shamir, S
1983. "Radicalism in Egyptian Historiography." In Warburg and Kupferschmidt, *Islam, Nationalism and Radicalism*. New York: Praeger Publishers.

Suleimân, H
1988. *Minil Qibṭiyya Ilal Islâm*. Cairo: Al-Maktab al-'Arabi Lilma'ârif.

Van Den Broek, R
1979. "Popular Religious Practices and Ecclesiastical Policies in the Early Church." In Vrijhof and Waardenburg. *Official and Popular Religion*. The Hague: Mouton Publishers.

Vatikiotis, PJ
1983. "Religion and State." In Warburg and Kupferschmidt, *Islam, Nationalism and Radicalism*. New York: Praeger Publishers.

Waardenburg, JDJ

1979. "Official and Popular Religion as a Problem in Islamic Studies." In Vrijhof and Waardenburg, *Official and Popular Religion*. The Hague: Mouton Publishers

Wakîl, M

1986. *Kubra Al-Ḥarakât Al-Islâmiyya*. Cairo: Dâr Al-Mujtama' Linashr Watawzî'.

Warburg, GR

1983. "The Evolution of Islamic Fundamentalism." In Warburg and Kupferschmidt, *Islam, Nationalism and Radicalism*. New York: Praeger Publisher.

Watt, WM

1973. *The Formative Period of Islâmic Thought*. Edinburg: University Press

1981. *Muhammad at Medina*. Oxford: Oxford University Press.

1988. *Islamic Fundamentalism and Modernity*. London: Routledge

Wellhausen, J

1978. *Al-Khawârij Wa Shî'a*. Kuwait: Wikâlat Al-Maṭbû'ât (Translation).

Youssef, M

1985. *Revolt Against Modernity. Leiden: E.J. Brill.*

Printed in the United States
2477

9 780878 08241